The Internment of Aliens

The Internment of Aliens

BY

François Lafitte

WITH

A NEW INTRODUCTION BY THE AUTHOR

Libris

1988

First published by Penguin Books, 1940
This edition, with introduction and index, first published 1988

Libris, 10 Burghley Road, London NW5 1UE

British Library Cataloguing in Publication Data

Lafitte, François
The internment of aliens.
1. Great Britain. Aliens. Internment
I. Title
940.4′72′41

ISBN 1–870352–95–5 (paperback)
ISBN 1–870352–55–6 (hardback)

Produced by Cinamon and Kitzinger, London
New material typeset by Wyvern Typesetting Limited, Bristol
Printed and bound in Great Britain by
Redwood Burn Limited, Trowbridge, Wiltshire

CONTENTS

No ordinary excuse, such as that there is a war on and that officials are overworked, is sufficient to explain what has happened . . . Horrible tragedies, unnecessary and undeserved, lie at the door of somebody . . . Frankly, I shall not feel happy, either as an Englishman or as a supporter of this Government, until this bespattered page of our history has been cleaned up and rewritten.

MAJOR CAZALET, in the House of Commons, *August* 22, 1940.

INTRODUCTION

Afterthoughts Four Decades Later

The only blessing for which we can thank Britain's rounding up of its "enemy aliens" in 1940 is that it unintentionally accomplished the genesis of the Amadeus Quartet. After the Second World War this talented and eventually internationally famous group delighted music lovers everywhere for nearly forty years until Peter Schidlof's death ended the partnership in 1987. For it was in a British internment camp that Schidlof, a youth of eighteen, made friends and first attempted to play music with two other gifted young men, Norbert Brainin and Siegmund Nissel. In the Third Reich, from which they had escaped to England, these three had belonged to the great host seen as a threat to the German "race" and way of life. Seen now by the *British* state as a possible threat to the nation's security in time of war, they found themselves fortuitously confined together – and plucked opportunity from adversity. Growing after the war, with the addition of Martin Lovett, from a threesome into a foursome, they proceeded to enchant the nation's heart and enrich its culture.

Little else can be pleaded in defence of the way in which Britain had then treated its refugees from Nazi persecution. Yet, given what we *now* know about the world war, it might seem that this book is concerned with a trifling and short-lived episode – hardly worth writing about at the time, certainly not worth reissuing nearly half a century later. Thus it is reckoned by Gil Elliot (*Twentieth-Century Book of the Dead*, Allen Lane, The Penguin Press, 1972) that the Second World War cost some 55 million human lives, including 15 million in China, between 1937 and 1945. 20 million were Russians and other Soviet nationalities, about 5 million were Jews deliberately exterminated, 5 million were Germans, 3 million non-Jewish Poles and 2½ million Japanese. For Britain's closest allies losses were much smaller: about 400,000 Americans and 570,000 residents of France; while the United Kingdom and its Commonwealth lost about 460,000.

Catastrophe and holocaust on this scale seem to dwarf into insignificance the subject matter of my book: the arrest and confinement in Britain of a large proportion of the 74,000 persons residing in the country whose original homes were in the Third Reich (of whom over 55,000 had been officially classified as "refugees from Nazi oppression"), and also of over 4,000 of our 19,000 resident Italians, including many known anti-Fascists; and the deporting to Canada or Australia of a substantial portion of those interned. All this was monstrously unjust. Yet if one uses man-made megadeaths as the measure of war-engendered misery, this whole lamentable operation comes close to the bottom of the scale. Not many more than a thousand of those affected are thought to have perished in the outcome: most by torpedoing of their deportation ships, some through despair leading to suicide, or by ill health succumbing to the shock of arrest, confinement and shipment overseas. Britain lost about a hundred times as many lives in the bombing of its cities, France at least four hundred times as many civilians killed by execution or privation in German concentration camps.

But this is not at all how we saw matters in the summmer of 1940. The major disasters and mass exterminations (outside Poland at least) still lay ahead in the unforeseeable future. We knew only three things: the uncertain present; the reasons why Britain was harbouring a small number – perhaps 70,000 – of the third of a million refugees who had succeeded in getting away from the Nazi terror; and the dubious chain of events that had led us into war against that terror. Those are the topics of Chapter I and the context of the whole book.

After years of compromise with, and highly dangerous concessions to, Hitler and Mussolini, Britain under Chamberlain appeared, but still uncertainly, committed to a war to overthrow Nazi tyranny in the name of human freedom and democratic values. The uncertainty about Britain's war aims was not removed while I was writing by the fact that Churchill had just replaced Chamberlain as the nation's leader, but had retained him along with Lord Halifax – the "Men of Munich" – as senior members of the new wartime Coalition Government. That uncertainty was deepened when that Government responded to direct aggression – the "Blitzkrieg" that overwhelmed Western Europe after Poland had been torn apart – by labelling the victims of Nazi oppression within our shores enemy aliens and herding them into confinement. This seemed to contradict all the war aims to which we were supposedly committed, to impugn Britain's honour and good name, to cast grave doubts on our Government's true motives. Had not the French, overwhelmed in June 1940, simply turned over their similar enemy aliens' internment camps to the victorious Nazis (see p. 208)? What might our own Government do, were Britain to be invaded?

All who cherished democratic values were bound to feel uneasy, if not to protest. Those who saw the war – as I did among millions of others – less as a conflict between nation states, more as an international civil war for the soul of civilisation, were bound to ask: Is internment a justifiable military precaution? Or the outcome of an uninformed and needless wave of hysteria? Or does it point to the influence of sinister political forces more in sympathy with the Nazis than with the Bolsheviks, hoping perhaps to accomplish a compromise peace with the former at the expense of the latter? These were the sort of questions I sought to answer in this book.

Forty-eight years later we know the answers probably as surely as we ever shall. A very substantial literature has explored almost every aspect of the events reviewed in this book and the reasons for them, compared to the rather tenuous information I could obtain, in conditions of war secrecy, when I was writing. For want of information, for instance, I could say little about why it was decided to pack internees off to Canada and Australia, still less about what happened to those who eventually reached those destinations. I could find out very little about the Italian internees. And I could make only shrewd guesses at exactly how and by whom and why the official decisions to intern and deport were taken. It was not possible to confirm or correct those guesses until most of the Government records of those days (save for many Home Office papers) were opened to public inspection over thirty years later. This enabled Peter and Leni Gillman to make a thorough study of the official archives – along with much other new material – and to publish their findings in '*Collar the Lot!*': *How Britain Interned and Expelled its Wartime Refugees.**

With the knowledge and hindsight of 1988 I find astonishingly little that I would wish to rewrite. But I permit myself two addenda. The first concerns the random list on pp. 78–81 of persons who were

---

* Quartet Books, 1980.

already distinguished when they were interned. Still taking names at random, I would now add others to that list and would supplement it with yet more who achieved either notoriety or (like the Amadeus Trio) distinction in later life.

Among the notorious *Klaus Fuchs* stands out: a German physicist and dedicated Communist, deported to Canada but later brought back to work for the British Atomic Energy Commission both at Los Alamos (on the atomic bomb) and after the war at Harwell, where he eventually became the Commission's deputy scientific director. It was only in 1949 that MI5 established that not long after his release from internment Fuchs had begun to pass crucial information to the Soviet Union.

The more conventionally distinguished include:

Professor Sir Hermann Bondi, FRS, Austrian research student at Cambridge when deported to Canada. Back in Britain wartime scientific work for Government launched him on a career culminating in his becoming in the 1970s successively chief scientific adviser to the Ministry of Defence and chief scientist at the Department of Energy, duties he combined with being Professor of Mathematics at King's College, London, and secretary of the Royal Astronomical Society. He finally returned to Cambridge as Master of Churchill College.

Francis Carsten, German historian, active in anti-Nazi resistance work in Germany from the twenties. Studying for doctorate in Oxford when interned. Became Masaryk Professor of Central European History in the University of London.

Richard Friedenthal, German writer and then editor of *Knaurs Lexikon*. Subsequently author of major biographies of Goethe, Luther and Marx.

Dr Hans Gal, Austrian composer and musicologist distinguished in Austria and Germany before gaining asylum in Britain. After the war was enticed by Donald Tovey to Edinburgh University where he enhanced his distinction over a further forty years, becoming one of the founders of the Edinburgh Festival.

Professor Max Grünhut, previously professor of criminal law at Bonn, subsequently an eminent criminologist in England.

Fritz Hallgarten, originally a judge in Germany. After the Nazis shot his father and brother he escaped to Britain and established himself as a wine importer. Since the war many Britons have savoured his famous firm's wines.

Pastor Franz Hildebrandt, famous, with Dietrich Bonhoeffer, for his defiance of Hitler in the name of Christian values.

Dr Werner Kissling, Prussian aristocrat and prominent diplomat. When posted at the German embassy in London, where his loathing of Hitler was unconcealed, made a dramatic escape when threatened with recall. Subsequently settled in Scotland, winning fame for his work on the preservation of Hebridean culture. "He not only studied the crofters," wrote *The Times* in his obituary in 1988, "immortalizing them with his camera and collecting their artefacts for the Dunfermline Observatory Museum; he also did much to reorganise and promote their fishing and weaving industries."

Jürgen Kuczynski, German economist and statistician who made significant contributions to the study of British social problems before the war. An active Communist, he settled after the war in East Germany.

Dr G. V. Lachmann, prominent German expert on aerodynamics who had worked for Handley Page in Britain since 1930.

Otto Lehmann-Russbüldt, German pacifist socialist, well known as general secretary of the International League for the Rights of Man (which included such famous Italian anti-Fascists as D. Anzani, drowned in the *Arandora Star*). Interned aged sixty-seven.

Uberto Limentani, working for the BBC Italian service when interned. Deported on, and survived torpedoing of, *Arandora Star*. Ultimately became Professor of Italian in Cambridge.

Sir Claus Moser, aged seventeen when interned with his brother and father (who had been a banker in Berlin). After release served three years in Royal Air Force. Eventually became Professor, Social Statistics at London School of Economics, head of Government Statistical Service for eleven years, Director of Central Statistical Office, and president of Royal Statistical Society. Also vice-chairman of N. M. Rothschild and Sons and chairman of Covent Garden Opera House, 1974–87, as well as Warden of Wadham College, Oxford since 1983.

Professor Hans Motz, Austrian expert in nuclear physics and microwave engineering who became Oxford's first Professor of Engineering.

Professor Max Perutz, FRS, Austrian working in J. D. Bernal's Cavendish crystallography laboratory at Cambridge when deported to Canada. After wartime government scientific work was for many years director of the Medical Research Council's Molecular Biology Unit. Awarded Nobel Prize for chemistry in 1962.

Professor Guido Pontecorvo, FRS, Italian Jewish scientist at Edinburgh Institute of Animal Genetics when interned. After important war work eventually attained international eminence in a varied career, including seven years on staff of Imperial Cancer Research Fund, ending as Professor of Genetics at Glasgow.

Eugen Prager, Austrian publisher working in wartime British Ministry of Information when interned.

Maryan Rawicz and *Walter Landauer*, popular musicians. Started with recitals for fellow internees in Isle of Man. In post-war Britain built up an immense following among those who liked light musical entertainment.

Emil Rich, Austrian engineer who developed a glove manufactory in Germany. Escaping early, he brought his machinery to England and started the production of Miloré gloves in Worcester. When interned he was under contract to make electrically heated pure silk gloves for the Air Ministry, for high altitude flying. After release he eventually established three factories, initiated the Glove Fairs of England, made the Queen's coronation gloves – and was awarded the Freedom of the City of London.

Kurt Schwitters, famous German Dadaist painter, collagist and bilingual poet.

Paolo Treves, son of a famous Italian Socialist leader. When interned was working as translator and announcer in BBC Italian service, like his interned cousin Uberto Limentani.

Walter Wallich, German post-graduate student when interned and sent to Canada. Subsequently ended up as chief producer for BBC radio.

Bernhard Weiss, had been deputy police commissioner in Berlin and was wanted by the Nazis.

Similar lists could be compiled of deported refugees who eventually made new lives in Canada, Australia or other new countries, rather than return to Britain.* Two examples may suffice. *Dr Ernst Kitzinger*, mentioned on p. 79, deported to Canada, remained across the Atlantic and ended his career – to Britain's loss – as Professor of Art History at Harvard. And

---

* For Canada this has been done, by Erich Koch, in *Deemed Suspect: A Wartime Blunder* (Methuen, Toronto, 1980).

according to Professor Sol Encel,* one prison ship alone, the *Dunera*, supplied Australia with at least five future professors as well as a future shipping magnate and several musicians and writers.

My second retrospective addendum concerns the speculations in Chapter IV about precisely why internment and deportation were embarked upon and who took the crucial decisions. Writing in August 1940 I concluded (pp. 189–90):

> Internment and deportation of refugees are a sordid and disreputable scandal, but in spite of our lengthy analysis of the reasons why this policy was adopted, we find it impossible conclusively to apportion the blame between Mr Eden, Sir John Anderson, Mr Chamberlain's Committee, the Army chiefs and the subordinate officials (Chief Constables, Home Office officials, Prisoners of War Department of the War Office, etc.) under these Ministers.

There followed a long list of questions that wanted answers. Most of them have at last been answered from their study of official records by Mr and Mrs Gillman, who have also corrected and supplemented my 'lengthy analysis' in various details. It is highly gratifying to find that in all essentials save one my analysis was correct.

The exception is that, rather astonishingly, I completely ignored the crucial role of Winston Churchill, Prime Minister from 10 May 1940, but a key Minister before then closely involved with the armed forces' chiefs as First Lord of the Admiralty. I had assumed him to be too busy rallying the nation and waging the war to be bothered at all about what should be done to refugees. So Churchill gets only two incidental mentions in this whole book; and the tenor of my analysis was to fix prime responsibility on the more obvious candidate, the Home Secretary, Sir John Anderson. The Government was under intense pressure from the War Office, various Army chiefs and a wide section of the Press to intern all 'enemy aliens'. It looked to me as though Anderson was not disposed to resist this pressure very firmly because he partly shared the same outlook, partly because other senior Ministers were fully persuaded of it. But I did not count Churchill among the latter.

He was not an old-fashioned xenophobic Colonel Blimp. But he was an impetuous, emotional upper-class rogue elephant. On

* In an article in *The Age* (Melbourne, Australia), 15 September 1972.

becoming Prime Minister, with Western Europe succumbing to the "Blitzkrieg", he made it almost his first business to visit France, then in the throes of military collapse. Immediately after his return, we know from the Gillmans, Chamberlain conveyed to the War Cabinet on 24 May "a request made by the War Office for the internment of all enemy aliens and the imposition of severe restrictions upon neutral aliens". Churchill then told the Cabinet that his view on internment had "greatly hardened . . . The German technique in the occupation of the Low Countries had shown the weaknesses to which we were exposed". And he added that *he was strongly in favour of removing all internees out of the United Kingdom*".*

A few days later the deportation exercise was started and on 3 June Churchill was demanding its speeding up, perhaps by using St Helena as an internment colony. On 10 June arrest and deportation were extended to the Italians in Britain, whether exiles or not, when Mussolini declared war. Churchill's response was the curt order: "Collar the lot!" Yet barely eight weeks later on 1 August Churchill told his Cabinet that it should "now be possible to take a somewhat less rigid attitude in regard to internment of aliens", and went on shortly afterwards to tell the Commons that he had always thought the "Fifth Column danger . . . somewhat exaggerated in this Island"!†

All the same it seems that my judgement was not widely at variance with the truth as now established when I wrote (pp. 178–9):

We are not entirely persuaded . . . that the 'Army' pressed so strongly for wholesale internment that the Government was forced to adopt this policy . . . We are not convinced that the Home Office in particular put up a very stubborn resistance when pressed by the military chiefs. We have the impression that it yielded with a good, rather than a bad grace . . .

It seems probable that some of our Army chiefs themselves succumbed to a panic unworthy of soldiers, and found the Home Office not unwilling to yield to a pressure inspired by a 'public opinion' largely created . . . by papers like the *Daily Mail*. Partly, no doubt, this was due to the subconscious belief lurking in their minds that 'once a German, always a German'. Too many

---

* Peter and Leni Gillman, op. cit., p. 133 (my emphasis, F.L.).
† ibid., p. 231.

of our Generals simply believe that this is a war of England against Germany (and Austria), so that all 'Huns' are enemies. Too many of our military chiefs appear to be so saturated with undemocratic traditions of discipline and obedience to established governments (*however* established) that they inevitably regard as the 'enemy' all those who speak the language of the enemy government, and cannot see the necessity of appealing to *peoples* over the heads of *governments*, or conceive of the possibility of positive action to encourage revolts in enemy territory against dictatorial regimes.

Sir Claus Moser has made the same point more simply:

I think the Government of the day panicked. Yes, of course, there might have been a few spies. But I can't believe it was necessary to lock up thousands of people, some of them great scientists and engineers who could have been so useful. Surely a couple of days checking backgrounds would have revealed that most of us had more reason to hate Hitler than the British (*TV Times*, 12 February, 1983).

As recorded on page 180, in seventy-four days the Nazis overwhelmed five neighbouring countries. Britain, soon under daily air bombardment and under threat of enemy landings, stood alone against the combined tyrannies of Hitler and Mussolini. So the military panic was understandable. What was far less understandable – and certainly not excusable – was the notion that our refugees from the dictatorships constituted a serious security risk. That can be explained only if we understand the mental make up of the Establishment of the day – that combination of ignorance and prejudice against foreigners so prevalent among the civil and military Upstairs-Downstairs set who had run Britain during the past decade, with their tendency to assume that foreigners who disliked Hitler (who had dealt with the "Bolshevik menace") and Mussolini (who had at least "made the trains run on time") were very likely to be Communists wanting to overthrow the established order.

In a crude form that is what the young refugee scientist, Max Perutz, found when working at Cambridge in those days: "In the colleges and among wealthy people Hitler was regarded as a bulwark against Communism and Jewish stories of Nazi atrocities as propaganda.''* In more subtle forms such sentiments were widely diffused, as this book records. More specifically, thanks to the Gillmans's research, we can now trace to its origins in official establishment minds that request which Chamberlain brought to the War Cabinet on 24 May 1940 to intern all enemy aliens in case some of them were Nazi Fifth Columnists. The request came from the War Office, pressed upon it by the Chiefs of Staff Committee. They in turn had had it pressed upon them by their own intelligence chiefs meeting together in the Joint Intelligence Committee under an upper-crust chairman, William Cavendish-Bentinck, an aristocratic diplomat and former Guards officer. And he made sure that they were kept fully apprised of the views of the Secret Intelligence Service (SIS or MI6), headed by 'C'.† 'The latter, according to his recent biographer (Anthony Cave Brown, *The Life of Sir Stewart Menzies, Churchill's Spymaster,* Michael Joseph, 1988), was a fine upper-crust specimen – Eton, Life Guards, White's Club, Beaufort Hunt and Royal Enclosure at Ascot – a way of life apparently approximated to in varying degrees by the members of the Joint Intelligence Committee and the rest of the military top brass who formed "the opinion of the Army" demanding internment. Shocked and bewildered by the British failure to prevent the Nazi occupation of Norway, followed soon by the Low Countries, they evolved from the flimsiest of evidence a muddled theory that Hitler's armed forces could not have accomplished these triumphs without the powerful aid of Nazi Fifth Columnists in all these countries . . .

* Quoted by Paul K. Hoch in 'No Utopia: Refugee Scholars in Britain', *History Today*, November 1985.

† Phillip Knightley, an authority on our security services, tells us that early in the war in Germany "there existed a loose alliance of politicians and military men anxious to prevent another world conflict and who looked to Britain for support. . . In no British department was the desire for a deal with the Germans more enthusiastic than in the British Secret Intelligence Service. It . . . expressed a general feeling that circumstances might come about in which it could be possible to achieve a quick end to the war. . . . SIS believed that the British government might have gone along with a settlement with the Germans even if it did not necessarily involve the removal of Hitler. This was because within SIS and certain sections of the British establishment there was agreement with the German view: that both countries were fighting the wrong war, and that the 'right' war would involve Germany and Britain fighting together against the Soviet Union" (*Sunday Times*, 3 April 1988).

Today with the hindsight of history all this is tolerably clear. It was less obvious when, as an ordinary member of the public with no special access to the corridors of power, I embarked upon this book, finding out only what any other man in the street with the necessary persistence could find out. Just completing my twenty-seventh year, I was enabled to undertake this inquiry because fortuitously I was not, like most of my contemporaries, serving in the Forces or in essential war work. (Called to the Army at the time of Dunkirk, to my surprised dismay my medical board had taken a poor view of my heart.)

In most attributes I was an Englishmen but in my emotions a European, seeing human and cultural values as transcending irrelevant concepts of nationality, and seeing – as I still do – nation states as obsolescent hindrances to progress. Though I was born in England there was much that transcended England in my upbringing and nothing directly English in my parentage – an unknown American father and a French mother who became Havelock Ellis's second wife. I was reared under his wise, intellectually wide-ranging, unpartisanly radical, cosmopolitan influence in a home replete with the world's finest literature. I had several years' schooling in France, spent later school summers in Weimar Germany (Bremen, the Harz, Breslau, Leipzig, Dresden) and student summers in Switzerland. Most important was my study summer of 1934 in Vienna, when Dollfuss was murdered by Nazis a few hundred yards from my lodging. Being then a Communist like many of the best of my generation, I found friends in Vienna in left-wing circles working underground for the restoration of Austrian democracy. (Most of those friends later had to flee Austria for their lives. Some got to England and stayed in my London house. Their friends followed, then their friends' friends; and my wife and I kept open house for them.) The flickering light of Marxism-Leninism was finally doused for me in 1939 by the Stalin-Hitler pact. But, like Eratosthenes, I continued – and still continue – to see all good men as my fellow countrymen.

In 1938 I had the good fortune to be recruited to the staff of PEP (Political and Economic Planning) where I gained a thorough grounding in research methods and values – scholarship, independence, impartiality. More important, research at PEP was infused with an overriding concern for the great policy issues besetting British society, handled in a fashion which afforded me the unforgettable intellectual excitement of involvement in almost daily discussions with many of the finest, most forward-looking minds of the day. PEP was born in the crisis year of 1931, brought into life by leading personalities – industrialists, financiers, businessmen, academics, scientists, civil servants, journalists, and just a few unusual politicians – with a common concern at the intellectual barrenness of governments confronted with economic slump and growing international tension. Located at the heart of Whitehall, it was a high-prestige institution *sui generis* – at once a West End club, a standing discussion group (or group of groups) and a research institute, yet not any one of these things as then conventionally understood. Its wide-ranging publications commanded high respect; and they were all anonymous, being the products of many minds. Meeting over meals in the club, the "working members" would discuss specific problems with the assistance of research staff, using and rewriting their material into papers or reports for publication.

(Even now, peering back from the distant shore of 1988, I find it hard to discern exactly what was so unique – and so thrilling – about PEP in the 1930s and 1940s. Its spirit and significance are best recaptured by some of its leading personalities in *Fifty Years of Political and Economic Planning*, edited by John Pinder, Heinemann, 1981. Among much else PEP can fairly claim to have been one of the major intellectual influences preparing the way for the National Health Service and the Beveridge social security system instituted in the aftermath of the war.)

My book was produced in that setting. But because it dealt with a very urgent problem demanding wide publicity and immediate action, PEP waived its normal procedures of thorough discussion by an expert study group (impossible to assemble during a military emergency) and of anonymous authorship. Instead, though I did in fact draw heavily on the knowledge and collective wisdom of PEP members, the book was to be my own and was to be issued as a "Penguin Special". ("Specials" were specially commissioned titles on current affairs, produced and published at speed, and with a higher print-run than most other Penguins.)

The bulky notes and documentation I proceeded to accumulate while preparing the book have long since vanished in the turmoil of war, apart from a few letters from the publishers; and so apparently have their relevant records. But in my seventy-fifth year I still vividly recall the salient features of what I was doing at the end of my twenty-seventh, though I may err in some details. As the "phoney" war in the West gave way to real warfare in the spring of 1940, my half-finished work for PEP – an inquiry into population problems and policies – had petered out. Fresh tasks for me had not been settled when late in May Leonard Elmhirst (of Dartington Hall), PEP's chairman, invited me as a matter of urgency to investigate, and write a Penguin book about, what was being done to refugees from Nazi persecution. He was enraged at the internment of Kurt Jooss, Sigurd Leeder, and many other talented dancers and musicians at the Dartington Arts Centre, for no better reason than that Dartington came within one of the "protected" coastal zones that had just been proclaimed (see pp. 154–55).

His request was supported by all the senior PEP personalities. These particularly included Kenneth Lindsay MP (then at the Board of Education), PEP's former general secretary; the (to me) "incomparable" Max Nicholson (then in government war work), Lindsay's successor as general secretary and my first chief; Israel Sieff (of Marks and Spencer), PEP chairman before Elmhirst, a leading Zionist actively involved in rescuing from the Nazis and caring for fellow Jews; Sir Henry Bunbury (retired Comptroller of the Post Office), treasurer of the Czech Refugee Trust Fund, Chamberlain's conscience money for facilitating Hitler's annexation of the German-speaking provinces of Czechoslovakia (see pp. 53–4); and Professor (later Sir) Alexander Carr-Saunders, Director of the London School of Economics. He was enraged by the same problem as Elmhirst: the LSE, evacuated to Cambridge, together with Cambridge University itself, had also suddenly found itself in a protected coastal belt and had just witnessed a wholesale round-up of scholars, however eminent, and of many students who happened to be of "enemy" origin.

Over lunch in the club, or by other means, as news of my assignment spread, I was spurred on and offered help by many others. Among these I particularly recall three associated with my population research: Dr C. P. Blacker, who (among much else) directed the Eugenics Society and the Population Investigation Committee; Professor (later Sir) Noel Hall, first director of The National Institute of Economic and Social Research; and (Sir) Julian Huxley. Just outside this circle and equally eager to help were Tom Harrisson of Mass Observation (see pp. 165–67); Dr J. J.

Mallon, warden of Toynbee Hall; Eva Hubback, principal of Morley College; and Graham White, a Liberal MP involved with both Eleanor Rathbone and Col. Josiah Wedgwood in relentless daily questioning of Ministers in Parliament about what they were doing to refugees.

So encouraged, I set myself five aims: (1) to present the public with a clear factual picture of who the "enemy aliens" were; (2) to give an account of what was being done to them, a picture rapidly changing as I wrote and rewrote; (3) to explain why this was being done; (4) to set the British "enemy alien" problem in the wider political and philosophic context of Hitlerism and our war against it; and (5) to conclude with practical suggestions on what should be done.

I accomplished the first two aims by visiting all the agencies concerned with refugees, as listed in Chapter II, as well as numerous other knowledgeable persons. With virtually no exception I found them dismayed by what was happening and, thanks to the respect commanded by PEP, glad to supply whatever information they could. Bloomsbury House in London, with its chain of provincial centres (pp. 48–52), was the headquarters of all the main refugee welfare organisations. As I noted in this book (p. 159), "when a major crisis occurs the Bloomsbury House organisations show a marked preference for relying solely upon private representations to the appropriate authorities, coupled perhaps with questions in Parliament and a few letters in the Press. When they are up against a scandal they hesitate to make the facts public for fear it would jeopardise their relations with the authorities". But on this occasion I found among their staff key individuals who, guaranteed confidentiality, were prepared to keep me posted regularly with news of fresh developments in internment and deportation. I made similar arrangements with key people in the Free German League of Culture and the Austrian Centre (pp. 54–8 and 159–60), with both of which through my exiled friends I already had some acquaintance. Less formally I received a steady stream of data from PEP members and from Members of Parliament associated with the Parliamentary Committee on Refugees (pp. 59 and 78).

Help of a different kind came from a Fleet Street journalist, hitherto unknown to me and working, I think, on the *Daily Mail*, who volunteered to read through the files of the leading refugee-baiting newspapers for several years back in order to supply me with a chapter-and-verse portfolio of their record. That portfolio (regrettably now lost) gave me the material for my review (pp. 168–73) of this disgraceful episode in British journalism, including my denunciation of Beverley Nichols. This latter passage was queried by Penguin Books' lawyers (Rubinstein Nash) as possibly holding Nichols up to "hatred, ridicule and contempt", though they helpfully added: "Assuming the author has stated his facts correctly, I think any fair-minded jury . . . would accept a plea of fair comment on matters of public interest." (No action for this or a dozen other possible libels was ever brought.)

Without the active support of a network of committed helpers the book could not have been written. In that sense it was a collective enterprise; and I felt that I was writing it on behalf of all in England who were decent, well-informed and enlightened and who cherished our nation's good name. Among those helpers Eva Kolmer played a vital role. I had met – and come to respect – Eva through the circle of my Austrian exiled friends. The daughter of a leading Viennese medical man, Eva was herself a medical student when she escaped to England in 1938. In that same year, using the pen-name Mitzi Hartmann, she published in English a partly autobiographical book, *Austria Still Lives*,* which still makes good reading – an impressive feat for a woman of twenty-five writing in a foreign tongue. Combining a political history of post-Versailles Austria with an account of her own experiences in the Austrian socialist youth movement and under Dollfuss, Schuschnigg and eventually the Nazis, the book left her final political stance in doubt ("I am not perfectly explicit about myself"). But in 1940 there was no doubt: she had become a committed Communist – just when Communism had turned to ashes in my mouth.

This difference in ultimate political ideals in no way impaired our will to collaborate in an enterprise about which we completely agreed. Among the information sources that I needed to tap were the refugees' own organisations (pp. 53–8); and of these the Austrian Centre was much the most efficiently managed. In its management Eva, sitting on its executive committee, played a leading part. At the very outset I discussed with her, along with her friend Dr Walter Hollitscher (one of the Centre's two vice-presidents), both the scheme for the book and the practical problems of information-gathering about internment camps and

* Michael Joseph, 1938.

deportations – at a time when even the names and locations of the camps and the ships, if not official secrets, were certainly not published. Very quickly Eva and her colleagues (I never inquired exactly how) built up an intelligence service which, through local informants, smuggled out of every camp almost every day the latest news of what was happening; and through part of June and all July and August copies of these reports, typewritten on flimsy paper, were passed to me through Eva.

I had of course numerous other sources, but the major flow – in quality as well as quantity – streamed through this Austrian channel. It was thus for instance that I got the first detailed information about the *Arandora Star* tragedy, as well as the first survivor's account of what had happened, which at the last moment I was able to append to Chapter III (pp. 139–43). And this accounts for a distinctly Austrian flavour in some passages. Thus we now know that Italians were the main group on this torpedoed ship and that among the German-speaking refugees on board (i.e. omitting German seamen and other prisoners of war) more probably hailed from Germany than from Austria. Yet page 127, based on what I then knew via the Austrian Centre, might give the impression that Austrian refugees predominated.

Gathering raw material and ideas occupied me up to mid-July. I then wrote the book flat out in six weeks, with frequent revisions to encompass fresh developments, and despatched the script to Penguin Books on the last day of August. I had worked by day on the book at PEP. In the evenings I had produced it on my portable typewriter at home in Dulwich, often continuing to type after dark, when the nightly air raid started, in the Anderson shelter (a steel-roofed hole in the ground) in the back garden in the company of wife and friends.

The publishers acted with remarkable speed: the book was out nine weeks later. Nevertheless, impatient for instant publication, I found those weeks somewhat irksome, although they were fully taken up with proof-checking and revision, making last-minute insertions, making cuts (since the publishers found the book too long), dealing with lawyers' queries about possible libels, and getting the final product printed – in 50,000 copies – bound and into the shops, with prior circulation of review copies. When the book appeared in the first week of November 1940 – and PEP, fairly enough, had knocked my £50 advance on royalty payment off my salary and switched me to fresh duties – the great invasion panic was subsiding and a new Home Secretary, Herbert Morrison, was feeling his way towards reversing the policies denounced in the book.

In bringing about the reversal I should like to believe that my book did exert a significant influence. But I do not know that with any certainty; and it is a matter for others, not the author, to assess. What I do know is that the book was quickly and widely reviewed, that not a single review was unfavourable, and that it brought me a large fan mail from (among others) Members of Parliament and others well placed to influence policy.* The book was smuggled into the internment camps – where internees organised reading sessions – from the Isle of Man to Australia. There are to this day, I gather, still several copies in the Diplomatic Branch of the US National Archives in Washington. And the book still has connoisseurs elsewhere. In 1980 one of these, so the Archive Centre for the Austrian Resistance reported to me from Vienna, had purloined the Centre's copy of the book!

But what I cherish most of all is a three-inch strip of the barbed wire which surrounded the Onchan internment camp in the

---

* This fan mail included a letter from Sir Andrew McFadyean, a prominent Liberal and public servant, who persuaded me that there was no justification for the doubts I had voiced (see pp. 197–98) about the membership and behaviour of the "Category 19 Tribunal" – to which he had been appointed – established in September 1940 to review cases of interned refugees with unquestionable records of public opposition to the Nazis. He assured me – rightly – that he could "state without breach of confidence that you should find little difficulty in learning from other sources that we have adopted the most generous possible interpretation of the terms of our mandate". That apart, he praised my book unreservedly. He added: "My own profound conviction is that nothing short of a complete reversal of policy will either cure the evil or restore our own self-respect, and I hope that you will continue your good work. The enclosed copy of a memorandum which I wrote some time ago, and which had an extensive private circulation, may interest you as it is a compressed statement of a case which you have so ably argued."

I replied regretting that I had not seen this memorandum, circulated (but not to me) in August when I was writing the book: "Ever since I wrote that passage I have felt uneasy about it." In September 1940 I wrote:

"I was correcting the proofs in a tiny Welsh village at the foot of Snowdon when I read one morning of the appointment of your tribunal. I was cut off from my customary sources of information . . . I had to insert a passage into the proofs at once, and so I wrote those rather unfortunate sentences to which you rightly object."

Isle of Man. On his release the writer and journalist, the late Heinrich Fraenkel (whom I had not previously known), presented this memento to me in a little cigar box on behalf of his fellow internees. That symbol of their "chains" has remained on display in my study bookcase ever since.

François Lafitte

Birmingham
April 1988

The Internment of Aliens

CONTENTS

5

CONTENTS

To

MR. HERBERT MORRISON,

Home Secretary and Minister of Home Security, formerly Ruler of London, in the hope that he will succeed where his predecessor, SIR JOHN ANDERSON, formerly Ruler of Bengal, has failed.

FOREWORD

THIS book is primarily a historical record. It attempts to describe the history of German and Austrian refugees in Britain from the outbreak of war down to August, 1940, and especially to describe how refugees were treated when the Government began interning them in May, 1940. But I attempt also to analyse the reasons for the official attitude to " enemy aliens," to suggest a better attitude, and to make constructive proposals for giving expression to that attitude. As a history this book tells a lamentable story of muddle and stupidity ; as a critique it attempts to show that the " refugee problem " now facing us in wartime is really a *British* problem, a problem of justice and personal freedom in which the reputation of Britain is involved. Fear and ignorance produced an anti-foreign scare in Britain in May-July, 1940, the results of which have been highly damaging. Fully recognising the urgency of the military situation after the collapse of France, and the difficulties confronting our authorities in a time of national peril, much of this book is nevertheless devoted to describing the effects of quite unnecessary panic and pig-headedness. It is not a pretty picture. But a mild injection of panic is not a bad thing, provided we understand what is happening and how to overcome it. It can serve to inoculate us against the real thing—the foul disease of demoralisation that paralyses a people's will to resist, inhibits all initiative, and leads straight to disintegration and defeat. If we look at this ugly picture with sober eyes and cool minds we shall learn one vital lesson : to discriminate intelligently between our friends and our foes.

Probably the book contains errors of fact or of interpretation. I have done my best to avoid such errors. If they are present, it will be mainly the fault of those who try to hush up unpleasant happenings because to publish the facts would be " doing Goebbels's work." There never was a more fatuous

9

argument. Anyone who commits or tolerates injustice is doing Goebbels's work. To conceal injustice is to help those who do Goebbels's work, for it prevents public opinion from insisting on a remedy of the injustice. The best proof that a democracy is active and virile is that it can tolerate public discussion of abuses and wrongdoings, and that it is prepared to remedy its shortcomings. I have striven earnestly to make sure of my facts, to break through the smoke-screen of secrecy which surrounds internment conditions, and to write down my conclusions objectively. I cannot claim to be impartial as well as objective. Writing this book was an education for me, as I hope reading it will prove an education for the reader. My indignation and amazement grew steadily stronger as I probed deeper into my subject and fresh facts came to light. And so my book takes sides—for common sense and personal freedom against panic and arbitrary arrest.

For the material used in this book I have to thank a large number of officials of refugee organisations, released refugees, Members of Parliament, civil servants, journalists, colleagues and friends. About half of these wish to remain anonymous, so I shall not name the other half. For the patient way in which these busy men and women provided me with information, checked my facts and criticised my manuscripts, they have my deepest gratitude. But they are in no way responsible for the opinions or the proposals of this book, which are my own.

F. L.

Beddgelert,
        September 14, 1940.

CHAPTER I

THE NATURE OF THE REFUGEE PROBLEM

1.—*Who is Hitler Fighting?*

THE Nazi war did not begin in 1939 when Hitler overran Poland, nor in 1933 when he seized power, nor even in 1920 when the Nazi Party was founded. There were " Nazis of the soul " long before the German Nazi movement began, and they were not, and are not to-day, to be found only in one country. Since 1918 especially Europe has more and more become split into two warring camps—the camp of anti-democratic authoritarianism and the camp of democratic tolerance and (implicitly) of social progress. This division of Europe has long existed. In the nineteenth century it took the form primarily of a division between reactionary and progressive States. Since 1918 it has increasingly assumed the form of an international civil war.

The peoples of Western Europe have been very slow in grasping this transformation of international relations. The traditional way of thinking of politics, international affairs and warfare in terms of nation States, coupled with the fact that in every country the growing reactionary movements were—in appearance—violently nationalist, impeded a quick under-standing of the fact that the new division of Europe cuts across all accepted national frontiers.

Reactionary totalitarianism scored its first major triumph when Mussolini's Blackshirts seized power in Italy, and pro-ceeded to stamp out the co-operative, trade union and socialist movements, the liberal and conservative parties, and to destroy all forms of parliamentary and local self-government. Every-one in those early days saw clearly that it was not the Italian nation as a whole which had gone violently militarist and chauvinist. It was generally admitted that a group of brutal and unscrupulous adventurers and demagogues who had gathered around them a movement of deluded ex-soldiers and malcontents, backed by industrialists and big landowners, had succeeded in establishing a reactionary dictatorship against the wishes of probably the majority of Italians, by the simple method of abandoning all decency and murdering or torturing all who opposed them.   But because the Fascist counter-revolution assumed an intensely nationalist and " patriotic " form, and loudly proclaimed that Fascism was not for export, the peoples of Western Europe tended to regard it as a purely internal affair for the Italians.   The international implications of Fascism were not grasped, and, apart from the Labour Movement and Liberals who read the *Manchester Guardian*, events in Italy aroused feelings of sympathy for the Italian people, rather than solidarity with them.

The coming to power of the Nazis in Germany aroused far greater apprehension.   The nationalism of the German counter-revolution was so bellicose as to produce a real fear that it might end in war.   Yet even those who feared a war of revenge tended for the most part to think of it as a war of the German *nation* against other *nations*, rather than a *Nazi* war against the lovers of freedom in all countries, including Germany.   Thinking in terms of nations still prevented a full appreciation of the changing character of European reaction. The Nazis had a so much greater popular movement behind them than the Fascists in Italy that many people tended to forget that the Nazis too had never won a majority of votes in a free election, and were also, like the Fascists, waging a savage and ruthless war against a large section of the German people. There was, moreover, a very powerful feeling that Britain and France, through the unjust provisions of the Versailles Treaty, were partly to blame for the triumph of the Nazis in Germany. The Nazi counter-revolution tended to be regarded as nothing more than an extreme reaction of the German nation against oppressive conditions for which we were partly to blame.   All these considerations helped to perpetuate the belief that, even though Nazism might threaten a new world war, it was nevertheless largely an internal affair of the German nation.

British official policy after the rise of Hitler was able to make use of this confused state of public opinion to encourage the Nazi Government and to assist it to strengthen its grip upon the German people.   Both in Britain and France men of power and privilege used their influence to ensure that nothing effective was done to prevent aggression by the Nazis and

later by the Axis because they hoped to guide aggression east-
wards in the belief that it would " save Europe from Bolshevism."
In Britain the Marquess of Londonderry, an outspoken and
influential inspirer of this policy, was arguing as late as 1938
that between Britain and Germany " there is a racial connection which in itself establishes a primary friendly feeling
between us which cannot be said to exist between us and the
French." He argued further that, although " we must have a
close understanding with the French," there was no need for
" complete concurrence in French international policy."

" Our Foreign Office appears to condone the associations
with Communism and Bolshevism through our affiliation
with France,* while paying but little regard to the robust
attitude of Germany, Italy and Japan which wholeheartedly
condemn Bolshevism and Communism. . . . That Germany,
Italy and Japan condemn Bolshevism is an attitude of mind
which is not properly appreciated in this country. We may
perhaps think we can afford to ignore Bolshevism as incapable of disturbing our political equilibrium because the
conditions in which Bolshevism prospers are practically
non-existent in this country. We fail to recognise that the
present condition of Spain is mainly the result of Red
machinations. We console ourselves with the reflection
that, owing to the Conservatism of the French peasant,
Bolshevism will not prevail to any serious extent amongst
the urban industrial population of France, although the
Communist representation in the Chamber has increased to
the number which Herr Hitler personally prophesied to me
over two years ago.

" Belgium is showing signs of Bolshevism, and *Germany
sees herself surrounded by Bolshevist countries and militarily
and economically hemmed in with what may well be disastrous
consequences*. We watch this movement with a strange
equanimity. We throw in our weight under ' non-inter-
vention ' on the side of the Reds in Spain, Belgium and
France do the same, and we wonder why Germany and
Italy appear more truculent and challenging as their strength
and prestige increase. . . . Why not make up our minds

* That is, through the Pacts of Mutual Assistance which France
had signed with the Soviet Union and Czechoslovakia, and which
were torn up at Munich later in the year.

that we condemn and oppose the international doctrine of Communism ? "*

Fritz Thyssen, the German Steel King, who was one of Hitler's most important financial backers, poured several millions of marks into the Nazi Party funds on the understanding that the Nazi regime should fight " Bolshevism." Now that Hitler has broken his contract by attacking Britain and France, Thyssen has fled abroad, whence he issues statements denouncing the *Führer* for breaking his word. The Thyssens and the Londonderrys in all countries are now—since the German–Soviet Pact—seeing the error of their ways. The Chamberlain policy of strengthening Hitler to fight " Bolshevism," of appeasing aggressors through approval of their apparent social and political objectives and in the secret hope of guiding their aggression in a certain direction, has ended in disaster. It has broken down because it misunderstood the nature of the " Bolshevism " that Hitler is fighting. National-Socialism may or may not be antagonistic to the political and economic system of the Soviet Union ; but to the Nazis " Bolshevism " includes the fundamental values of all culture and civilisation—the belief in the value of the individual personality, in freedom of thought, speech and government, in the " rule of law " and " fair play," in the impartiality of justice, tolerance, equality of opportunity and peace.

Yet it is only in the course of the present war itself that we are coming fully to appreciate the significance of the totalitarian international. The Fifth Columns led by Seyss-Inquart in Austria and by Henlein in the Sudeten territory, were not simply " nationalist " phenomena among German-speaking communities wishing to rejoin their Reich. Captain Vidkun Quisling, Commander of the Order of the British Empire until he betrayed Norway, is not a German nationalist ; nor are Mussert in Holland, Laval, Bonnet, Flandin, Tardieu in France, or the Czech and Slovak leaders who assisted the Nazi seizure of Czecho-Slovakia. These men are natives of their own countries, super-" patriots " who betray their countries, " Nazis of the soul."

The collapse of five countries in seventy-two days of *Blitzkrieg* aided by internal treachery has now made it as clear as

* Marquess of Londonderry: *Ourselves and Germany* (1938. Penguin Special, No. S21).

daylight that National-Socialism, its Fascist jackal and all who secretly admire or encourage anti-democratic reaction in all countries, including Britain, are the enemies of all in Europe, whatever their nationality, race or religion, who believe in freedom, tolerance and common decency. *In this sense the war is not a war of conflicting nations (although this is its outward form), but an international civil war. Hitler's allies and Hitler's enemies are to be found in every country.* There are " Nazis of the soul " and there are bold, freedom-loving spirits in every country engaged in the present conflict. Wherever they mee they are on opposite sides. The division cuts right across all frontiers, all accepted divisions of nationality. An understanding of this principle and its implications is fundamental to any sensible handling of the " aliens " problem in our own country.

2.—*Hitler's Victims*

It is useful at this stage to remind the reader of the methods used by the Nazis against their own " aliens " and of the type of people who were made the scapegoats of German reaction.

The Jews were the main, but by no means the only, victims. The German Jewish community was economically ruined by a " cold pogrom " lasting over years, th e main features of which were expropriation, trade boycott, direct prohibition of working in various trades and professions, and looting and wrecking of shops and dwellings. Jewish cultural activity was largely brought to a standstill, synagogues destroyed, the Jews themselves debarred from the normal cultural facilities of civilised people, branded and reduced to a laughing stock. Many smaller towns and villages drove out all their Jews and proudly proclaimed themselves *judenrein*.

Out of innumerable cases of revolting brutality we mention two which were the causes of major refugee movements out of the Reich : the Vienna pogrom in the spring of 1938, and the great pogrom which began in the winter of the same year. When the Nazis seized Austria Goering announced in Vienna : " We don't like Jews and they don't like us. We will make them glad to go away." They did. The terror unleashed upon the 170,000 Jews of Vienna was so ghastly that in April, 1938, Jews were committing suicide at the rate of 130 a day, and in one single day in July 800 are said to have taken their lives. At least 7,000 suicides are estimated for the first four months of Nazi occupation. Many readers will remember the following instance of the " wandering Jews on the Danube," described by Louis Golding :

> " Fifty-one were put on a breakwater in the Danube, near the Czechoslovakian border, without food or money. . . . Czechs rescued them and provided them with temporary shelter and food ; but they could not venture to let them have permanent hospitality, and so deported them to Hungary, who in turn sent some back to Austria.   Others were shipped on a barge and were afloat for weeks on the Danube, a human flotsam and jetsam, until at last they were allowed to anchor outside a Hungarian river port.   (The Middle Ages were kinder, when Viennese Jews placed on the Danube in oarless boats were at least suffered to disembark when at last they drifted ashore)."*

These outcasts were finally allowed to enter Palestine and start a new life.   They were fortunate.

The pogrom of the winter of 1938 began with the mass expulsion of Jews across the German frontiers in October and November.   Jews of Polish origin, for example, were rounded up all over Germany, many clad only in night attire, and driven across the German-Polish frontier.   Fifteen thousand Jews, including 2,000 children, were marched across the frontier, driven from behind by soldiers with machine-guns.   On October 29, 7,000 were left stranded in no-man's land between the German and Polish frontiers at Zbonszyn.   A man who went through it all, and who later came as a refugee to England, described his experience of the first week thus :

> " On Friday, October 28th, at five o'clock in the morning, we were dragged from our beds and arrested. . . . Since the prisons were already overcrowded with Polish Jews we and many hundred others had to stand in the pouring rain in the prison yard.   Here an ' S.S.' leader addressed us and informed us that we had been ejected and would be deported from Germany at seven o'clock in the evening.   We were not allowed to return home.   And thus we had to quit

* Louis Golding: *The Jewish Problem* (1938, Penguin Special, No. S10).

Germany with only the clothes we wore. All our linen, furniture and money we had to leave behind in Germany to be confiscated by the Gestapo.

" In a cattle truck we were transported, and for hours we sat or stood tortured by hunger and cold. From the German frontier ' Neu Beuschen ' to the Polish border, a distance of ten kilometres, was covered by us on foot. . . .

" Hardly had we stepped off the train when we were pushed, driven, chased and beaten. To the right and left German soldiers with fixed bayonets on their rifles marched, and the rear was covered by a detachment with machine-guns. . . .

" We finally reached the Polish border, exhausted. Old men and women, children and sick collapsed and dropped, remaining lying where they fell without any medical attention. The Polish soldiers did not let us proceed, and so our contingent of about 8,000 people from Hamburg, Berlin. Cologne and Essen had to remain in the forest there.

" Nobody attended us, the pangs of hunger and cold demanded always further victims. We are now in a small border village for the last eight days guarded by Polish troops. . . . We are quartered in stables. In two stables where ordinarily 100 horses were kept, now 8,000 human beings have to camp. We sleep here, terribly cramped, on straw, freezing in a dreadful cold.

" We have very little to eat. In the morning and in the evening we get from an aid committee one slice of bread and a little soup, which does not satisfy our hunger. . . .

" The number of sick rises rapidly. They are housed in tents lying on straw. Seven tents are already filled and a further ten tents are just being erected. A hospital does not exist here. Many develop stomach trouble due to bad and insufficient nourishment.

" But the number of typhoid cases has soon reached the 100 mark. The water in our camp is undrinkable, being contaminated. But since no other water is available, from utter despair the people drink it."*

This was written after one week. Five thousand of these miserable outcasts remained at Zbonszyn for over two months,

* " A Man Writes in Despair from a Stable," *News Chronicle*, November 14, 1938.

assisted by Polish-Jewish relief agencies which collected funds from all over the world.   On December 20th the *News Chronicle* correspondent in Zbonszyn reported :

> "An eleven-day-old baby was frozen to death to-day in a provisional shelter in ' No Man's Land ' at Zbonszyn, on the Polish-German frontier where 5,000 Jewish refugees, driven out of Germany on October 28, are still living. The child's mother was severely frost-bitten and taken to hospital.   They were found lying on a straw sack in the shelter.
>
> " Twenty-seven other children kept in a children's home are reported to have lost limbs owing to frost-bite, and the whole camp population is suffering terribly from the frost, which is reaching 30 degrees (Centigrade) below zero (equal to 54 Fahrenheit degrees of frost).
>
> "About 2,000 people are crowded in an old stable with only one stove to keep them warm.   Five hundred are living in an old mill with no heating facilities whatever. . . . Three hundred are reported to be suffering severe hunger in Drawski Mlyn, near Zbonszyn.   They have to walk four miles in the cold to fetch such food as they can get.   About 1,100 of the refugees are reported to have fallen ill in the last two days."

The following *News Chronicle* report from Berlin on November 15, 1938, shows how people became refugees :

> " Invalid Jews in Berlin, it is reported, are dying from want of medical attendance, as their doctors have been taken to concentration camps.   Weeping women, some with children, stand outside the British Consulate and beg British subjects : ' Can't you get me a visa ?   Can I go to England ? ' "

But Jews are not Nazi Germany's only " aliens."   Political opponents of every description were equally savagely dealt with.   " Shot while trying to escape," " committed suicide," such were the formulæ which covered the deaths of thousands of Hitler's political opponents.   Gerhart Seger, who knew Oranienburg Camp from the inside, gives an account of conditions there which has been summarised by E. O. Lorimer :

> " The dark cells were stone-floored cubicles painted black

inside, with only such light and air as came from a small grill in the door. At most they could hold three or four men, but fourteen were crowded in, and would be kept there twenty-three hours out of twenty-four, for four and a half weeks. The oldest of the Friedrichstal men was confined for twenty-eight days in such a cell after his seventeen-hour march (barefooted). This form of 'strict arrest' was too luxurious. Schäfer (the commandant) invented the upright, stone coffin. The floor-space of this cell was less than 2 feet by 2 feet 6 inches. A man could just stand upright, unable to stoop, unable to move leg or arm, bearing the whole weight of his own body in one unalterable position. After fourteen hours of it, he emerged half mad, his knees cut to pieces from sagging against the stone. Neumann spent eight days and eight nights in one of these stone coffins. . . .

"A man would be thrashed, taken half dead to a cell, made to attach a halter to a hook provided, while the warder left him with a recommendation to lose no time in using it. Every step outside might portend another flogging, and at intervals the cover of the peep-hole would be shot back with the mocking question : ' What, not hanged yet ? ' One man in Oranienburg was flogged nine nights in succession until he attempted suicide."*

The story of Pastors Niemöller and Müller, in the parish of Dahlem near Berlin, who struggled to maintain a free Lutheran Church against the Nazi propaganda machine which calls itself the " German Christian Church," is an inspiring epic of that better Germany which not even to-day has been extinguished. Dr. Niemöller's long struggle for religious freedom culminated in March, 1938, with his acquittal before a civil Court on the charge of " underhand attacks on the State and Party." The verdict was, in fact, a vindication of the whole " Confessional Movement " within the Lutheran Church. Released by the Court he was promptly arrested by the Gestapo and sent to Sachsenhausen Camp. There he was presented with a " contract " undertaking to renounce his Dahlem living and to refrain from " all political activity." If he signed he could, go free. He did not sign.

* E. O. Lorimer : *What Hitler Wants* (1939, Penguin Special, No. S13).

Dr. Müller, rightful head of the " Provisional Administration " of the Church (which the Nazis would not recognise), took Niemöller's place at Dahlem.   Many of his fellow pastors suffered persecution and imprisonment.   At the time of the Munich crisis in September, 1938, Müller and his colleagues conducted peace services in their churches.   Müller attacked the morals of leading Nazis and stressed the fact that the German people were being forced into war by the Nazi leaders. On Dr. Niemöller's forty-seventh birthday in January, 1939, Dr. Müller preached in Dahlem denouncing Hitler's " German Christian Church " as the " whore of the Government. . . . What is the use of a Church that is bludgeoned by decrees ? . . . Pastor Niemöller will know that his parish is gathered at this hour to think of him in his solitude and confinement." For these " crimes " Dr. Müller was brought up for trial in February, 1939.   On his birthday Niemöller, the ardent German patriot who had been a U-boat commander and became a minister out of deep inner conviction, was released for half an hour to see his wife and his brother.   He attempted to send his children to England, but the Nazis forbade this.

Such atrocity stories could be repeated a thousand times over about the treatment of leaders of all German political parties, trade union officials, religious leaders and clergymen of all denominations, members of local authorities, civil servants, any German who had distinguished himself in any way by opposition to reaction or advocacy of tolerance and free speech.

Writers, artists, scientists, men of learning of every description suffered heavily.   Hitler's movement has always been afraid of " intellectuals " because it glorifies the irrational and cannot tolerate argument.   Nazis " think with their blood " because they are afraid of the integrity of the educated human mind.   Symbolically Hitler's reign of terror began with the ceremonial burning of " un-German " books.   This was followed by the persecution of their writers.   There began that exodus of men and women of talent in every field of art and learning that has denuded Germany of its finest minds and reduced the intellectual life of the German universities to a low ebb.

It has been estimated, according to Melvin Rader, that

" of the one hundred writers who were most highly regarded before the advent of Hitler only twelve are now living within

Germany. Even if one includes, to be completely objective, the most famous Nazi authors, Hitler, Rosenberg, and Goebbels, the number is only fifteen. Of the eleven writers who enjoyed the greatest international reputation before Hitler's advent, only two are still living within German boundaries. These estimates are based upon purely objective criteria— the size of the editions, the number of translations and the number of reviews exceeding fifty lines."*

What applies to writers applies also to almost every field of endeavour. To be a refugee became an honourable profession. Whether they ·were humble, inoffensive persons, wishing only to be useful citizens and good neighbours, or whether they were men and women with outstanding achievements to their credit, the refugees from Germany and Austria were, and remain, citizens of that other better Germany which Hitler is striving to destroy. Only a small minority of those who hate Hitler were able to get away, both because it was difficult for them to leave German territory and because it was equally difficult to enter the territory of any other country.†

3. *The Flight from the Nazis*

Beginning as a steady trickle the flow of Hitler's " aliens " out of Germany became a flood after the invasion of Austria in March, 1938. The flood has not ceased through the whole course of the war. Although we choose to give the name of " friendly aliens " to the war-time refugees from the most recent countries to suffer Nazi aggression—the Poles, the Norwegians, the Dutch, the Belgians and the French—the new refugee problem is not essentially different from that of the " enemy aliens " who fled in peace-time from Germany and Austria, or the " friendly aliens " who fled from Czechoslovakia. The distinction between " peace-time " and " war-time " refugees is in fact largely erroneous. Many of the refugees from Holland, Belgium and France were themselves men and women who had previously fled from Germany and Austria or from Czechoslovakia to find shelter in a friendly

* Melvin Rader : *No Compromise : The Conflict between Two Worlds* (1939), quoting Lion Feuchtwanger.
† Further details of how Hitler's " aliens " are treated will be found in the British White Paper.

country. In any case, all groups of refugees have fled from Hitler's war against freedom. It was not peace-time for any of them ; it was only peace-time for us until Hitler was ready to include us in his war.

This book deals, however, primarily with the so-called " enemy aliens." We have shown that Hitler's victims needed little encouragement to take leave either of their country or indeed of the world. Stripped of their possessions, of their citizen rights, of their nationality, they were in thousands of cases literally thrust out over the frontiers of the Third Reich. In thousands of other cases, when would-be emigrants were given time to prepare their departure, the obstacles to be overcome were innumerable. They could take only a few shillings with them, and few countries were anxious to admit penniless refugees. To gain visas for foreign countries—even transit visas—they had to find sponsors in those countries, either benevolent individuals or charitable societies, who would undertake full financial responsibility for them, to prevent them becoming a charge on public funds. Few of those who wished to leave had friends or connections in other countries. Nevertheless, willy-nilly, legally or illegally, when it was a matter of life and death, they did get out. In the five years from Hitler's rise to power to December, 1937, probably about 150,000 refugees left Germany, most of them through the magnificent work organised by Jewish relief societies out of their own funds. The flood which followed the seizure of Austria and Czechoslovakia and the terrible pogrom of the winter of 1938–39 resulted in a wave of emigration amounting to nearly another 150,000 in the twenty months before the outbreak of war.

In the early months of 1939 the Press was full of stories of boatloads of Jewish refugees wandering around the world in search of a " port without a visa." Shanghai was the only one, and thousands were finally dumped there. A typical case is that of the Hamburg-America liner *St. Louis*, which sailed to Cuba in June, 1939, bearing 922 Jewish refugees who had spent their last pennies to escape from the Third Reich. Arrived at Havana, they were refused permission to land. The husband of one woman on the ship had already settled in Cuba, with all their furniture and belongings. His wife was not allowed to land, although she had paid 160 dollars to get a landing permit. During the liner's ten days' stay in

Havana harbour the husband three times came alongside in a small canoe and spoke to his wife and his two little children through a porthole. Relatives of other refugees on the ship did the same. Finally came a cable from the shipping company's Hamburg head office instructing the captain : " If unable to land alternative port return Germany immediately." Two refugees committed suicide on the spot. A refugee doctor severed a vein and was carried ashore on a stretcher. On leaving Havana 100 refugees (mostly men) decided to throw themselves overboard if they were forced to return to Germany. Captain Schroeder had to maintain an armed watch day and night to prevent this. An attempt to land in the Dominican Republic failed, because the Dominican Government required £100 landing tax per person. The ship then wandered around the Gulf of Mexico and finally made for Hamburg, where the passengers were to be sent to the hell of a concentration camp. Three days off Cherbourg came the good news that Britain, France, Belgium and Holland had agreed to offer the refugees a temporary haven. Transhipped in mid-stream at Antwerp, the contingent destined for England set sail. That is how 249 Jewish outcasts from Nazi Germany arrived in this country two months before war broke out. Pending a final settlement of their ultimate destination, they were maintained at the expense of Jewish charities.

Not all these stories ended so happily.

Of the third of a million refugees from the Nazi terror who succeeded in escaping abroad prior to the outbreak of war, only about 70,000 were actually in Britain when war broke out. A somewhat larger number had passed through Britain, possibly staying a year or two, on their way to other countries, but it must be frankly stated that Britain's record in providing a haven of refuge to the persecuted of other countries has not, of recent years, been impressive. A very large proportion of the 70,000 refugees who were caught here at the outbreak of war were in fact on their way to other countries. Over 5,000 of them did, in fact, re-emigrate from Britain between September, 1939, and the end of April, 1940, as their plans for re-emigration matured (most of them were waiting in Britain for their turn to come on the U.S.A. immigration quota ; others were intending to proceed to Palestine). Very few had been admitted into this country with permission to settle down and start a new life in a peaceful, tolerant atmosphere.

In the early part of 1939, when the great pogrom was proceeding in Germany, there was a general demand in Britain
for refugees to be allowed to enter *en masse*, and put into
interim internment camps until they could be sorted out and
their ultimate fate decided.   It was argued that this was the
only way—in co-operation with other countries—to save the
lives of the thousands who were threatened with massacre in
Germany.   If they had to wait until they could find financial
guarantors in Britain and then go through all the red tape of
getting British visas (which often took three to six months of
negotiating), many of them would never survive to leave
Germany.   But the Government definitely refused to depart
from the method of " individual infiltration " and continued
to insist that the number of refugees admitted must be limited
by the capacity of voluntary organisations to select, receive
and maintain them.   Regulations were relaxed somewhat, the
granting of visas speeded up and admissions made somewhat
easier.   The Government had many difficulties which must
not be overlooked ; on the other hand, it is impossible to avoid
the conclusion arrived at by Sir John Hope Simpson in his
monumental and objective study of the refugee problem,
published early in 1939 :

" Great Britain's record in the admission of refugees is
not distinguished if it be compared with that of France,
Czechoslovakia or the United States of America.   The
strictly enforced restrictive and selective policy of immigration which she has pursued since the war,* particularly the
emphasis placed on the admission only of aliens with economic resources adequate for their re-establishment, has
kept the number of admissions to figures that have little
significance in the total numbers of post-war refugees.   The
one possible exception to this generalisation, the admission
of Jewish refugees from Germany, is the result of the extraordinary effort and generosity of the Jewish community in
Great Britain in undertaking unconditional responsibility for
their support.
" Great Britain has played a more prominent part in the
general international work for refugees. . . . It is doubtful,
however, if this international work, largely personal and

* i.e. The war of 1914–18.

periodic, is a sufficient contribution when measured by the standard of that made by other countries. Owing to the excessively cautious post-war immigration policy, Great Britain has ceased to be a country of asylum on a large scale. Her initiative and role in international work would be greatly strengthened if she could show a braver record as a country of sanctuary."*

Such is the sober judgment of one of our greatest authorities on " aliens " problems. Possibly it was an advantage to have such a small number of " enemy aliens " in our country after war broke out. Since there are inevitably a number of doubtful cases among the great mass of genuine refugees from the Third Reich, the small number of " enemy aliens " in our country is no doubt an advantage when we have to track down actual or potential enemy agents among them. The problem is far simpler than that which France, Belgium or Holland had to face, both because our " enemy aliens " are few and because they have been far more carefully sifted and checked, both before and after admission into this country, than were the refugees in France and the Low Countries. But the very fact that our " enemy alien " problem is so much smaller and simpler than that of other countries surely makes it all the more imperative that we should adopt an intelligent attitude to the problem and not lose our heads. Hitler's " aliens " problem is colossal. He has enslaved " aliens " by the million in Poland, Czechoslovakia, France, Belgium, Holland, Denmark and Norway. Yet he is able to use those " aliens," most of whom are bitterly hostile (unlike our own), to manufacture his tanks and aeroplanes in Czech arms factories, to grow his food (Danish, Dutch and Polish farm-workers are being drafted into German agriculture), and even to build his fortifications (the Siegfried Line was built by conscripted labour which included large numbers of anti-Nazi Austrians). Compared with Hitler's problem ours is minute. We have " ceased to be a country of asylum on a large scale." Let us at any rate be sensible about those refugees we *have* welcomed to our shores.

* Sir John Hope Simpson : *The Refugee Problem* (1939).

4. *The Anti-Foreign Scare*

The policy of " intern the lot," which was inaugurated in mid-May, 1940, *and which has caused so much needless suffering and dislocation, was not due to anything that any of our " enemy aliens " had done or to any change in their attitude towards us.* This is freely admitted by Government spokesmen, but has not been clearly understood by the public. The " intern the lot " policy was mainly adopted because certain military chiefs and certain Ministers succumbed to momentary panic when all the defences of Holland and Belgium proved to be of no avail against Fifth-Column activities and parachute troops (*see* Ch. IV, Section 3).

The anti-foreign scare which followed, and which captured a large section of the public for some weeks, was mainly due to two factors. In the first place, the true significance of events on the Continent was *not* explained to the public. At a critical stage in the development of the war our leaders failed to face up to one of their responsibilities as leaders. They made no attempt to educate the public by putting the plain facts before it, in spite of the fact that an entire Ministry of Information was there to do the job. They allowed a widespread feeling to grow up, directed against *all* foreigners, but especially against the unfortunate " enemy aliens," without making any real effort to stress the fact that most " enemy aliens " are neither enemies nor even suspect (*see* Ch. IV, Section 2). They unwittingly encouraged the growth of antiforeign feeling by the rather mysterious and definitely wholesale and indiscriminate manner in which the internment round-ups were organised.

Mr. Peake (Under-Secretary for the Home Department) has himself explained how *the mere fact of internment creates suspicion*. On July 10, 1940, he explained that the Government had not " interned the lot " at the outbreak of war, amongst other reasons because

" the mere internment of an individual creates suspicion about him in the minds of those who know him. In the second place, when I reflect upon the number of letters that I got from the general public and from Members of this House protesting about the internment of the few hundreds that we did intern, I confess that I am terrified at the thought

of what my correspondence might have been had we gone in
for general internment."

The second part of this statement bears out our assertion
that public opinion was, prior to the collapse of Holland, on
the whole, friendly to " enemy aliens."

The second reason why a large section of the public temporarily lost its sense of discrimination is to be found in the
behaviour of a section of the Press (unchecked by any hint
from official quarters). Certain newspapers went out of their
way to treat the internment round-ups in a lurid fashion.
Headlines such as " Police swoop on aliens and Fifth
Columnists " were freely used. There is evidence that some
newspapers systematically fostered anti-foreign feeling by
inflammatory articles and misleading news items, and that
this was done in many cases by men with uneasy consciences.
Both in the Press and in public speeches certain gentlemen
whose pro-Nazi views were notorious in peacetime were
among the loudest in the clamour to " intern the lot."
Protestations of super-patriotism in this cheap and easy form
have often been the rather obvious defence-mechanism resorted
to by men about whose patriotism there was some doubt
(see Ch. IV, Section 2).

There is yet another factor, the importance of which is
difficult to assess. We cannot escape the conclusion that more
is involved in this matter than public ignorance and panic in
high quarters. We cannot blind ourselves to the fact that an
authoritarian trend has been developing recently in our home
life, a trend which manifests itself not merely in the treatment
of " enemy aliens," but also in the indefinite detention in
custody of British citizens without charge or trial, in attempts
at widespread censorship of opinion (ranging from wholesale
threats to the freedom of the Press to silly prosecutions for
" insulting words and behaviour " and for spreading " alarm
and despondency ") and in other ways. In this sense the
" enemy aliens " problem cannot be dissociated from the
problem of the British community itself, in its struggle for
personal liberty, democracy and a new order (see Ch. IV,
Section 4).

Such, in our opinion, are the main causes of the stupid and
ill-conceived policy of indiscriminate internment and deportation of " enemy aliens " which took place in May, June and

July of 1940.   The damage—moral still more than material—
which has been done is considerable.   In Chapters III and IV
we attempt to assess the extent of this damage, and sub-
stantiate in detail the statements made in this section.

5. *The Fundamental Issue*

Now that public common sense is reasserting itself, and
pressure of well-informed opinion is compelling the Government—as happens in a democratic country—to modify its
attitude, we can look back on our period of panic and consider
its lessons.

The basic problem that arises is to decide whom *we* are
fighting against.   Are we fighting the Germans as a people, the
Austrians as a people, the Italians as a people?   Or are we
fighting Nazis and Fascists wherever we meet them, all who
seek to reduce the whole of Europe to a condition of slavery,
whatever their nationality or mother-tongue?   Do we regard
every German, Austrian and Italian as our enemy, or do we
believe that in every country there are people who think like
us and who are *not* our enemies?

The collapse of France has made an answer to these questions
an issue of supreme importance.   The leaders of France have
betrayed their own country and left Britain to fight alone.
But our Government is perfectly aware that there are *two*
Frances—the France of the traitors and pro-Fascists, the
counterparts of the men who betrayed Germany to Hitler,
and the France of the people, which loves freedom, peace and
social justice.   Our Government knows that millions of
Frenchmen are hoping and praying for the destruction of
Hitlerism and its French agents, and are straining every nerve
to hamper the enemy from within.   Our Government recognises General de Gaulle as " Leader of all Free Frenchmen."*
It also recognises the existence of two Belgiums, two Hollands,
two Norways, and two Polands.   Even the Czechs and

* Sir Archibald Sinclair, Air Minister, told Parliament on
August 15, 1940, that Prince Starhemberg was an officer in General
de Gaulle's Air Force.   Starhemberg was a leading Austrian Fascist
who conspired with Mussolini to destroy Austrian freedom.   At a
later stage he was prepared to come to terms with Hitler over the
surrender of his country to the Nazi Reich.   Mr. John Parker,
M.P., asked the Air Minister whether he was aware of " the unfortunate effect this appointment would have among the democratic
people of Austria."

Abyssinians, who have never been Britain's allies in battle (in fact, the British Government threatened military action *against* Czechoslovakia during the Munich crisis) are now recognised as " friendly aliens." In January, 1939, Mr. Chamberlain drank to the health of the " King of Italy *and Emperor of Ethiopia* " in Rome, but now Mr. Churchill has rushed Haile Selassie out to Khartoum to encourage by his nearness Abyssinian resistance to Fascist domination.

All these things are done, and yet our Government will not recognise that Germany, Austria and Italy also contain their " friendly aliens," men and women whose entire outlook on life chimes in with that of the British people, who are, therefore " aliens " to all that Nazi-Fascist tyranny represents. Because we are fighting barbaric dictators whose native tongues are German and Italian, must we therefore regard all who speak German and Italian as their supporters and abettors ? Do we really believe that there is some magic about German and Italian which makes those who speak these tongues automatically into enemies of freedom, and some magic about the English language which makes us, who speak it, of necessity lovers of peace and justice ? Have we abandoned all hope of *any* goodness surviving in the hearts of any Germans, Austrians or Italians ? Apparently our Government has done so. In his reply to Hitler on July 22, Lord Halifax said in his broadcast speech that " in Germany the people have given their consciences to Hitler, so that people have become machines, merely fulfilling orders without considering whether they are right or wrong." Our Foreign Secretary seems to have lost all hope of the German people. Although he appeals to " all those who love truth and justice and freedom " as allies, he does not, apparently, believe that any considerable number of such people remain in Germany.

This pessimism is not justified. There are thousands upon thousands of men and women in Germany, Austria and Italy who have never surrendered their consciences to Hitler or Mussolini. They have been silenced, but their spirit is not broken. They, too, believe in all the ideals of freedom and democracy and are striving to realise them. The men and women who struggled to build up democratic forms of life in Germany, Austria and Italy, and their millions of supporters, have not all been driven out, massacred or converted to the principles of racialism and brutal chauvinism. They are the bearers of our democratic faith, as Hitler and Mussolini know only too well ; *they are the people who will reconstruct Germany, Austria and Italy when tyranny has been shattered.* Throughout the post-1918 period their task was rendered more difficult by the burden of the Versailles settlement which we, with the French, imposed on them. It has become fashionable in recent years to regret the Versailles Treaty. Having admitted the harm done by Versailles, let us not add to the injury we thus dealt our best friends in Germany the final insult of locking up their relatives and colleagues in Britain, as though they were agents of the enemy.

Only a small minority are active ; the great mass are waiting for something to happen, and need powerful encouragement from outside. But the most fearless and determined fighters against tyranny *are* still continuing the struggle within Germany, Austria and Italy. The *New Statesman* of July 20 was able to report the following details which have filtered out of Germany :

"From the beginning of this year in many German towns, especially in Northern Germany, houses and fences and walls were decorated with posters against the Hitler war. Though the Nazis every morning destroyed these posters, they always appeared anew the day after. In spite of the most searching inquiries, the originators and distributors of these posters could not be found. The illegal fighters could only dare this daily play with death with the silent connivance of large parts of the population. . . . Resistance is especially strong in industrial areas. . . . In November, 1939, there was an 'accident' in Hall F of the German works in Spandau. The machinery in this hall was used for making gun barrels. Shortly before six o'clock a severe explosion shook the hall. Machinery and tools were flying about, the workers thought they had been caught in an air raid. Sixteen revolving lathes were completely destroyed and other machines were rendered useless for a long time to come. More than two-thirds of all the machinery was put out of action. . . .

"Even in the *Reichswehr* we can find signs of resistance. In a Silesian garrison illegal leaflets were distributed. Twenty soldiers were court-martialled and shot for conspiracy and for keeping up illegal political connections. Walls and gates of a Saxon barracks were plastered with leaflets. As the police could not find out who had been responsible for this, the Gestapo took severe measures against the civilian population. Hundreds of members of the former free trade unions and of the parties of the Left were jailed for so-called examinations. During such an imprisonment-action in December, 1939, alone, about 4,000 people were put into concentration camps in East Prussia, which have been fitted out as arms factories . . . . In the concentration camp Schorfheide . . . one detachment of political prisoners that had been subjected to especially mean and cruel treatment, mutinied on the 4th of November. The mutiny was instantly suppressed by machine-gun fire. In the face of the dead lying on the ground the camp commander had every fifteenth man shot. These few incidents may suffice as examples of countless others."

The same authority reminds us that the Gestapo itself estimates that in Germany and Austria alone there were, in 1939, 35,972 persons detained for political reasons, 126,308 persons punished for political reasons, and 211,650 others in concentration camps. This gives a total of 373,930 political prisoners, to which must be added 62,649 prisoners in the Sudeten territory and the " Protectorate " of Bohemia, making a grand total of 436,579. In Germany and Austria alone there are thus over a third of a million enemies of tyranny who were not driven out, and who have been brave enough to risk torture and death, and unfortunate enough to have been found out. How many hundreds of thousands of others are there who have not been found out, who are waiting and hoping for the day when they can unite to destroy their oppressors ?

If we hear little in wartime of the struggle of freedom-loving people in Germany, Austria and Italy, it is not solely because of difficulties in getting news out of those countries. Is it not partly because the conduct of Britain and France has not so far inspired in them any burning hope and belief that they may look to us for freedom and a new way of life ? In the first days of the war, Mr. Chamberlain clearly recognised the need for seeking allies within the dictatorship countries. In his broadcast speech to the German people he told them :

" In this war we are not fighting against you—the German people—for whom we have no bitter feeling—but against a tyrannous and forsworn régime."

Since those early days there has been a tendency for our Ministers to forget this vital distinction, and above all there has been a complete failure to develop the implications of Mr. Chamberlain's statement. Although we have no bitter feelings against that large section of the German, Austrian and Italian peoples which hates tyranny, but waits passively for " something to happen," the Government has done little to develop among them a spirit of active resistance to Hitlerism and Fascism. To steel human beings to resist the savage terror that lies in wait for those who resist oppression we must seek to fill them with a fanatical faith in the cause of freedom and social justice.

Is it not time that the Government followed up its declarations of whom and what it is fighting *against* by a definitely clear and concrete statement of the kind of world it is fighting *for* ? The great majority of Hitler's enemies in Germany, whose confidence we must win, have bitter memories of the aftermath of the first world war. They remember the *promises* made by Britain and France, and they remember what happened in practice after they had driven out the Kaiser and set up a democratic régime. The language of 1914–18 does not appeal to them now. Vague phrases about truth, justice and freedom, and a " community of nations freely co-operating for the good of all," no longer suffice. We must have *concrete plans* for the practical realisation of the new world order our Foreign Secretary speaks about. We must make those plans public and win for them approval of the friends of freedom in Germany, Austria and Italy.

And because, in this *second* world war, our actions count far more than our words or promises, we must see that in our conduct we live up to our plans for a new world order, so as to spur on resistance to tyranny. Especially in our attitude to our " enemy alien " refugees can we prove that we mean what we say, and give fresh determination to those who fight Hitler and Mussolini from within.

It is precisely because these vital principles are not yet fully appreciated by our Government, because there is official confusion both as to whom and what we are fighting *against* and whom and what we are fighting *for*, that the " enemy aliens " policy of recent months has been possible. At bottom it derives from the pessimism expressed by Lord Halifax in his statement that " in Germany the people have given their consciences to Hitler."

6. *Why the Problem is Important*

Why make all this fuss about 70,000 Germans and Austrians and 19,000 Italians? In the first place, because the attitude underlying the Government's "aliens" policy is increasing the difficulties of those who are working to destroy Nazism and reaction in their own countries.

Nothing could be more calculated to dishearten our friends and allies in Germany and Austria than the news that Britain has put under lock and key her own anti-Nazis of German and Austrian origin. It has also caused dismay among thinking people in Britain and cast doubts in many minds as to the genuineness of our stated war aims. Continuance of this policy of treating as suspects all "aliens" who fought Nazi aggression whilst Britain was still officially tolerating it, may cause serious damage to Britain's good name in other countries. To lock up prominent anti-Nazis simply because their mother tongue is German instead of English, to deport overseas Germans and Italians whose sons are fighting in the British armed forces, is liable to damage Britain's prestige far more than the wildest and most irresponsible of "Blimpish" speeches could ever do.

Our treatment of "enemy aliens" has given a weapon to Goebbels to forge that very national unity in Germany which democrats wish to avert. It is disconcerting to Britain's supporters in America, who have to answer critics who cast doubts on the honesty of British war aims and ask how British methods differ from those of the Gestapo. The problem is important in the first place, therefore, because it is far more than a question of the fate of 90,000 unfortunate foreigners. It is a question of Britain's prestige and good name, of our sincerity about the way of life for which we profess to be fighting. If we need the approval and assistance of other countries, we cannot be too careful about framing our policy so as to win the support of "all those who love truth and justice and freedom."

In the second place the problem is important, because xeno-phobia and the more subtle attitude of mind which regards as "enemy aliens" all who speak a certain language or who have been citizens of a certain country involve implicit accept-ance of one odious Nazi doctrine—the doctrine of the eternal "alien." What, after all, is the basic difference between the

Nazi argument : " Once a Jew, always a Jew," and the " patriotic " British attitude expressed in phrases like " once a German, always a German," " The only good German is a dead German," " The Hun is a natural killer " ? At bottom they are all expressions of the same sort of infantile anti-foreign feeling that civilised adults are expected to grow out of.

On July 23, Mr. Eden explained to Parliament that " enemy alien " men were going to be discharged from internment for enlistment in the Pioneer Corps. Whereupon Lieutenant-Colonel Acland-Troyte, C.M.G., D.S.O.,* shouted : " Will my right hon. Friend bear in mind that you cannot trust any Boche at any time ? " This is the voice of Colonel Blimp. In *spirit*, in the frame of mind such a statement reveals, it does not differ from Dr. Goebbels' denunciation of Jews :

> " The deed of murder falls on all Jewry. Every individual must account to us for every pain, every crime, every nasty action of this criminal race against the Germans ; each individual Jew is responsible without mercy."

This outburst was provoked by the death of a Nazi official, murdered by a half-crazed Polish Jewish boy, who had seen his parents driven out of their home towards the end of 1938. The action of one Jew was blamed on to an entire people.

Lt.-Colonel Acland-Troyte's outburst was provoked by the action of a section of the German people, the Nazis, who have plunged Europe into war. He, too, blames an entire people. In the case of the Member for Tiverton this anti-German attitude is no doubt mere prejudice and nothing more. In the case of Hitler, Goebbels and Streicher, hatred of the Jews has been developed into an entire " philosophy " and " science," which form the basis of systematic and deliberate persecution. But fundamentally all suspicion of " aliens " *as such* springs from a common, undemocratic, un-Christian and wholly deplorable state of mind. Under the Nazis it has become an organised system of racialist doctrine. In Britain it remains a mere individual prejudice.

To maintain their spurious " community of the German people " (*Volksgemeinschaft*), the Nazis need " aliens " *against* whom they can unite. The Nazi concept of a community united for war, for the destruction of the " alien antagonist,"

---

* M.P. for Tiverton, educated at Eton and Cambridge ; recreations (according to *Who's Who*), hunting and shooting.

who is and must be human, makes " aliens " a necessity. If they do not exist, they have to be (and are) invented. Such a way of life is totally repugnant to the tolerant, free and peace-loving traditions of the British people. The real enemies of mankind are ignorance, poverty, insecurity, disease and fear. The real community of mankind is that of co-operative struggle to defeat these enemies, and to make ourselves masters of our environment and of Nature. Let us be careful not to import into our thought any trace of the Nazi doctrine of " aliens." To make concessions to Nazi ideas cannot but damage our own morale. To fight tyranny with a half-formulated belief in any of the doctrines of tyranny deep in our hearts can only lead us, as it has led the French, to disaster.

In conclusion we may sum up the doctrine of this book in four points. A constructive attitude to the " aliens " problem demands :

1. That we understand the nature of the war we are fighting.

2. That we discriminate, not between Britons and " aliens," or between " friendly aliens " and " enemy aliens " in the present way, but between those who stand for freedom and those who stand for tyranny in every country. This division cuts right across all nationalities. The real " aliens " are the " Nazis of the soul " of all countries, including our own—the Quislings, the Lavals, Baudouins and Weygands, and our own English-speaking Fifth Columnists and reactionaries, some of whom, like Mosley, are under lock and key, others of whom, because they have become " enemies " of Hitler for the dura-tion, are still at liberty. Our real friends are not to be deter-mined by tests of birthplace, nationality or language, but by their past and present conduct in the struggle against authori-tarian forms of government.

3. That genuine refugees be allowed at least the same free-dom to lead their own lives as all other foreigners in this country enjoy ; and that we recognise that unwarranted attacks on the freedom of " enemy aliens " who are genuine refugees, and who were becoming a part of the British community, cannot be dissociated from attacks upon our own civil liberties.

4. That as far as possible we should create opportunities for our " alien " friends (whether officially " enemy " or officially " friendly ") to develop and use their ability, skill and man-power both for our war effort and generally to enrich our economic, social and cultural life.

CHAPTER II

1. *Who are the " Enemy Aliens " ?*

THE great Nazi pogrom in the winter of 1938–39 inevitably led to a rapid increase in the number of refugees admitted into England during the last months of 1938 and all through 1939 down to the outbreak of war. During the six years 1933–38 the Jewish Refugees Committee, upon which the bulk of the cost of maintaining refugees fell, spent £233,000 on refugees in Great Britain. In the first seven months of 1939 alone it spent more than £250,000. The trickle had grown into a torrent ; 9,000 children were brought over by the British Movement for the Care of Children ; 1,000 permits a month were issued for women to enter the country as domestics. Over 10,000 people with definite plans for re-emigration were admitted, as well as some 3,000 old people over sixty. After much pressure, especially from Jewish relief organisations, the Government agreed to permit the organisation of an interim camp for men aged 18–45 with definite prospects of re-emigration. The Central Council for Jewish Refugees got this camp going in February, 1939. The site consisted of the derelict army buildings (used for training Kitchener's Army in the last war) at Richborough, near Ramsgate. The men were mostly selected by the Jewish organisations in Germany and Austria, and fulfilled not only the age and re-emigration qualifications, but were also men who had no other chance of coming to Britain and who were in urgent need of leaving the Reich. By the outbreak of war the Kitchener Camp contained its full complement of 3,500 men (including small groups of refugees from Belgium, Italy and Czechoslovakia). The Camp had become a small town on its own, thanks to the energetic spirit and the communal activities of the men themselves, who, without barbed wire or armed guards, constructed an entire new community almost from nothing and were busy being re-trained for new jobs and a new life in their countries of final destination.

Right down to the outbreak of war the Government had clung to the policy of limiting admissions to the number which could be financially guaranteed either by societies or individuals, although in 1939 it was obliged somewhat to relax the strictness of its policy. The main categories for admission were therefore (*a*) transit emigrants, with definite plans for further emigration within two years, (*b*) children under 18, usually to be prepared for re-emigration, (*c*) persons aged 16–35 for training, (*d*) persons over 60. Apart from these groups only domestics, nurses and a few agricultural workers could gain admission, because their work was needed.

This immigration policy largely determined the character of our refugee population at the outbreak of war, when persons of German and Austrian origin and *not* of British nationality had risen from the normal 15–20 thousand to no less than 74,000 (excluding children), in addition to about 8,000 Czech refugees. There were also at least 10,000 refugee children under 16. A very large proportion (perhaps half) of these persons of German and Austrian origin had definite plans for further emigration, mostly to the U.S.A., and at least 5,000 did leave the country between September, 1939, and April, 1940.

Who, then, are our " enemy aliens " ? Some were Nazi citizens ; others were Germans and Austrians who came here before 1933 and, not daring to return to their own countries, were in fact refugees. But the great majority of them were genuine refugees, and at least four-fifths were Jewish. When war broke out 73,400 out of 74,200 " enemy aliens " appeared before tribunals, who examined their bona-fides and classified them in two ways. They were put (not too consistently) into one of three classes : A Class were interned, B Class were subject to restrictions of liberty, C Class were left entirely free. They were also classified into " refugees from Nazi oppression " and non-refugees. The work of the tribunal is examined later, but the statistics resulting from their work are presented now.

Out of 73,400 " enemy aliens " examined, no fewer than 64,000 were put in C Class, and 55,500 were classified as " refugees from Nazi oppression " (51,100 of these being in C Class). Half of the men over 18 years of age were 41 or older, and one-third were 50 or older. Forty-four per cent. of the women were 41 or older, and over a quarter were 50 or older.

Just over one-third of the men were manufacturers, employers and business men. No less than 27 per cent. of the men and 17 per cent. of the women were professional workers. One-quarter of all the women were domestic servants (a considerable, proportion of these were not actually domestics by trade, but had only been able to enter the country on permits for domestic work). The following tables show some of the occupations of German and Austrian " enemy aliens " :

	Total (excluding stateless, etc.)	Total Classed as Refugees.	Total Classed as Refugees and also put in Class C.
Professional Workers :			
Doctors :			
Men - - - -	964	910	876
Women - - -	73	65	60
Dentists :			
Men - - - -	284	267	254
Women - - -	179	171	169
Pharmacists :			
Men - - - -	255	231	217
Women - - -	67	58	53
Oculists (Men) - -	24	22	21
Psychologists :			
Men - - - -	29	28	28
Women - - -	24	21	21
Teachers :			
Men - - - -	689	571	518
Women - - -	1,539	1,008	960
Architects :			
Men - - - -	129	108	98
Women - - -	8	5	5
Consulting Engineers (Men)	115	97	86
Employers and Manufacturers :			
Clothing :			
Men - - - -	836	700	632
Women - - -	237	201	188
Textiles :			
Men - - - -	1,040	983	890
Women - - -	63	53	52

	Total (excluding stateless, etc.)	Total Classed as Refugees.	Total Classed as Refguees and also put in Class C.
Employers and Manufacturers—contd.			
Leather Goods :			
Men - - -	502	467	430
Women - - -	30	27	26
Metals (Men) - -	287	259	236
Chemists, Chemical Industry (Men) - -	225	191	165
Instrument Makers :			
Men - - - -	67	32	26
Women - - -	20	18	18
Farmers :			
Men - - - -	361	335	300
Women - - -	11	9	7
Workers :			
Engineers (Men) - -	871	720	642
Tailors :			
Men - - - -	780	375	328
Women - - -	882	706	656
Farm Workers :			
Men - - - -	371	345	298
Women - - -	46	40	35
Domestics (Women) -	9,624	6,628	6,132

These figures give a rough idea of the character of our " enemy alien " population at the outbreak of war. Apart from the domestics and nurses, a few professional workers, and the men and women who were being trained for re-emigration, the majority of the refugees were not working, because they were not allowed to. Their maintenance was shared in roughly equal proportions between the organisations which had assisted them to enter this country and private individuals (friends or kindly people) who had offered hospitality to refugees. There was, however, a considerable group of refugee employers who had been able, because of special skill or good luck, to start enterprises (for the most part manufacturing semi-luxuries and industrial accessories) which employed quite a large total of British workers. No precise data on this question are available, but we do know that 223 employers interned in one camp in the Isle of Man in mid-July had been employing between them 6,500 British workers. We also know that *entrepreneurs* who started eleven factories on the Treforest Trading Estate (some had been officially encouraged to come over to Britain and given special facilities to start enterprises in a depressed area) employed between them over 1,000 British workers.

But the majority of refugees were not able to work, and depended, in fact, on charity (however disguised) in one form or another. The Chamberlain Government, because it was bankrupt of constructive ideas for tackling the unemployment problem, clung to the outmoded " fund of labour " theory which holds that there is only a fixed amount of work which can be done, so that if the number of workers available is increased the number of unemployed is also increased. Refugees in general were forbidden to earn a living out of fear that they might thereby deprive British workers of jobs. This fact, that charity rather than democratic solidarity was the atmosphere in which the majority of " enemy aliens " were obliged to live, must be borne in mind if an understanding of the reaction of refugees to internment is to be achieved. By virtue of their living in this country and sharing its fate, by virtue of the fact that they could not claim the protection of any other Government, they were in fact becoming part of the British community. This does not apply to the same degree to the considerable group of transit emigrants, but even in their case many would have to wait for two years or longer before their turn on the U.S.A. immigration quota arrived, and the outbreak of war made it impossible for many to re-emigrate to countries like Palestine or Australia, and involved a postponement of plans for many intending to go to America. Willy nilly, war strengthened the ties of the refugees with the British community, so that the sudden reversal of official policy which ended in mass internment came as an even greater shock to them.

Finally it must be noted that the refugees are not an unknown and well-hidden body of potential Fifth Columnists, but men and women about whom far more is known than about most British citizens. As Mr. Peake told the House of Commons on July 10 :

" Practically all the (German-Austrian) aliens who have come to this country in the last five or six years have been sponsored either by a refugee organisation or by a private individual. . . . Apart from that vouching of character by the organisation or the individual, there was then an examination by the British Consul abroad of the bona fides of the individuals who wished to come. Then there was a scrutiny by the immigration officer when the alien came into this country. After landing, the alien had to report and register with the local police, and since the outbreak of war every alien has been before a tribunal of some kind or another; many of them have been before two tribunals. . . . *I can only say, on behalf of the Home Secretary and myself, that I wish we knew half as much about many of the neutral aliens and many British subjects as we know about the enemy aliens now in this country.*"

Most individual refugees, before they even left Nazi territory had (a) to find an individual or organisation in Britain to sponsor them and to take full financial responsibility for them, and (b) to persuade a British consular official that they were desirable immigrants. Then they had (c) to pass the port immigration officer, (d) to satisfy the local police of their genuineness, (e) to lodge full details of their life history, present situation and future prospects, with their appropriate refugee committee, and (f), on the outbreak of war, to go before at least one tribunal for " enemy aliens " and give good reasons why they should not be interned. Over 47,000 of the refugees at present in this country are registered with the Jewish Refugees Committee alone, which has a dossier about each one; the police also have a dossier about each " enemy alien " in the country. There are very few British citizens about whom so much is known. Although there may be a dozen or two enemy agents and disguised Nazis among the refugees, the refugee disguise is the last one which an enemy agent would adopt, because it would be a hindrance to any spy worth his salt to have to speak English with a foreign accent and to have so much information about himself lodged with official bodies. The real enemy agent most usually possesses an English passport or that of a neutral country, speaks English perfectly and mixes with the " best people," who have the information he is after. The real British Fifth Column *is* British. If our authorities treated the British public in the same way as they now treat refugees from Nazi oppression, they would have to put the majority of us under lock and key, because comparatively they

know so little about us. As Mr. Peake said in the same speech
from which we have quoted :

" You can never obtain absolute, guaranteed 100 per cent.
security. If we were to aim at that we should have to lock
up an immensely large number of people, and the numbers
engaged in guarding them would be so great that there would
perhaps be only a minority of the population left to proceed
with the war effort."

The refugees, then, are well taped. Not only the police
but the refugee organisations know almost all there is to know
about most of them. When the authorities began to intern
" enemy aliens " on a large scale they completely ignored those
organisations, and continued to do so right down to the end of
July. They thereby not only caused tremendous damage,
much of it irreparable, but threw out of gear the important
and valuable work the refugee organisations were doing.
Because the man in the street knows so little about refugee
organisations and their work, we propose to give a picture of
them in the next section.

2. *The Refugee Organisations*

So many societies and committees have been created for
refugees or by refugees that it is quite impossible to give more
than the barest outline of the work done by the most important.
Jewish Bodies.—In 1933 the first Jewish refugees were only
a small band, and it was natural that the Jews' Temporary
Shelter, in the East End of London, should be their refuge.
For fifty years this institution had looked after transmigrants
from Poland, Hungary, Rumania and many other Eastern European countries, and had always opened its door to those persecuted through no fault of their own. Now it was to fugitives
from Nazi persecution that the door opened. By May, 1933,
it was evident that the problem was likely to become larger and
lasting, and it was felt wise to segregate the activities for
German refugees from the regular work of the shelter. The
Jewish Refugees Committee was, therefore, created with the
President of the Jews' Temporary Shelter as its chairman.
It was soon evident, however, that there would be many
thousands who would seek asylum in other countries, and

Anglo-Jewry felt that it must play its full part, if the British Government agreed, in assisting entrance into the United Kingdom. Consequently four leaders of the Jewish community saw the Home Office and gave the undertaking that if German Jewish refugees were allowed to come to England the cost would be borne by the Jewish community here and they would not become a charge on public funds. On the Government's acceptance of the proposals submitted by the deputation, a fund-raising and policy-directing body was created. This new body, known as the Central British Fund for German Jewry, launched its first appeal in May, 1933. This produced a sum of approximately £200,000. Subsequent appeals made at various intervals between 1933 and the spring of 1940 produced some £3,000,000 for general refugee work and special work for women and children, and such bodies as the Society for the Protection of Science and Learning, etc., which dealt with specialised categories of refugees. In 1936 a special appeal was launched to facilitate the emigration from Germany of 100,000 Jews within four years. At this stage the Central British Fund became known as the Council for German Jewry ; after the outbreak of war its name was changed once more to the Central Council for Jewish Refugees. Apart from the financial contributions, which ranged from the large donations of the wealthier members of the community to the few pence of the poorest, innumerable offers of hospitality and practical service were received, the value of which can never be accurately estimated in financial terms, but which cannot have been less than £7,000,000.

By September, 1939, 60,000 refugees representing 80 per cent. of all the refugees in this country had registered with the Jewish Refugees Committee, and of these some 47,000 were still in Great Britain. A moment's reflection will enable the reader to envisage not only the enormous growth of the work involved in caring for these refugees, but also its many-sided aspects. The main part of the Council's funds went to the Jewish Refugees Committee which dealt with individual cases, whilst other allocations were made to the Richborough Camp, for 3,500 male refugees awaiting re-emigration, to agricultural training schemes and to other organisations dealing with children, domestic servants, academic and professional workers. Money was also spent on assisting and training refugees for emigration to Palestine and elsewhere. This was perhaps the most constructive of all the work undertaken by the Jewish refugee organisations.

Christian Bodies.—On the Christian side the story also began early in 1933, when the Society of Friends set up a Germany Emergency Committee to cater for those refugees who did not come within the scope of the activities of the Jewish organisations.   Members of the Society of Friends had been working in various parts of Germany and Austria ever since 1919, and their centres in cities like Berlin, Frankfurt, Vienna and Prague were recognised by the Nazi authorities as the main bodies for assisting the emigration of non-Jewish refugees and of Christian refugees of Jewish origin.   Through these and other centres in France, Holland and elsewhere the G.E.C. carried on all the usual activities of applying for visas and labour permits, assisting refugees to emigrate and providing them with relief, training and advice.

Other Christian bodies engaged in work for refugees were the International Hebrew Christian Alliance, the Church of England Committee for " non-Aryan " Christians and the Catholic Committee for Refugees.   The first of these bodies is mainly concerned with the linking together in all parts of the world of Jews professing the Christian faith.   It began its work for " non-Aryan " Christian refugees early in 1933 and has both emigrated and maintained in this country a considerable number of outcasts from the Nazis.   The Church of England Committee for " non-Aryan " Christians was formed under the Chairmanship of the Bishop of Chichester in November, 1937.   Its work has consisted mainly in the care of old people and " non-Aryan " Protestant pastors and their families.   The Catholic Committee was set up under the Presidency of Cardinal Hinsley in March, 1938, and has been primarily concerned with the well-being of the " non-Aryan " Catholics who fled from Austria immediately after the annexation in March, 1938.   Its children's section is responsible for nearly 300 children in British schools or homes.

Overlapping in the case-work of these and other Christian bodies was overcome by increasing co-operation between the various case-working committees and the German Emergency Committee, until this latter body came to be recognised as the Christian counterpart of the Jewish Refugees Committee.   Since its inauguration it had handled 22,000 cases and had about 5,000 refugees registered on its books in June, 1940.   Prior to the outbreak of war it had assisted in the re-emigration of well over 700 refugees, while a further 300 were re-emigrated between September, 1939, and August, 1940, the whole at a cost of some £30,000. The Committee has technical and industrial training schemes, and had developed eleven agricultural training centres and one for carpentry by the outbreak of war. In these centres about 200 trainees were being maintained. In October, 1938, the Christian Council for Refugees from Germany and Central Europe was founded under the Chairmanship of Sir John Hope Simpson, to inform Christian opinion on refugee matters in general and on the problem of the " non-Aryan " Christian refugees in particular, and to raise funds for the work of the Christian refugee organisations. Shortly after its formation the Christian Council co-operated with the Central Jewish Council in the launching of the Lord Baldwin Fund, which between December, 1938, and the following June raised £550,000. This sum was divided between the two main Councils which, in their turn, allocated just over half the amount to the Movement for the Care of Children from Germany. On the winding-up of the Baldwin Fund the Christian Council accepted responsibility for its outstanding affairs, including the general administration of Bloomsbury House, which in January, 1939, became the headquarters of all the major refugee organisations. Collaboration between the Christian Council and the Central Council for Jewish Refugees has resulted in some effective pieces of co-operative work. It is one of the few bright spots in an otherwise very dark picture that a tragedy which had its rise in the exploitation of anti-Jewish prejudice in Germany should have resulted in so much co-operation both between the various sections of the Christian community and between the Jews and Christians in this country.

Undenominational Bodies.—Of the many undenominational bodies for the assistance of refugees we mention only four of the most important. The Movement for the Care of Children from Germany (Chairman, Lord Gorell ; Director, Sir Charles Stead) has an exciting history. It began as an Inter-Aid Committee linking the Children's Departments of the various Jewish and Christian refugee bodies. In November, 1938, during the great pogroms, it decided to attempt to rescue children from the Nazis on a mass scale. The Government allowed it to bring in children without passports, but with

identity cards issued by the Movement itself, on the understanding that the Movement should be financially responsible
for the children and that they should be re-emigrated before
the age of eighteen or when their training was finished. A
public appeal for funds and hospitality met with a great response,
and the Movement decided to bring over 10,000 children from
the Third Reich. As soon as the news became known in
Germany and Austria the Children's Movement was flooded
with thousands of letters and photos and pathetic appeals,
mostly from Jewish parents who had decided, for their children's
sake, to make the supreme sacrifice of sending them to a foreign
but friendly country where they could grow up in peace and
happiness.   The children were chosen by the central organisations of the Jewish and " non-Aryan " Christian communities
in Germany and Austria, and by a British Committee in
Bohemia and Moravia.   Those in most urgent need were taken
first, and then children for whom English sponsors had been
found.   The first transport arrived in December, 1938, the
last on the day war was declared. All through this period
a new shipload arrived on average every four days ; 9,354
" enemy alien " children were thus rushed into this country
before war stopped the movement.   On arrival the children
were temporarily put into camps on the east and south-east
coasts, and gradually sorted out and distributed among private
families, hostels and training centres.   Over 6,000 are cared
for by private families and were so well placed that up to
December, 1939, only fifty children had to be removed on
gounds of incompatibility.   The younger children, in English
homes and schools, are growing up with an English background.   Over 2,000 of the children were over sixteen and
needed training for work.   After the relaxation of restrictions
on the employment of " aliens " about 600 boys and 200 girls
were placed in private employment as trainees.   The magnificent work done by the Children's Movement gave Britain
the lead over all other countries in the rescuing of children
from Nazi persecution.   It is something to be proud of.
   The Society for the Protection of Science and Learning
(President, the Archbishop of York ; Chairman, Sir Frederick
Kenyon), which began life in 1933 as the Academic Assistance
Council, exists for the purpose of assisting " university teachers
and other investigators of whatever country, who, on grounds
of religion, political opinion or ' race,' are unable to carry on

their work in their own country." The Society set itself the task not merely of rescuing scientists and scholars who were persecuted in their own countries, but also of finding new posts, research facilities and scholarships to enable them to continue their work in harmonious conditions. By the end of 1938 it had placed 524 scholars in permanent positions, 378 in academic institutions and 146 in industry or general research. By April, 1940, the Society had found posts for 380 refugee University teachers and research workers in Britain, and about 720 had been placed in other countries (350 in the U.S.A.). In addition to these activities the Society has organised courses of lectures by distinguished refugee scholars, and raised funds to provide research fellowships or grants for refugees. In 1939 103 maintenance grants were awarded. Five fellowships are also administered by the Society for the assistance of distinguished scholars. The Society made a full register of the qualifications and offers of service of the refugee scholars and scientists resident in Britain, which was found very useful by the Government after the outbreak of war. But that did not save most of these scholars from internment in the summer of 1940.

Among students the International Student Service has performed a function similar to that of the Society for the Protection of Science and Learning for research workers. The I.S.S. began its life in 1919 as European Student Relief by bringing £450,000 to the relief of starving students in Central Europe. From 1933 to 1937 work was carried on for German refugees, of whom some 8,000 were suddenly forced to leave their Universities in Germany, and in 1938 assistance was extended to Austrian and Czech refugee students. I.S.S. aims at helping to frustrate the Nazi policy of stamping out the national culture of countries under its domination and at seeing that the abilities of the refugee students are not wasted by giving them a chance to finish their academic careers in British Universities or by giving constructive technical training to those whose ability lies in that direction. Financial assistance over a period of time has been given since 1938 to some 250 students. Emergency grants and/or assistance in kind have been given to well over 1,000 students (free places in English Universities or technical institutes, free hospitality, cheap hostel accommodation, etc.). The majority of students helped have been Germans, Austrians or Czechs, and 65 to 75 per cent. of them are Jewish. Most Universities in the

British Isles have given I.S.S. a generous number of free places to be put at the disposition of refugee students.

A fourth fund for refugees is the International Solidarity Fund, controlled by the Labour Movement, which is devoted mainly to assisting refugee Socialists and trade union officials who have had to flee from torture or death at the hands of the Nazis.

Bloomsbury House.—All the aforementioned refugee organisations have built up networks of provincial committees and centres of which some 200 are now in existence. Early in 1938 the need for co-ordination of refugee work became so acute that a Central Co-ordinating Committee—now the Joint Consultative Committee on Refugees—was set up in London, with Lord Hailey as Chairman. In 1939 it was decided to centralise in one building the offices of the main organisations under the Committee, and the Executive of the Baldwin Fund leased a hotel in Bloomsbury, which was renamed Bloomsbury House and became the headquarters of all the major organisations working for refugees. The Co-ordinating Committee in London established closer contact with the many refugee committees outside London, who also joined forces with one another and set up local co-ordinating committees in some of the larger towns.

The various organisations at Bloomsbury House, although continuing to handle individual case-work of refugees registered with them, set up joint committees for each particular type of refugee work in order to exchange views, develop policy and avoid overlapping. As far back as 1938 all work in connection with domestic service had been concentrated in a single department, the Domestic Bureau. Up till the end of November, 1939, domestic service was the only form of employment open to refugees, who were permitted to enter the country otherwise only if arrangements were made to train them for re-emigration, and on condition that they took no work, paid or unpaid, while in Britain. Prior to the outbreak of war thousands of women who had no experience whatever of domestic service sought to enter this country in the only way open to them—by obtaining permits for domestic service. The Domestic Bureau became the main channel of entry, and brought over 14,000 women, accompanied by nearly 1,000 children. By arrangement with the Home Office the refugee organisations themselves selected the women to be brought over, through the channel of approved continental organisations, and obtained the permits for them. The " domestics " brought over by the Bureau included doctors, lawyers, radiologists, teachers, chemists, economists, social welfare workers, clerks, dressmakers, milliners and hosts of women with every conceivable background. Those with no previous experience were given a short course in housewifery and domestic work before coming over, and the majority turned themselves into good servants, though looking forward to the day when they could do something better and more useful. In 1939, 7,000 other women came over on permits issued directly by the Ministry of Labour without reference to the voluntary organisations. These organisations pointed out the dangers of such an uncontrolled influx, and the authorities decided, in July, 1939, that the Ministry of Labour should transfer to the Domestic Bureau all applications received from refugees wishing to enter the country as domestics, so that the Bureau might vouch for them and provide for their welfare. The outbreak of war produced three months of dislocation and unemployment among the Bureau's domestics, between 7,000 and 8,000 of whom lost their jobs. This was not due to anti-German or anti-refugee feeling, but to the evacuation of householders from the cities leaving their refugee servants without jobs. For a time the Bureau suffered a rush of women wanting maintenance, medical assistance, clothing or advice. The Bureau met the situation by establishing five depots and twenty-eight training hostels (housework and English) in London suburbs. From November, when restrictions on the employment of " aliens " were somewhat relaxed, the women's employment situation improved steadily.

The Nursing and Midwifery Department, started in December, 1938, brought into Britain 950 women and girls to take up nursing and midwifery before war broke out. The Department also found midwifery openings for refugee women doctors who were not allowed to practise nor to work as nurses. At the outbreak of war the Department had placed 1,000 women in British hospitals. The Medical Department, started in March, 1938, deals with all refugee doctors and dentists, and since May, 1938, has been assisted by the Jewish Medical and Dental Emergency Association which raised funds from the Jewish medical profession in England to assist refugee doctors, as well as by the Central Council for Jewish refugees, the

Christian Council and the Czech Trust Fund. (In January, 1940, the Czech Trust Fund assumed all responsibility for Czech doctors, and the Christian Council became financially responsible for Christian doctors.) The Department tried to bring medical men to Britain to make a fresh start in their profession. It was in touch with no less than 10,000 doctors, of whom 2,000 were actually brought over to this country before war broke out, 500 subsequently emigrating to other countries. The Department placed in medical schools the fifty Austrian doctors and forty Austrian dentists who were permitted to take English qualifications as a preliminary to practising in this country. It arranged for fifty Czech doctors to qualify for practice in the same way, and sixteen psychotherapists and six female radiographers were also allowed to work.

Employment and Welfare Work.—The cancellation or postponement of thousands of re-emigration plans faced the refugee organisations at the outbreak of war with the prospect of maintaining a great number of persons who never intended to stay in this country at all. Those who had means would gradually become destitute, while none of them were able to offer their services to the country in any capacity, either in civil employment or at the Army recruiting offices. At the end of November, 1939, however, the Government relaxed the rules regarding the employment of "aliens" under certain conditions (*see* Section 4), and the refugee committees immediately set up employment bureaux, co-ordinated by a Consultative Employment Committee. Although British unemployment remained at a high level for several months, and although no official encouragement was given to the employment of refugees, there occurred a rapid absorption into employment of refugees with experience and ability. Every month after November 2,000 to 3,000 refugees found jobs, and this absorption into employment continued at growing speed until May, 1940, when the Government reversed its whole policy and began mass internment.

This reversal of policy compelled the refugee organisations to overhaul all their machinery and concentrate on the wives and children who were left stranded when the wage earner was spirited away at a few minutes' notice from his work, his home and his family. The welfare department of each Committee undertook this new task. The Central Welfare Department had been established in January, 1940, as a joint body of all the Bloomsbury House welfare departments, to co-ordinate the work of establishing contacts with refugees in their own homes, and it had promoted the establishment of " Refugee Friendship Committees " in a number of areas for the purpose of providing social life and entertainment for refugees, especially for the domestics. When general internment began the Central Welfare Department organised the visiting of relatives and dependants of internees in their homes to assist them in solving their new difficulties. For the welfare of internees a special department of Bloomsbury House was set up in June, 1940 (see Chapter III, Section 5).

The work of the Welfare Department of the Jewish Refugees Committee is typical of that done by each of the welfare departments of refugee organisations. In the middle of 1940 it was giving personal interviews to 100–200 refugees daily and sending money through the post to about sixty people daily. It investigated and recommended cheap accommodation to 200 persons daily, and arranged special care for convalescents, maternity and problem cases. It issued clothing and shoes (one pair in three months) to needy refugees, and sent sick people for examination by the Medical Department (the English doctor in charge personally examined 959 refugees in the second quarter of 1940). The J.R.C. Welfare Department also maintains several hostels in London : one at Highbury for expectant and nursing mothers and children, one at Belsize Park for factory apprentices and trainees (girls), another for aged and infirm men and women (run by a refugee superintendent, whose husband, a doctor, lives on the premises), and a hostel for nurses.

A New Social Service.—There has thus grown up an entire new voluntary social service system, unobserved by and unknown to the majority of the British public. The Bloomsbury House organisations have all the defects and irritating inefficiencies which exist in even the best organised voluntary social work, but their efficiency and cheerfulness are nothing short of amazing in view of the repeated successive expansions of the refugee problem which they have had to face, ill-equipped, understaffed and chronically short of cash. Mainly because of the successive waves of refugees created by Nazi persecution, but also because of the uncertainty and vacillations of British official policy, the refugee organisations have always laboured under immense difficulties, and under the circumstances have a splendid record of humanitarian achievement to their credit. Full official recognition of the value—indeed the indispensability—of the refugee organisations was given early in 1940. The financial strain on the refugee organisations had become insupportable in the first few months of the war (in the autumn of 1939 the main Committees were spending more than £14,000 a week on maintenance alone), and Bloomsbury House therefore made an appeal to the Government for a grant in aid. The Government agreed more or less to share half the cost of maintaining refugees. A retrospective grant of £100,000 (about 85 per cent. of which went to the Jewish Council) was made to cover roughly half the expenses of the Committees from the outbreak of war to the end of 1939 (£5,000 earmarked for provincial committees). A monthly grant with an upper limit of £27,000 was given, to be administered by a Central Refugee Committee set up at the request of the Government for the distribution of the grant (Chairman, Sir Herbert Emerson). This amount was fixed on the assumption that, on a pound-for-pound basis, it would cover the expenses of the refugee organisations. These sums were apportioned between all approved organisations caring for refugees from Central Europe, except the Czech Trust Fund and the Children's Movement. The first six months of this scheme showed that the sum of £27,000 was not sufficient to meet half the expenditure of the voluntary organisations (for several months it met only about one-third of actual expenditure) ; and that the average maintenance allowance paid to refugees in almost all cases was several shillings a week less than that paid by the Assistance Board to British subjects in distress.

The Government, by financially assisting refugee work in 1940, at long last gave a clear public recognition to seven years of splendid unaided work by the voluntary organisations for refugees. When Mr. Peake explained on July 10 that internment of refugees was necessary because their unemployment was likely to increase the Government's financial burden, we simply cannot fathom his meaning. The Government did *not* avoid any financial burden by interning 10,000 or more breadwinners and throwing their dependants on to relief. At first sight it may appear to be cheaper to lock people up as if they were cattle than to leave them at liberty and give them allowances. But the " economy " excuse looks very like an afterthought with no basis of fact, for even in May and June,

1940, after the evacuation and internment orders were applied, 500 to 600 refugees were still obtaining employment *every week*.

The Czech Trust Fund.—Outside the Joint Consultative Committee on Refugees, though working in close collaboration with it, is the Czech Trust Fund. This originated in the British Committee for Refugees from Czechoslovakia which was set up in September, 1938, to administer the various funds raised for refugees from the Sudeten territories (including Germans and Austrians). After the seizure of Czechoslovakia by the Nazis in March, 1938, there was a second wave of refugees, and the Committee's scope was extended to cover Czechs and Slovaks ; but its funds were quite inadequate. A portion of the " gift " which Mr. Chamberlain's Government had put at the disposal of the Government of Czechoslovakia in January, 1939, was set aside by the British Government for refugees and the Czech Refugee Trust Fund was created in July, 1939, to administer those funds. It took over all the functions of the original British Committee. The Fund has 8,000 refugees under its care, of whom about 3,500 are Czechs and Slovaks, 2,000 are Sudetens, 850 are German refugees, and 475 are Austrians. The Fund spent about £7,000 a week in the first half of 1940, of which £5,500 went on maintenance allowances and another £1,000 on services (medical, educational, clothing, etc.). The Czech Trust Fund is unique in that it is an organisation *for* refugees which works in closest collaboration with an organisation *of* the refugees themselves. The majority of Czech Trust Fund refugees are political victims of the Nazis, and in Britain they are organised in their appropriate political groups. There are also Jewish groups and various professional groups, so that almost every refugee from Czechoslovakia belongs to a group which represents him. The representatives of the political groups, together with those of the Jewish groups, and of the Thomas Mann Society (artists, dramatists, writers) meet together as a Working Committee (*Arbeitskreis*) which works together with the Trustees in the interests of the refugees. In addition there exists a *Landsmannschaft* (Association of Fellow-Countrymen), which is a cultural and social organisation for the Czechs and Slovaks. The Trustees and the *Arbeitskreis* set up a number of refugee hostels in various parts of the country, the Groups appointing the wardens. Their most successful piece of work was the organisation of a mass emigration of Sudeten German refugees to Canada to work on a farm scheme. The value of this dual organisation is evident, and the group organisation of the refugees has been very successful in wartime in keeping up the morale of the refugees. The London organisation has a cultural committee which has done good work organising classes and entertainments, gives advice on legal and personal problems, and seeks to inform the British public about Czechoslovakia. It has done much to maintain friendly relations between the Czechs and the British people.

Organisations of Refugees.—A number of other organisations *of* refugees exist. There are—or were—a number of self-aid committees, mainly founded by residents or early arrivals among the refugees to provide guidance and advice for later arrivals. The best surviving body of this type is the *Notgemeinschaft Deutscher Wissenschaftler im Ausland* (Emergency Association for Exiled German Scholars, under Dr. Fritz Demuth), which is the refugees' counterpart to the Society for the Protection of Science and Learning. It works in close collaboration with the Society, supplying it with detailed information about refugee scholars who need assistance. Originally it limited itself to helping German scholars, but later its assistance was extended to Austrians and Czechs, and it has even helped Spanish and Italians.

The Austrians.—The most important organisations of refugees are cultural and social in character. By far the most successful of these are the Austrian Centres in various towns built up under the auspices of the Council of Austrians in Great Britain. Representative refugee bodies are almost impossible to organise, since the mass of refugees are scattered and large numbers of them (in the case of the German refugees, the great majority) dislike to take part in organised activities for fear their British hosts might take offence. Apart from the Czech Working Committee under the Czech Trust Fund, the Council of Austrians can claim to be more representative of a refugee community than any other body in this country ; it can probably speak for over half of the 12,000 Austrians in the country, and certainly for the majority of Austrian refugees who do not wish to lose their Austrian identity because they look forward one day to being free citizens of a regenerated Austrian democracy. The Council of Austrians was constituted in September, 1938, under the patronage, amongst others, of the Archbishop of York, Lord Hailey, Mr. Duff

Cooper and Viscountess Rhondda. Its chairman is Professor Walter Schiff (former Professor of Statistics at Vienna University and President of the Austrian Federal Bureau of Statistics). Unlike the Czech Working Committee the Council of Austrians decided to work on a strictly non-political basis. It has been very energetic in working for the social, cultural and economic interests of Austrian refugees and in striving for improvements in their general status. It began by negotiating with the Home Office to ensure that Austrian refugees whose passports expired should be given a British travel-paper, and not be forced to apply for German passports. Immediately after the pogrom of November, 1938, it took the lead in pressing for interim immigration camps to save refugees from death or starvation. In January, 1939, it opened two homes where Austrians in London could meet on Sundays, and in March it opened the Austrian Centre in London. After war broke out the Council compiled full records of some 3,000 Austrians to supplement the material supplied by the relief organisations about refugees for the Aliens Tribunals. In October, 1939, it issued a memorandum, which aroused much comment, analysing the first fortnight's work of the tribunals and pointing out a number of inconsistencies and weaknesses. The Home Office later issued new regulations which resulted in a marked improvement in the tribunal's work. In November and December, 1939, the Council devoted attention to all the new refugee problems created by the war and organised a conference which resulted in the establishment of a Studio for Arts and Crafts, and classes for re-training in welding, engineering (with the assistance of the Polytechnics an engineering workshop was organised) and other subjects to fit refugees for useful employment. The Austrian Self-Aid Committee, formed originally by residents and naturalised British subjects, played a considerable part at first in giving advice and technical assistance to refugees. When refugee work was centralised at Bloomsbury House its functions were greatly reduced, although it continues as an advice and information department of the Austrian Centre. Amongst other things, it succeeded in bringing 162 Austrian children and 520 domestics to England before the outbreak of war, as well as 40 prisoners released from Nazi concentration camps. It also raised funds and clothing for Austrian International Brigaders interned in France. After the outbreak of war the Self-Aid advised the refugees who went before tribunals, attempted, together with the Council, to rescue Austrian refugees from France after the French surrender, and assisted interned refugees in Britain.

The Austrian Centre was started in a house waiting to be demolished put at the disposal of the Council and Self-Aid by the Paddington Estate. A dozen young Austrians with £15, voluntary labour and unbounded enthusiasm, built it up in a year into the finest centre of refugee culture in Great Britain. Before the year was out, with the help of a £200 grant from the Christian Council, the Centre had expanded into two adjoining houses. Facilities restricted to members of the Austrian Centre Club (about 2,500 paying members, and another 3,500 " floating " members) include a library (about 2,000 German books, and 1,500 English books, etc.) ; a reading room containing leading British and Continental papers ; the *Zeitspiegel*, a weekly digest of the British press in German (large postal circulation) ; classes on a wide range of subjects (especially English language, literature, shorthand, etc.) ; and performances and entertainments. An initial series of lectures on various topics by distinguished Austrian scholars was so successful that the Centre instituted three-month courses of lectures on a large number of scientific and topical subjects. Twenty-three musical and variety evenings were held in the Centre's first year (in a theatre hall fitted out by voluntary workers) at which well-known pianists, singers and musicians gave their services. In June, 1939, a group of playwrights and actors who had worked formerly at the Vienna *Kleinkunstbühne* (Little Arts Theatre) revived it at the Austrian Centre under the name of *Das Laterndl* (The Lantern). They began with short sketches dealing with topical subjects both satirical and serious, in pantomime, song and parody ; and the PEN Club later became patrons of new ventures. The outbreak of war suspended the *Laterndl's* activities until November, 1939, when it put on a new programme, *Beacons*, at the Hampstead Concert Studio, which in three months was seen by 6,000 people. Apart from frequently changing variety programmes, Jura, the gifted young Austrian author murdered by the Nazis in Buchenwald concentration camp, was commemorated by the performance of his three most beautiful sketches. A dramatised version of *The Good Soldier Schweik* (including *Schweik under the Republic* and *Schweik under the Protectorate*) and a German version of the *Beggar's Opera* were their last, highly successful productions. Internment killed the *Laterndl*, but in May, 1940, a new theatrical venture, the *Kammerspiele* (Club Theatre) was launched at the London Centre with the well-known Czech producer Lewitt in charge. Owing to internment the cast are mostly Czechs and Sudetens, and include such well-known actors as Richter, Demel and Josef Almas. This highly successful company has survived internment, presenting, in addition to a number of cabaret shows, Offenbach's *Salon Pitzelberger*, Nestroy's *Freiheit im Krähwinkel*, René Fauchois' *Achtung, Frisch Gestrichen !* (translated from the French), Molnar's *Spiel im Schloss* and Schoenthan's *Raub der Sabinerinnen*.

Other activities of the London Centre include a restaurant providing Viennese menus at the cheapest prices to 13,000 guests a month ; co-operative workshops for the repair of members' clothing, underwear and shoes ; a hostel, started after the outbreak of war to provide temporary shelter ; Self-Aid services ; an Employment Department and Domestic Agency. The Austrian arts and crafts workers formed a co-operative guild and launched the Austrian Studio for Arts and Crafts at the London Centre, which aimed at turning out products in the best traditions of the famous *Wiener Werkstätte* and *Werkbund*, on a scale sufficient ultimately to ensure its members a livelihood. Outside London a large number of Austrian groups and several actual centres (sometimes embracing Germans and Czechs too) were established.

The Germans.—Among the mass of refugees from Germany proper no organisation corresponding to the Czech Working Committee or the Council of Austrians exists. The most important German refugee organisation is the Free German League of Culture, founded in December, 1938, for the purpose of " building bridges between German culture suppressed in our homeland and the spiritual life of England." Its English patrons include Mr. Wickham Steed, Mr. J. B. Priestley and Professor Gilbert Murray. Its Hampstead centre, in a house put at its disposal by the Church of England in December, 1939, resembles the premises of the London Austrian Centre on a smaller scale. The League also has a number of branches in provincial towns. Berthold Viertel, the writer, was the League's first president, followed by Vincent Brun, whose most recent novel, *Untimely Ulysses*, was published in August, 1940, after his internment. Other well-known artists, writers and actors associated with the League include Oscar Kokoschka, Stefan Zweig, Ludwig Renn, Hanne Norbert, Lilly Kann, Annemarie Haase, John Heartfield, Alan Gray, Erich Freund and Gerhard Hintze.   The League organised a number of concerts and theatrical performances, notably the Cabaret *Four and Twenty Blacksheep* at the Arts Theatre in London, and two one-act plays of Barrie (March, 1940), a number of variety shows, and, in July, 1940, a series of special perform-ances to raise funds for interned members of the League (the actors, singers and musicians were mostly Czechs and Austrians, as most of the Germans were interned).   The League also organised a memorial meeting for Ernst Toller and Josef Roth, at which Mr. Wickham Steed told the refugee audience :

" Please do not attempt to become hundred-per-cent Englishmen.   You will never succeed. . . . Remain rather good Germans, for in the coming years the world will have need of good Germans.   And if you can absorb something of the English spirit into your Germanness, you will render good service to both peoples."

A highly successful exhibition of works by German artists in exile was held at the Wertheim Galleries.   In February, 1940, some of England's leading actors and actresses took part in a special performance at the Embassy Theatre, London, to raise funds for the League's work.

As the war progressed the League took up other forms of activity, necessitated by the worsening position of German refugees.   The Hampstead Centre started a canteen, serving 40–50 meals daily.   In March, 1940, an office for advice and information was started ; it had plenty to do when internment began.   Two evenings a week were devoted to entertainments for German domestic servants.   The League's membership in London was increasing steadily in the early part of 1940, and had passed the 1,400 level when general internment suspended all further progress.

Semi-Official Bodies.—Apart from these voluntary organisa-tions of or for refugees, two semi-official bodies must be mentioned.   The British Council appointed a Resident Foreigners' Committee in October, 1939, which sought to promote the social and cultural welfare of people from other countries resident in Britain for the duration of the war.   It held a number of receptions for people of different nationalities and a very successful course of lectures on British life and Institutions by distinguished British authorities (January to April, 1940). Lectures on English Art and Life were also arranged. The Committee also distributed over 2,200 free tickets for theatres in the first five months of its work, over 550 concert tickets, and large numbers of tickets for lectures, art-shows and film performances. A different kind of body is the Parliamentary Committee on Refugees (Secretary, Miss Eleanor Rathbone, M.P.), a group of M.P.'s of all parties which watches over refugee problems and raises issues in the House of Commons and in representations to Ministers. It works in close co-operation with Bloomsbury House and other refugee organisations, and has a record of good achievements as protector of refugee interests.

The High Commissioner for Refugees.—Finally some reference must be made to the League of Nations High Commissioner for Refugees. Up to the end of 1938 the Nansen International Office for Refugees, working under League auspices, acted as protecting power for Russian, Armenian and other groups of refugees. It built up in the most important countries a machinery of local representatives who fulfilled semi-consular functions and had powers of defining who was and who was not a refugee. Refugees under the Office's protection were issued by the Governments of their country of refuge with " Nansen passports " which were recognised as valid travel and identity documents and guaranteed their holders definite rights and status under the Convention Relating to the International Status of Refugees of 1933. When the Nazis created a new refugee problem the Nansen Office was not put in charge. Instead the League of Nations appointed a separate High Commissioner for Refugees (Jewish and other) Coming from Germany, late in 1933. In order to avoid offending the susceptibilities of the Nazi Government (still a member of the League) the High Commissioner functioned in semi-detachment from the League, which accepted no responsibility for his actions, and a special Governing Body was appointed by interested Governments to which the High Commissioner was answerable. Lord Cecil was Chairman of the Governing Body and Mr. James G. McDonald, an American, became High Commissioner. Without funds, without local offices in different countries, without the weight and authority of the

League behind him, the High Commissioner was in a weak and isolated position and was able to achieve very little. He had none of the semi-consular or definition powers of the Nansen Office and no " McDonald passport " was issued for the refugees under his care. His functions were almost exclusively limited to diplomatic intervention with various Governments. Through his Advisory Council and an Experts' Committee co-operating with academic committees in a number of countries, Dr. Walter Kotschnig, under the High Commissioner, was however able to promote work on a large scale for the placing in new posts of exiled scholars. After two years of frustrated effort Mr. McDonald resigned, following Hitler's anti-Jewish Nürnberg Decrees, stating in a famous letter of resignation that the refugee problem was beyond the power of private organisations to solve.

The new High Commissioner, Sir Neill Malcolm, a League official, was made directly responsible to the League, and the independent Governing Body was abolished. His tasks were to work for improvements in the legal status of refugees coming from Germany, and to support and encourage co-operation between private organisations conducting relief, emigration and resettlement work. His position was stronger than Mr. McDonald's, since he had full League backing. His Office was in London, and he too had no administrative machinery in various countries. In May, 1938, the League placed refugees from Austria under his protection. When his period of office expired at the end of 1938 Sir Neill Malcolm was able to claim —in spite of the weaknesses of his position—that 5,000 refugees, groups or individuals, had benefited from his personal intervention with various Governments. In February, 1938, a Convention concerning the Status of Refugees Coming from Germany was adopted at Geneva. This Convention extended to refugees most of the rights (personal freedom, access to courts of law, etc.) accorded by the 1933 Convention to refugees under the Nansen Office, and bound the Governments to issue some sort of travel document to refugees in their territories. (This had been done since July, 1936, under an informal Inter-Governmental Arrangement).

In 1938 the Nineteenth Assembly of the League decided to liquidate both the Nansen Office and the High Commissioner's Office, and to appoint a League High Commissioner for Refugees who should take over both " Nansen " refugees and refugees coming from Germany. The powers of the new office are rigidly limited. It cannot commit the League in any way, it is restricted to questions of legal status and social protection ; the High Commissioner has severely limited funds and machinery, diplomatic standing only, and a staff restricted to one Deputy, two secretaries, four shorthand typists and one office-keeper. In 1939 Sir Herbert Emerson was appointed High Commissioner, with Dr. G. G. Kullmann as Deputy, and headquarters in London. He is assisted by a Liaison Committee of the principal private organisations, but is entirely free to establish contacts as he thinks fit with voluntary bodies or Governments. In 1938 representatives of 31 Governments met at Evian to consider plans for international assistance of refugees, and an Inter-Governmental Committee of 27 Governments, with headquarters in London, was finally established to consider plans for the emigration of would-be refugees from Germany and for their final settlement in other countries. Its functions were, however, purely diplomatic and limited to conducting negotiations. The plans would have to be carried out by voluntary bodies or benevolent Governments. The High Commissioner for Refugees coming from Germany attended its meetings, and after the resignation of Mr. Rublee in February, 1939, Sir Herbert Emerson became Director of the Evian Committee.

From his London office in Northumberland Avenue the High Commissioner is supposed to act as protecting power to the former " Nansen " refugees and to refugees from Germany, Austria and the Sudeten territories (Czechs were provisionally added in 1939 pending a final League decision). He has the task, in all countries where League authority is recognised, of seeing that the provisions of the Conventions of 1933 and 1938 are operated for the benefit of refugees. As Director of the Evian Committee he has (or had until war work made such work quasi-impossible) the responsibility of negotiating for practical emigration and settlement schemes. In addition, as Chairman of the Bloomsbury House committee which allocates the Government subsidy to refugee organisations, as vice-chairman of the new Advisory Council on Aliens (under Lord Lytton) appointed by the British Government to advise it on measures for " maintaining the morale of aliens in this country " and on internment conditions, and as a member of the Committee of Three which assists Sir John Anderson in " dealing

with this problem of aliens of enemy nationality," Sir Herbert
Emerson has important duties to the British authorities.   The
international protector of refugees in Britain operates from a
small office without any international machinery, and at the
same time occupies official and semi-official positions under the
auspices of the British Government which may or may not
be compatible with his functions as an international authority
independent of any Government.   The urgent need of the
refugees is precisely for an independent Protecting Power
which can ensure to them some of the rights and backing
which the ordinary citizen enjoys when in a foreign country,
by virtue of having a Government of his own to protect him.
This question is discussed in Chapter V.

3.   *Measures on the Outbreak of War*

As is well known, after the war broke out the Government
felt it necessary to make all " enemy aliens " go before special
tribunals which examined their bona fides and attempted to
decide whether they were genuine refugees.   The tribunals
were asked to order the internment of any individual of whom
they had serious doubts (A Class), to exempt from all restrictions (except those which apply to all foreigners) those about
whom they were certain (C Class), and to place other individuals, whose record did not justify either internment or
complete liberty, into a special group (B Class) with restricted
freedom.   The main restriction on B Class individuals was
that they could not travel more than five miles (except in the
London area) without first obtaining police permission.   The
tribunals were also asked to classify " enemy aliens " into
" refugees from Nazi oppression " and   non-refugees, a
classification which to some extent cut across the A, B, C
classification.   Out of 62,200 Germans and 12,000 Austrians
in the country, about 73,400 were examined by the tribunals.
The remaining 1,000 were not examined either because
they were about to re-emigrate, or were ill, or because
some mistake had been made about their nationality.
The following table gives the results of the tribunals'
work (like most official statistics they are not 100 per cent.
consistent) :

Class.	Men.	Women.	Total.	Total classed as "refugees from Nazi oppression."		
				Men.	Women.	Total.
A	400	200	600	130	30	160
B	3,200	3,600	6,800	2,150	1,950	4,100
C	26,500	37,700*	64,200	21,850	29,350	51,200
	30,100	41,500	71,600	24,130	31,330	55,460
Miscellaneous (Stateless, Danzigers, etc.) - -	1,300	900	2,200			
	31,400	42,400	73,800			

* Includes 2,600 British-born women.

In the main the 120 tribunals did their work well. But although they relied largely upon information provided from the files of the refugee organisations (without whose co-operation they would have had a hopeless task), there were many instances where they went astray through sheer ignorance or through prejudice. In particular there was no consistency about the placing of people in B Class. A few suspicious tribunals took the line of putting all "enemy aliens" whom they did not intern into B Class. Several tribunals adopted the practice of placing all domestic servants in this Class (which made it much more difficult, in provincial towns and country areas, for them to leave their jobs or go on journeys in their free time). Others put all unemployed refugees or all living in refugee hostels in B Class, sometimes telling the unemployed to come back and apply for transfer to C Class when they got employment. This particular practice made it more difficult for the individuals concerned to find work, and led to unfortunate incidents when B Class men were interned when just about to be transferred to C Class. Some tribunals also failed to understand that a non-Jew might nevertheless be an anti-Nazi and put many non-Jewish victims of Hitler into B Class. To be in B Class did not therefore necessarily mean that an individual was in any way suspect.   On the other hand, although the bulk of C cases are undoubtedly genuine, we know of tribunals who placed certain highly suspicious gentlemen in C Class.   These were usually men with relatives or connections with the German officer class or with the various German-Austrian royal families, but who had English connections among the " best " people to speak for them.

This snobbery or class prejudice also worked the other way. There were tribunals who regarded brave anti-Nazis who had fought Hitler and Mussolini in Spain as " dangerous Bolshevists " and ordered their immediate internment.   Others could not understand why a genuine anti-Nazi should have stayed in Germany for years after Hitler came to power in order to take part in underground trade-union or political opposition movements, and, scenting something " fishy " about such men, ordered their internment.   Genuine refugees who in desperation had smuggled themselves into this country, or had overstayed the period their visitors' permits entitled them to, were often put in A Class.   In some cases men were put in A Class for trivial and incidental reasons.   Two young Austrians were put in A Class because their employer had had trouble with them.   The tribunal decided that internment " might be a good lesson to them."   Later one was drowned on the *Arandora Star*, the other rescued from it.   The majority of A Class men thus sent for internment in civilian war prisoners' camps were undoubtedly of Nazi sympathies, but the anti-Nazi minority in those camps—consisting usually of left-wing " politicals " and International Brigaders—suffered terribly from being locked up with Nazis . . . until they were all deported to Canada together.   Thus even A Class cases were by no means all Nazi sympathisers or suspects, and the Home Office was persistently pressed from many quarters for the release of the anti-Nazis among them.

So general was this confusion over B cases especially (discussed twice in the House of Lords in October, 1939) that soon after the tribunals had finished their work, new tribunals (Regional Committees) were set up to begin a review of all B Class and other cases about which there might be some doubt. After some delay the review of B cases began in May, 1940. The men had begun to appear before the new tribunals (about a quarter had passed through them), when internment of B Class men was ordered and carried most of them off.   The extension of internment to B Class women similarly interrupted the review of their cases. Many men who might have been placed in C Class were shipped overseas because they were still B Class " suspects " when interned.

Apart from these measures the authorities naturally lost no time when war broke out in arresting and locking up all individuals about whom they had definite information or very strong suspicions as to their possible connections with the Nazi Government. As Mr. Peake explained on July 10 :

" On the outbreak of the war we interned every man and woman who was on the security list. Some who were on that list had gone back to Germany ; some had been permitted to go and others had been prevented from going, *but every known suspect who was still in this country was interned on the outbreak of war, and our policy at that time was, rightly or wrongly, to submit every enemy alien to individual examination.*"

About 350 were on the security list, and, apart from some 2,500 foreigners arrested on arrival at ports (many of whom were *not* suspects but refugees from the *Blitzkrieg*), probably nearly another 1,000 suspects had been interned by the end of June, 1940. The authorities cannot therefore be blamed for any lack of vigilance.

4. *The Position of the Refugees*

Employment.—The outbreak of war upset many plans for re-emigration. Almost all countries except the U.S.A. closed their doors to immigrants, and there were shipping difficulties. Thousands had steamship tickets for which they had paid in German currency and which now were valueless. Nevertheless, in the first six months of 1940 alone 3,763 persons registered at the Jewish Refugees Committee re-emigrated, all but 188 of them going to the U.S.A. This total is larger than that of any entire preceding year (1939 : 3,412 ; 1938 : 1,377 ; 1937 : 1,013). It would have been even greater if internment and deportation had not temporarily upset re-emigration plans. About 27,000 of the German and Austrian refugees in Britain in June, 1940, had definite arrangements to go sooner or later to the United States to start a new life as free men and women.

In August, 1940, re-emigration began again, as the original internment muddle began to be cleared up.

The attitude of the public to refugees when war came was generally sympathetic, since they were known to be victims and enemies of Hitler.   Consequently, after an initial wave of dismissals of refugees from employment, due to the same dis-location that threw many British workers out of their jobs, the employment situation of " enemy aliens " did not change very much in the first months of the war.   They were still not allowed to work, except in rare cases (highly qualified chemists, engineers, etc.) or as domestic servants.   Their papers were endorsed : " Not to take employment paid or unpaid."

Only a very small number were accepted into national service work like A.R.P. or first-aid organisations.   This situation continued until the end of November, 1939, when Sir John Anderson issued an Order in Council modifying the existing restrictions on the employment of " aliens."   Foreigners could not be employed in certain key industries (power plants, arms works, etc.) and in certain other trades directly connected with the war effort.   Apart from this a foreigner was allowed to register for work at employment exchanges and, wherever work was available and there were no British workers to do it, the employment exchange itself issued a labour permit, provided the conditions of work were not below those of British workers. In the prohibited employments a foreigner could only get work by first obtaining a permit from the Auxiliary War Services Department, which carefully examined the applicant's creden-tials.   Although the Order defined the prohibited trades in a very loose way, so that much depended upon the interpretation adopted by the A.W.S.D., the effect of this change of policy was to allow the refugees to enter the labour market.

In the following six months it is estimated that nearly 20,000 actually found work.   The German Emergency Committee placed about 500 men and women in jobs, including electrical engineers, industrial chemists and tool-makers.   Employment of Czech Trust Fund refugees rose steadily until internment began.   At the end of May 505 of its men and 101 of its women had been placed in industry (metal workers, textile workers, mechanics and precision workers, fitters, turners, tool-makers, etc.), 222 were in agriculture, 160 in forestry and 73 in professional occupations. Placings by the Employment Department of Bloomsbury House rose steadily until June, when a heavy fall began. The Domestic Bureau of Bloomsbury House similarly reports a considerable absorption of women into employment after November, 1939. It placed about 250 a month in domestic service, and as many more each month found domestic work by their own efforts. In addition large numbers of women, now that other work was permitted, got jobs as machinists and factory hands, usually earning better wages than domestic servants. Another indication of what was happening is given by the fact the number of refugees fully supported by the Jewish Refugees Committee fell steadily from 5,320 in January to 4,150 in May, 1940, while partly supported cases fell from 1,370 to 770. German Emergency Committee maintained cases had been reduced to a few hundreds. Finally, the Government decided in November to recruit up to 2,000 refugees into labour battalions of the Auxiliary Military Pioneer Corps. A thousand men were enlisted at the Kitchener Camp at Richborough by the end of the year, and Lord Reading became Commander of a Depôt at the camp for the training of Pioneer Corps recruits.

Thus by April, 1940, absorption into employment and re-emigration had gone some way towards mitigating and reducing the refugee problem. Probably a little imagination could have produced constructive schemes for affording almost every refugee wanting work with opportunities for using his abilities, skill or labour power in some useful sphere or another of our national life. Internment shattered all these tendencies, and it was only in August, 1940, that a new Minister of Labour, Mr. Ernest Bevin, revealed the imagination necessary for drawing refugees fully into the life and work of the British community. (*See* Chapter V, Section 4.)

Public Opinion.—Generally speaking the attitude to refugees both of the public and of the authorities right down to May, 1940, was thoroughly friendly. This general atmosphere of friendliness was disturbed, although not seriously damaged, by a campaign against refugees which began quite suddenly in the third week of January in several newspapers. " The fact that the same charges were put forward at the same moment and almost in the same words in many papers," writes " Onlooker " in the *Contemporary Review* (August, 1940), " suggests that the campaign emanated from one centre." Among the worst offenders were the *Sunday Express* and the *Daily Sketch*, which published lurid and totally unsubstantiated allegations about refugees acting as spies and saboteurs, and accused the tribunals of neglecting their duty because they had only interned a few hundreds of suspicious " enemy aliens." The *Daily Sketch* on January 20, 1940, actually accused refugees of being responsible for the explosion at the Royal Gunpowder Factory at Waltham Cross. Many similar stories appeared in a section of the press, often pretending to give the opinions of the police themselves. Scotland Yard finally took the unusual step of issuing the following statement on behalf of Sir Philip Game, the London Police Commissioner :

" The attention of the Commissioner of Police of the Metropolis has been called to articles that have appeared in certain newspapers, purporting to represent the views of Scotland Yard on the subject of the internment of enemy aliens. In these articles it is alleged, *inter alia*, that Scotland Yard is gravely concerned by the leniency of Aliens Tribunals. The Commissioner desires to take the earliest opportunity of stating publicly that such articles are completely unauthorised and do not, in fact, represent the views either of himself or of the responsible officials at Scotland Yard who are concerned with this problem."

As the campaign continued in the following months Scotland Yard issued a similar statement on April 15, 1940. In spite of this unprincipled campaign no considerable hostility to refugees was aroused. In Chapter IV, section 2, we give evidence that at the end of April less than one person in a hundred thought that all refugees should be interned. The campaign certainly made no visible impression upon the authorities. In March, when M.P.'s expressed anxiety about the employment of German domestics at Aldershot, Sir John Anderson told the House that neither he nor the Chief Constables concerned were worried in the slightest, and went on :

" In my view there would be no justification for a policy under which all aliens of German or Austrian nationality were treated alike without regard to the fact that the majority of them are refugees from Nazi oppression and are bitterly opposed to the present régime in Germany."

Even after the first internment measures were taken in May, the Duke of Devonshire, speaking for the Government on

May 23, 1940, reminded the House of Lords that " it was important, when wholesale internment was advocated, to remember that the vast majority of aliens and refugees here hated Germany* more than we did." Thereafter the Government's attitude changed rapidly, and the press campaign, limited hitherto to a few newspapers, became widespread and inflammatory, and general internment began. In examining what happened then and why it happened it is important to remember the fact that for the first eight months of the war the Government's attitude to refugees was sensible and friendly. As Mr. Peake, Under-Secretary of State for the Home Department, explained to Parliament on July 10 :

" My right hon. Friend (Sir John Anderson) and I realised the risks we were running in leaving these refugees and enemy aliens alone. We knew that if a serious act of espionage or sabotage were attributed to and proved against any of them, both he and I would be blown sky-high by the House of Commons and the country. However, we felt fairly confident, and *I should like to pay my tribute to the behaviour of these refugees in that they have shown themselves worthy of the confidence which we placed in them.* Apart from one or two petty, isolated instances, such as the undergraduate, Mr. Solf, who photographed a burning aeroplane, and one or two black-out offences, there have been no serious cases of acts hostile to the State which can be attributed to these people."

This statement should be borne in mind. Two months after the policy of forced removals, wholesale internment and deportation began, the Home Office spokesman paid a tribute to the " enemy aliens." There is no doubt about it : our " enemy aliens " *have* " shown themselves worthy of the confidence which we have placed in them." They cannot be charged with anything worse than " one or two black-out offences " and " one or two petty, isolated instances " such as photographing forbidden objects, offences which have been committed by far greater numbers of British citizens.

* Meaning, presumably, the Nazi regime ?

CHAPTER III

1. *The New Policy*

ON Sunday, May 12, 1940, the third day of the battle for Holland and Belgium, the first step in the new " aliens " policy was taken. A wide coastal belt, stretching from Inverness to the eastern edge of Dorset, was declared " protected." *All* male Germans and Austrians aged 16–60 (" excluding the invalid and the infirm ") in this belt were rounded up for " temporary internment." This round-up, which brought in 2,000 men, was carried through irrespective of the personal character or the type of work of the individuals concerned. (Both the University of Cambridge and the London School of Economics, now in Cambridge, lost important members of their staffs, because Cambridge fell within the coastal belt). Many " enemy aliens " who simply happened to be spending Whitsun week-end in a seaside town were taken off. Male Germans and Austrians outside the coastal belt were forbidden to enter it. Male foreigners aged 16–60 of all other nationalities were only allowed to remain in the coastal belt on conditions : (*a*) that they reported daily and in person to the police,* (*b*) that they observed a curfew from 8 p.m. to 6 a.m., and (*c*) that they used no motor vehicle (other than a public conveyance) or bicycle for travelling.

The Home Office announcement was apologetic in tone :

" These measures are to be considered as measures of urgency applied to areas where for military reasons special precautions are required for the time being.

" It is recognised and much regretted that these necessary measures will involve for a period great hardship in individual cases. Those persons, however, who are affected by them

* Repealed on May 28.

70

and who are in fact faithful to the vital interests of this country will give the best proof of their attitude by submitting freely and uncomplainingly to the restrictions which the exigencies of the situation for the moment require.

" It is intended that the rigour of these measures should be mitigated as soon as circumstances permit."

It will be noted that military necessity was the only reason given, and that great stress was laid on the temporary character of the measures taken.

On the night of the following Wednesday, and on Thursday, May 16, when the battle of the Meuse was raging in Belgium and Holland had surrendered, all male Germans and Austrians aged 16–60 in B Class, numbering about 2,200, were rounded up for internment. *The Times* (May 17) reported that

" the whole of Scotland Yard's fleet of motor-cars from headquarters and police stations in divisions were mobilised, and chief officers were on duty throughout Wednesday night. . . . The greatest secrecy was maintained by Scotland Yard and even the officers concerned had no idea of what was afoot until they were given instructions when reporting for duty yesterday morning. . . .

"At Sheffield two motor-coach loads were rounded up and they were accompanied by two lorries manned by soldiers."

Justified or otherwise, the official stress on secrecy and the mystery inevitably associated with " midnight arrests " (so urgent that they couldn't wait till morning) did not fail to assist in fostering a certain anti-" alien " feeling. So much so that on the following day (Friday, May 17), the Christian Council for Refugees from Germany and Central Europe issued a letter to all clergymen, signed by the Bishop of Chichester and the Bishop Auxiliary of Westminster, pointing out the serious danger that

" with the intensification of hostilities public antipathy may be aroused towards all people of German origin, in spite of the fact that these refugees are themselves victims of the ruthless oppression of the Nazi Party. May we therefore appeal for your help in averting such a tragedy by keeping your people well informed as to the facts of this rapidly changing situation ? "

On Monday, May 20, began the re-examination by the new Aliens Advisory Committees of all female Germans and

Austrians who had been placed in B Class. This review of B cases had been planned since the beginning of May. As we have seen, the men had actually been started on, but their internment left only the women to be dealt with. A week later, on Monday, May 27, when fighting on the Somme line was beginning, and General Ironside had been transferred to the chief command of the Home Forces, the review of B cases was interrupted by the internment of the 3,000 B Class women aged 16–60. " In some instances in London," says *The Times*, " the police had to wait until the women were dressed." (Fancy keeping the police waiting!) The Home Office again stressed that internment was to be *temporary*.

As from Monday, June 3, after King Leopold's surrender, and when the Dunkirk withdrawal was being completed, all foreigners over the age of 16, except the French, were subject to a curfew from 10.30 p.m. (midnight in London) to 6 a.m. In this same week the " protected " areas were further extended, and in many of them foreigners were not allowed to remain or to enter at all except by special permit. Notice to remove ranging from a few hours to three days was given to all resident foreigners in these areas.

Later in the week internment of the 300 B Class " enemy aliens " aged 60–70 (and who were not too ill) was carried out. By mid-June about 7,000 men and 3,800 women (including A Class) were stated to be in internment camps.

On the evening of June 10, following Mussolini's entry into the war, the interviewing and rounding-up of Italians began. Anti-Italian feeling in many towns led to disturbances and attacks on Italian shops and cafés. About 4,100 Italians (including women) were interned. As Mr. Peake explained on August 6, " the general principle was to intern Italians known to be members of the Italian Fascist Party and *all male Italians between the ages of* 16 *and* 70 *with less than twenty years' residence.*" A number of anti-Fascist refugees from Mussolini's terror were included in this round-up, some of whom lost their lives on the *Arandora Star*.

In the second half of June, internment of German and Austrian men became general, and no further apologies or references to its *temporary* character were made. On June 20, when the French delegates were proceeding to Compiègne to hear the *Führer's* armistice terms, Sir John Anderson stated in Parliament :

" I have authorised chief constables to arrest for internment any German or Austrian in Category C about whose
reliability the chief constable feels doubt from the point of
view of national security."

In answer to a question whether refugees were being interned
without any reason being given, he replied :

" That is perfectly true, and when it is represented to me
that as a matter of military necessity action should be taken,
my desire must be in the present circumstances to take that
action unless there are overwhelming arguments to the
contrary."

At that time the public had the impression that only men
suspected in any way by the chief constables were being
interned.   But round about June 25 an order was issued to
intern all C Class men under 70, with the exception of certain
supposedly exempted categories (invalids, key workers, etc.).
Sir John Anderson finally made it clear on July 11 exactly
what discretion had been given to chief constables :

" The discretion given to chief constables is not a discretion to exempt enemy aliens from internment, but a
discretion to intern individuals falling within the exempted
categories if as regards a particular individual the police have
special information showing that his immediate internment is
necessary on security grounds."

Instead of interning only those men about whom the chief
constables entertained some doubts, the great majority of
C Class men, including " suspicious " individuals in the
exempted categories, were taken away.   The question of who
was interned and who was spared will be discussed in the next
section.   Here let it only be said that the chief constables in
most areas appear to have discovered " special information "
or to have developed " doubts " about large numbers of men
who had every right to be exempted.   Nor is there any
evidence that they strove officiously, if at all, to ascertain
whether there were " overwhelming arguments to the contrary " in individual cases.   Certainly they did not consult the
refugee-relief organisations, government-subsidised though
they are, or the organisations of the refugees themselves,
although they possess information about the vast majority of
genuine refugees.

By mid-July, in addition to the 7,000 men and 3,800 women already interned, about 13,000 C Class men had been rounded up. This makes a total of 20,000 men interned out of a maximum of no more than 30,000 male Germans and Austrians in the country.* There were thus at most 10,000 males remaining at liberty in the middle of July. Since four to five thousand of these were in the Auxiliary Military Pioneer Corps, and since rounding-up continued throughout July, only a few thousand must have been still left in freedom by the end of July. In other words, the vast majority of genuine refugees from Nazi oppression were considered too potentially dangerous—i.e. *too well disposed towards Hitler*—to be permitted any kind of freedom at all.

In July came the news that male internees were being deported to Canada (and later to Australia) together with civilian and military prisoners of war. On August 22, Sir John Anderson announced the following deportation totals :

Germans and Austrians :
A Class	-	-	-	-	-	- 2,358
B and C Classes	-	-	-	-	4,206
						6,564
Italians	-	-	-	-	-	1,100
	Total	-	-	-	-	7,664

The total for A Class is far above those put in this class by the Tribunals, apparently because it includes Nazi civilian prisoners of war captured during the war mainly from German ships. For some unexplained reason Sir John Anderson was unable, a month after deportation, to give " precise information " about the number of deportees in B and C Classes respectively.

News began to filter out about the indiscriminate character of internment and deportation and about the bad conditions in the internment camps. The main feature of July was the growth of a mighty feeling of dismay and indignation among well-informed people in all walks of life, not against the principle of interning and deporting *suspects*, but against the tactless, stupid and unimaginative measures which had actually

* According to Sir John Anderson, 5,000 C Class " enemy aliens " re-emigrated from Britain in January–May, 1940, alone. These probably included at least 1,000 men, who must be deducted from the total of 31,000 in the country at the outbreak of war.

been adopted. The lumping together of Nazis and non-Nazis, of enemies and friends, soon made it clear that measures had been taken which were tinged with panic, and which were so wholesale and so lacking in common sense as to extend far beyond what national security required.

This spontaneous outburst of public indignation came to a head in the House of Commons debate on July 10, in which Members of all parties joined in pressing for the adoption of a sensible attitude. In this debate—in spite of the stone-walling of the War Office spokesman, Sir Edward Grigg—such a sorry picture of muddle, ignorance and lack of responsibility was disclosed, that the Government was subsequently compelled to beat a slight retreat. Changes in policy were later announced, and some of the worst features of internment conditions are now being cleared up. In a second debate on August 22, further concessions were made, but at the time of writing the Government had still not departed from its policy of keeping locked up or of deporting the vast majority of German and Austrian men. There is as yet very little indication that the authorities are intending to adopt that constructive attitude which we believe to be necessary.

2. *Who was Interned, and How it was Done*

Round-up Methods.—On the whole there is no doubt that, in arresting individuals for internment, police officers behaved with courtesy and kindliness. But they had their orders to carry out, and in far too many cases the police chiefs who gave those orders appear almost to have imagined that they were swooping on criminals. Was it necessary, when arresting B Class men in mid-May, to proceed with such secrecy that even the police officers were not told until they came on duty, paying visits *at all hours of the night,* in some cases with lorry-loads of soldiers accompanying the police vans ? Was it so often necessary to give such short notice that in many cases the individuals concerned had no time to put their affairs in order or even to communicate with relatives ? Let the reader work out for himself the minimum time he would require for settling his personal affairs and making his farewells, if the police came to take him off to an unknown destination (possibly on the other side of the world) for an indefinite period, especially if he had done nothing at all which might lead him to expect arrest.   We have knowledge of many incidents that were deplorable.   We mention only what happened in Hampstead, with the fervent hope that it was exceptional and not typical.   On July 13, about 1.30 p.m., a group of C.I.D. men walked into Hampstead Public Library and asked all Germans and Austrians to go with them.   Escorted to their homes, they were allowed a very short time to pack and were then taken away.   They were only able to take leave of such of their relatives as happened to be at home at the time. · People were also stopped in the main streets of Hampstead and, if found to be " enemy aliens," taken off to the police station.   Having spirited away thousands of harmless " enemy aliens," the authorities simply left the job of storing their furniture, terminating their leases, paying their bills, and settling a hundred-and-one other personal matters, to the refugee organisations or to personal friends who happened to be on the spot.

A Census of Internees.—On June 11, when 10,000 Germans and Austrians had been interned, Mr. Peake explained to the House of Commons that to publish a list of their names was " impracticable," as " waste of paper is a consideration at the present time and it would involve considerable expenditure." By the end of July about 30,000 " enemy aliens " (including Italians) had been interned, but it was still felt to be " impracticable " to give detailed information about internees, because, as Mr. Peake explained on July 31,

> " The staff of the Home Office are devoting all their attention to going through the categories of persons who have been interned by mistake, and I do not want to divert them from that job in order to procure statistical information of an elaborate character."

In the absence, not merely of " statistical information of an elaborate character," but even of lists of internees, we cannot attempt a comprehensive survey of the kind of people who have been interned.

By great good fortune, however, one valuable statistical survey has come our way.   In the third week of July a census was held of the 1,500 inmates of one typical men's camp by statisticians interned in the camp.   The results are highly interesting.   Two-thirds of the men came from Germany, and over one-tenth from Austria.   Another 17 per cent. were

stateless ; 82 per cent. of all the men were Jewish. Elderly
men predominated, since 58 per cent. were over the age of 40,
and 27 per cent. over the age of 55. Just under three-quarters
were married men, and another 5 per cent. were engaged to be
married. Half of the wives of these men were of German
origin, one-fifth of Austrian origin, and 13 per cent. were
British women. Over one-third of the men who were married
or engaged had wives or fiancées who were also interned. Over
one-third of the married men had children under 16 ; of the
fathers of children under 16, four-fifths had British-born
children, and one-third had children under 16 who were also
interned. Ninety per cent. of the men had been before one
tribunal, and 5 per cent. had been before a second tribunal ;
84 per cent. claimed to be refugees, and 70 per cent. had
actually been classed as " refugees from Nazi oppression " by
the tribunals ; 30 per cent. stated that they had been in prisons
or concentration camps or had suffered other forms of Nazi
persecution. Eleven per cent. were found to be either seriously
ill or cripples ; 44 per cent. had definite plans for re-emigration,
mostly to the U.S.A., and just under 10 per cent. had applied
for British naturalisation. Nearly one-quarter of the men
had been living in England for six years or more. Before they
were rounded up, just under three-quarters had volunteered
either for the Army, the Pioneer Corps, or some other form
of National Service. Only a tenth of those who volunteered
had been accepted. One-tenth of the men had near relatives
serving either in the Army, the Pioneer Corps, or in some other
form of National Service. No less than 87 per cent. of the
men, i.e. practically everyone except the seriously ill and the
crippled, were willing to volunteer for such service now. As
to their occupations, 223 (15 per cent.) had been employers of
British labour, and had employed between them no less than
6,500 British workers. The camp also included 38 physicians,
12 dentists, 113 scientists and teachers, 68 lawyers, 67 graduated
engineers, 22 graduated chemical engineers, 169 engineers and
mechanics, 46 chemists and chemical workers, 5 dispensing
chemists, 103 agricultural workers, 253 export merchants,
121 artists and literary workers, 19 clergymen and 97 political
refugees. About 600 of the rest were commercial and black-
coated workers, and some 300 were industrial craftsmen.

We make no comments on these statistics. They speak for
themselves. We have every reason to believe that this

particular camp is fairly typical of all the men's camps.   Since 70 per cent. of the men in this camp were officially regarded as refugees, we also have every reason to believe that the great majority of the internees are genuine anti-Nazis against whom the authorities have no evidence or suspicions.

Full details concerning the overwhelming majority of German and Austrian internees are to be found in the records of the various refugee organisations.   Individual Members of Parliament, especially those connected with the Parliamentary Committee on Refugees, were deluged with cases by every mail. From such sources, from the press and from Parliamentary reports, and from the scores of authenticated cases that were reported to us privately during the six weeks this book has taken to write, we can clearly show (a) that in most cases the police used their discretion to intern individuals in the supposedly exempted categories in a very " liberal " fashion ; (b) that " overwhelming arguments to the contrary " were commonly ignored ; (c) that many " friendly aliens " were mistakenly interned, and even deported ; (d) that the authorities appear to have had little idea of whom they were rounding-up and that, until recently, they generally failed to keep any reliable records even of the names of the individuals they were locking up and deporting, let alone the names and addresses of their next-of-kin.   We do not have to prove these assertions, because they have all finally been admitted by the authorities themselves.   We can, however, select a few individual cases to illustrate what has been going on.

Culturally Valuable Men.—To begin with, here is a brief selection of eminent writers, artists and professional men who were interned (a few have since been released) :

Dr. Franz Borkenau (Austrian), distinguished historian, sociologist and anti-Nazi propagandist.   Latest book : *The Totalitarian Enemy*.

Siegfried Charoux (Austrian), sculptor.   The Nazis removed his works from the Vienna State Gallery and destroyed his statue of Lessing in the Judenplatz.

Georg Ehrlich (Austrian), famous sculptor ; very successful in England.

Heinrich Fraenkel (German), well-known journalist.   Author of *The German People versus Hitler* and contributor to newspapers.   A lifelong opponent of the Nazis.   His wife was also interned . . . in a different camp.   *Dr. Martin Freud* (Austrian), son of the founder of psycho-analysis, Sigmund Freud, a distinguished writer and Fellow of the Royal Society.   His son was taken from an English college and shipped overseas. His wife and daughter were in France, whereabouts unknown.

Sebastian Haffner (German), lawyer and journalist.   Author of the famous book, *Germany, Jekyll and Hyde*.   His wife was also interned.   *Hamann* (Austrian), distinguished painter. Walks with crutches on account of rheumatism.   Wrote from Huyton Camp that he had not *seen* a chair for six weeks. *John Heartfield* (German), pioneer of photomontage.   His anti-Nazi cartoons are world-famous.   Adopted an *English* name during the 1914–18 war to express his hatred of Prussian militarism.   Devoted his whole life to fighting reaction in Germany, of which he made a classic exposure in his photo-book, *Deutschland Über Alles*.   Fled to Prague where he carried on his struggle.   Had the honour of being included in the second list of prominent Germans whom Hitler formally deprived of their nationality.   Came to England in 1938, where he continued his anti-Nazi photo-cartoons which appeared in *Picture Post, Lilliput, Reynolds News*. etc.   (C Class). *Heinz Heckroth* (German), well-known stage designer and principal authority in Germany on projection in the theatre for scenic decoration.   The Nazis removed his paintings from the galleries.   Became principal designer to the Ballets Jooss and head of the Dartington Hall Art Studios.   Shipped overseas on July 10 without warning to his wife and child or to the Dartington Trustees, his employers.   *Bruno Heilig*, anti-Nazi author of *A Man Crucified*.   *Gerhard Hintze* (German), well-known actor ;   secretary of the Free German League of Culture. *Spent years in a Nazi concentration camp ; now shipped overseas.*

Kurt Jooss (German), world-famous ballet master.   Became Germany's leading choreographer.   His anti-Nazi achievements in the sphere of art (see later, p. 154) are universally known. Came to England in 1934 and founded the Jooss-Leeder School of Dance at Dartington Hall.

Dr. Ernst Kitzinger (German), a young art historian of outstanding abilities, specialist in medieval art.   Had been working in the British Museum with the financial. assistance of the Society for the Protection of Science and Learning, and assisted in evacuating the Museum's art treasures from London.

Theodor Kramer (Austrian), lyrical poet of outstanding quality.

Fritz Lampl (Austrian), founder of the famous factory for " Bimini " artistic glass ware, very frail and delicate glass figures. Had opened a shop in England with two Austrian fellow-craftsmen (one was Bettina Ehrlich, wife of the interned sculptor).

Sigurd Leeder (German), co-director of the Jooss-Leeder School of Dance ; an outstanding teacher of dancing and an accomplished choreographer.

Ludwig Meidner (German), prominent expressionist painter.*
Dr. Ludwig Münz (Austrian), most famous Austrian art historian ; also specialist in the psychology of blind children.

Robert Neumann (Austrian), well-known writer with long anti-Nazi record. Hated by the Nazis who killed a man of the same name in mistake for him. Founded the Austrian PEN Club in Britain in 1938. Many of his books available in English. Had applied for naturalisation. *Dr. Otto Neurath* (Austrian), world-famous pioneer of pictorial statistics, fled from Vienna in 1934 because he was a Social-Democrat. Started a new life in the Hague ; escaped with his chief statistical assistant, to whom he is engaged, in a rowing boat when the Nazis overran Holland. Far out in the North Sea they were picked up by a British destroyer, brought to England and promptly interned. They were both in the Isle of Man. The news that he was in England at all was only revealed when a fellow internee, released at the beginning of August, began efforts to get him set free.
. *Rudolf Olden* (German), lawyer, journalist and life-long opponent of German reaction. Defended Ossietzky, who published details of illegal German rearmament under the Republic. Edited the *Berliner Tageblatt*. Sought refuge in England, where he founded the German branch of the PEN Club. Author of many books, including biographies of Stresemann, Hindenburg and Hitler. Latest book : *Is Germany a Hopeless Case ?* †

* On page 153 we explain what happened to the works of art he left behind him at his room in London.

† Released late in July, 1940, when he undertook to leave the country and gave proof that he was about to go to the U.S.A. to take up a University post which he did not want, but which was offered to him to get him out of internment. He and his wife set out on their unnecessary journey to America on the Ellerman Liner *City of Benares*. They were both drowned on September 17, 1940, together with nearly 300 other people (including other refugees and British children), when the liner was sunk by a Nazi torpedo.

Hans Oppenheim (German), conductor and musician ; founder of the *Deutsche Musikbühne*. Conducted at the Glyndebourne Festival Opera in 1934 ; Director of Music at Dartington Hall from 1937.* *Franz Osborne* (German), distinguished pianist, pupil of Schnabel.

Franz Pixner (Austrian), well-known sculptor. This " enemy alien " fought against the Nazis in Spain, and suffered over 200 injuries from grenades and a land-mine, which he was never expected to survive. After fourteen months in Benicasim hospital, and innumerable operations, he emerged with otitis media, continually inflamed eyes, permanent abdominal pains (due to embedded shrapnel), and general weakness of the left side (he had paralysis for some time). He entered France in the general retreat of February, 1939, and was interned in the notorious camps at Argeles and Gurs. Came to England in August, 1939. A visitor saw him at Huyton Camp on July 11, when he had a high temperature, pain in his left side, and eye and ear trouble (C Class). *Professor E. Pringsheim* (German), distinguished authority on Roman Law. Was at Oxford. His four sons, aged 16 to 26, were deported without his or their consent, and he was unable to take leave of his youngest son, although he was interned in a neighbouring camp on the Isle of Man.

Peter Stadlen (Austrian), distinguished pianist and a " modernist." Deported to Australia. *Professor E. Stern* (German), film painter and specialist in camouflage. Collaborated with Max Reinhardt, the theatrical producer.

Fred Uhlman (German), lawyer and artist, see later, p. 187.

Professor Egon Wellesz (Austrian), famous composer of operas and songs and authority on Byzantine music. Held a fellowship provided partly by prominent British musicians and partly by the Society for the Protection of Science and Learning. Elected Honorary Fellow of Lincoln College, Oxford, in 1939. He happened to be in England when the Nazis seized Austria, but his daughter was made to scrub pavements in Vienna. She later got away to England.

Most of the men in this list were in C Class ; many of them have records of consistent struggle against reaction and tyranny that cannot be equalled by any of the Ministers of the present Government. Space prevents us from giving similar selections of eminent men in other fields of endeavour. Lists

* Finally released in August, 1940, because he is diabetic.

of scientists and technicians running into hundreds could be compiled from the records of the refugee organisations.

The " Useful."—But the eminent are only a small fraction of the internees. There is a much larger group which may be described as " useful." They have fared no better. We quote a few cases from the *Manchester Guardian* (July 9) :

" The Cambridge scientist working for the Government on gas gangrene, the agricultural students at Reading University who were taken by the police whilst they were sitting for their final examinations, the authority on Germany's export trade who has been working for the Minister of Economic Warfare, the expert on agricultural chemistry who was called in by the Ministry of Agriculture to advise on the extermination of the Colorado beetle. . . . The fifty German and Austrian Jewish youths who formed an agricultural training camp at East Grinstead, had had more than a year's training, and had been helping local farmers. . . . One of Germany's best-known cloth manufacturers who had been encouraged to open an export business and a factory in Yorkshire, Marconi's chief technical adviser, the leading international authority on the gramophone industry."

The following are a few Lancashire cases (*Manchester Guardian*, July 17) :

" A chemist who has held an important position at a chemical works in the Manchester district for three or four years was dismissed at a moment's notice (his hat and coat were brought out to him ; he was not allowed to go to his office to bring them) when the factory was taken over by the Government. Two days later he was interned as an unemployed enemy alien. A highly qualified chemist, who specialises in a branch of industrial chemistry in which qualified men are rare in this country, employed by a firm engaged on sub-contracts for Government orders has been interned. . . . An ' Aryan ' German who has been with the same firm for more than three years and before that was in a German concentration camp as a punishment for having tried to help his Jewish employer when the employer was expropriated by the Nazis. . . . A slipper manufacturer who established a new industry employing 250 people in a

Lancashire town, together with his key men. All the directors and chemists of a works near Manchester engaged on chemical manufacture for the leather industry. . . . A pathologist in the pathological laboratories of Manchester University. A distinguished German Jewish dentist who had to leave the west coast town where he was practising, and, as he was therefore without a practice, was interned. A young chemistry research student of six years' standing at Manchester University, son of a famous German Jewish doctor."

In the debate of July 10 Miss Eleanor Rathbone mentioned the case of a " man who is managing director of a company which at this very moment is carrying out contracts for four different Ministries of a total value of nearly £500,000." There is the noteworthy case of Mr. H. W. Singer, a well-known German Jewish refugee economist, on the staff of Manchester University. He is an authority on British unemployment and labour questions ; he worked on the famous Pilgrim Trust Survey of the life of the unemployed, and published a book, *Unemployment and the Unemployed*, shortly after war broke out. He has conducted inquiries for the Government, and had applied for naturalisation. In spite of protests from distinguished people he was interned. *After his internment came a request from the Ministry of Labour for his help in the man-power survey organised by Sir William Beveridge.**

Dr. O. S. (aged 69), was Germany's foremost ophthalmic surgeon, consulted by people all over the world. Working in Edinburgh for a British qualification, he was forced to remove to Glasgow, where he was interned as unemployed. Dr. E. G., a distinguished neurologist, was helped over to England in 1934 by the Rockefeller Foundation, and worked in the Clinical Research Department of Maudsley Hospital. On June 4 he was dismissed under a general order discharging all " enemy aliens " from L.C.C. hospitals. They took him away. Professor E. A. (aged 65) was one of Austria's leading physicists. The Gestapo would not permit him to leave as they feared he would be valuable to other countries. He escaped under great difficulties—and was interned in Britain. K. is a brilliant Jewish research worker who was doing original and highly promising work on pituitary glands at a Scottish University. If successful his work will remove much suffering and unnecessary

* Released at the end of September, 1940.

deaths. He was taken away. And so on and so on and
so on.

" *Politicals*."—Anti-Nazi political and trade-union leaders
and workers, many of them with years of experience of illegal
opposition work or of actual military struggle against Nazis and
Fascists, were not better treated. The most scandalous case
known to us is that of *Max Braun*, the Saarland Social-Democratic leader. For twelve years he led the struggle against reaction
in the Saar, and thrilled the world by his magnificent and
heroic organisation of the anti-Nazi campaign during the Saar
Plebiscite. When the Saar returned to Germany the Nazis
wanted him dead or alive. He fled to Paris, where they made
four attempts on his life. When France collapsed he escaped
to Morocco and then came to England. Towards the end of
July Mr. S. S. Silverman, M.P., was allowed to visit Max
Braun for two hours . . . in Pentonville Gaol. Others who
were interned include *Hans Gottfurcht*, Chairman of the German
Trade Unionists in London ; *Karl Olbrisch*, a metal worker
and former Communist member of the German Parliament
(the Gestapo caught him doing underground propaganda and
locked him up in prison for three years and then in a concentration camp. In 1937 he escaped to Czechoslovakia, and later
to England. . . . He was drowned on the *Arandora Star*.) *Louis
Weber*, a leading anti-Nazi in the German Seamen's Union,
who worked on neutral ships after Hitler came to power.
Coming to England as an anti-Nazi, he was sent to the Seaton
Prisoners of War Camp (Devon), where he was one of the leaders
of the anti-Nazi trade union group. (Drowned on the *Arandora
Star*.) *Valentin Wittke*, a German trade union leader with a
long record of underground struggle, also sent to Seaton
(survivor from the *Arandora Star*). *Mr. Czernitz*, leader of
the Austrian Socialists in Britain.

Large numbers of lesser known people were taken. Alfred
Ruzicka, a Czech Socialist worker who lived in Austria and
who fought in the International Brigade in Spain, became
leader of a company and distinguished himself at Teruel,
Brunete and the rout of the Italians at Guadalajara, was interned,
as was Alfred Hrejsemnou, member of a well-known Socialist
workers' family in Vienna, who fought in Spain with his
brother (who died at Brunete) and became a *teniente* in the
Republican Tank Corps. Both these men were rescued from
French internment camps and brought over to England by the

National Joint Committee for Refugees from Spain. Miss G.
is a German Jewish refugee. The Gestapo trapped her working
in the underground trade union movement, and she suffered
three and a half years in a concentration camp. She succeeded
in getting away to England, where she was quite rightly put in
C Class by her local tribunal. She taught in a school in Suffolk ;
when Suffolk was declared a " protected " area she moved to
London, where she had no English friends. A fortnight later
she was brought before a second tribunal because a local shop-
keeper had denounced her as a Nazi sympathiser. She was
supposed to have said that Goebbels was a clever man, or
something similar. The tribunal was suspicious of her because
she could not name English people with whom she could stay
in London, but above all because four years of her life in
Germany were " unaccounted for " ! It ordered her internment. . . . At the end of July she was in Holloway Prison
hospital suffering from a complete nervous breakdown. This
case illustrates the difficulties which " political " internees are
up against. In their own countries they were fearless fighters
against tyranny. When they were caught they knew
there would be no mercy and expected none. They were up
against an enemy who would torture them and probably murder
them. They were ready for death. Their morale was not
shattered by the Gestapo ; but the gentler methods of British
" Blimpism " and stupidity *can* destroy their morale, because
they are not prepared for such senseless treatment at the hands
of people whom they regard as friendly.

Wenzel Jaksch, Leader of the Sudeten-German Socialists,
reports the following cases (*New Statesman*, August 3) :

" H. L. was the leader of the Tyrolese workmen in 1934
in the revolt against the breach of the Constitution by the
Dollfuss Government. He was sentenced to death, the
death penalty being commuted to imprisonment. By a
general amnesty he regained his freedom and lived in Czechoslovakia for some time. I am in a position to certify that *in
spite of a physical defect acquired in prison, this man repeatedly
went to Germany as a ' courier ' of an anti-Nazi organisation*,
and that he has risked his life innumerable times in the service
of his cause. Most unluckily, however, he is not a ' key
man of war production,' and although the very type of fearless

fighter against Nazism and dictatorship, has no hope of being released while the war is on. . . .

"When I lived in Vienna as a young Socialist, before the last war, I met a Social-Democratic lawyer, Dr. M., whose work as an organiser of mass education was most remarkable. Later on, he·held high office in the Social-Democratic administration of Vienna. A few months ago I met Dr. M. in London. He had spent more than a year at the Dachau concentration camp. Now he has been interned. I am afraid that Dachau may have failed to break his health thoroughly enough to qualify him for release as a person 'suffering' from an incurable disease. If Dr. M. had brought to this country a sum of money sufficiently large to enable him to open a factory, he would be considered as a person deserving release from internment."

"*Friendly Aliens*."—"Friendly aliens" were not spared. At least a hundred political refugees from post-Munich Czechoslovakia, men and women who spoke very little English, were classed as "enemy aliens" because they stated that they were *born* in Austria . . . in the days when *all* Czechoslovakia was part of the Austrian Empire. Some of them were deported. Other friendly aliens were detained in gaol under deportation orders; for example, two men whom the *Spectator* (July 26, 1940) described as "Sudeten-Germans of unimpeachable records." *Gustav Beuer*, Communist member of the Czechoslovak Parliament for a Sudeten constituency, was one of the leaders of the minority in the Sudeten territory who fought tooth and nail against Henlein's Nazis and the Munich settlement. He was rescued from certain death by English friends.[*] *Karl Kreibich* is a veteran Socialist leader of the pre-1914 Austrian Empire, and a Communist Senator in the Czech Parliament for many years. His daughter Ilse was seized by the Gestapo in Prague, with the words: "So you're the daughter of that old scoundrel Kreibich," and thrown into a concentration camp. No charges have been laid against these "friendly aliens." Will these men be released to attend the meeting of the Czech Parliament which is being talked of? *Dr. E. Synek*, leading member of Dr. Benes's Party in Czecho-

[*] It was reported in August that Beuer was detained under ordinary prison conditions and refused even a pencil to make notes as he read.

slovakia and former editor of Dr. Benes's newspaper, the *Prager Tageblatt*, was put in Pentonville prison in August and later transferred to Liverpool prison. It is alleged that he was arrested because of material he published exposing certain officer-adventurers connected with the Czech Legions in France and questioning the integrity of certain politicians connected with the Czech National Committee in Britain whom he accused of betraying the spirit of Masaryk by artificially fomenting race and class antagonisms among the Czech Legionaries.*

The Humble Majority.—But the great mass of internees are neither eminent, nor " political," nor even " useful " in the narrow sense. They have neither reputations, nor influential friends, nor special abilities falling within the narrow limits of Sir John Anderson's " usefulness," to ensure their release. They are humble harmless folk, mostly Jewish, whose only wish is to be left in peace to reconstitute their shattered lives in a country free from the atmosphere of Gestapo and pogrom, to settle down and have homes of their own and work of their own which will give them back their independence and self-respect. Granted the opportunity the majority of them can, each in his own way, enrich our economic, social or cultural life by their work, even if what they can do is definitely not " work of national importance " in the Home Secretary's definition. Of such " enemy alien " men internment has made a clean sweep. They can show no good reason why they should *not* be interned, except common sense, common decency and human solidarity. These are categories which unfortunately are not to be found among the score of exempted categories in the Home Office list.

We give only a few examples, chosen out of hundreds, to show how indiscriminate was the internment of men, women and children of " no importance." Thousands of invalids were taken away and interned, often in camps without even an adequate supply of thermometers for their treatment. The transfer to hospitals of these invalids to recover from the effects of internment, and in many cases their actual release, was under way by mid-August, but at a very slow pace. Medical provision in the camps has also somewhat improved. Were there

---

* From prison he wrote to friends : " It is a year since I had news of my wife and daughter. I have lost all. I am in prison. But I am still a democrat! "

ever any " overwhelming reasons of national security " for
interning people of the following types ?

Dr. L. H. (C Class), elderly Jewish headmaster of an
Austrian school, suffered five imprisonments under the Nazis,
and escaped to England to avoid being sent to Dachau. His
" Aryan " wife and his daughter were prevented from
following. Arrived in a state of nervous collapse and suffering
from a duodenal ulcer which requires strict dieting and
avoidance of worry. Health slowly improved until fear of
internment caused a relapse last May. Spent at least three
weeks in Prisoners of War Camp No. 3, where he was in
contact with his Nazi enemies and getting more and more
ill without his special diet. His English friends feared
internment would be a death sentence for him. (*Spectator*,
July 19.) Dr. E. R. (Austrian Jew, 28) suffers from grave
diabetes and requires daily insulin injections. Was interned
in a Prisoners of War Camp from October, 1939, to April,
1940. Was released when an Advisory Committee found him
to be innocent of hostile intentions and put him in B Class.
This meant re-internment on May 16, a fortnight before his
intended marriage to Miss H. K. at Birmingham registry
office. Repeated applications for permission to marry during
his internment were in vain. All formalities were complete
for the couple to re-emigrate to U.S.A. a few weeks after
their marriage. Dr. R.'s fiancée finally got news from the
camp commandant that he had been deported overseas
without money or luggage. Miss L. T. (60), a cook-general,
suffers from pernicious anæmia, and requires injections and
a liver diet if she is to survive. Interned on June 13, she
spent over a month being shifted around to four different
camps, at none of which she received her special treatment.
Although her condition was deteriorating, she was sent to
the Isle of Man in the third week of July, where, officials
in London " had no doubt," she would be properly treated.
Mr. J. K. (52), operated on for war wounds in 1938, suffers
from angina pectoris. Had to spend many weeks in bed in
1939, and his doctors doubted whether he would survive.
Unable to walk quickly or to carry anything. This dangerous
" enemy alien " was sent to Huyton Camp. Dr. F.H. (35),
had been attending the London Chest Hospital since September, 1938, for left Artificial Pneumothorax treatment of

pulmonary tuberculosis.   The hospital doctor wrote to his internment camp giving instructions for carrying on the treatment, with weekly refills, in order to avoid a relapse in Dr. H.'s condition.   The instructions could not be carried out at the camp.   Mr. P.S. was due for an operation for severe hernia a few days after he was arrested.   The police ignored a written medical certificate to this effect.   He was transferred from camp to hospital, where the operation took place.   As the hospital had no censor he was forbidden to write or receive letters.   His anxious wife sent telegrams to the camp which were not answered.   Finally she heard incidentally from a discharged patient that her husband had been operated on ten days previously, and that complications had occurred.

Many boys just past the age of sixteen were removed without notice from their parents or their schoolrooms and locked up.   In many cases their fathers were interned in different camps.   Most of these boys have now been released, but a large number were sent overseas, and many promising school and university careers have been interrupted.   Mr. George Strauss, M.P., gives an instance of another common type of case : " P., a boy of sixteen, son of an English mother and German father, was born in Germany and brought to England when he was a few months old.   He has lived here ever since.   He is an exceptionally bright boy, highly spoken of by his employer. He is the main support of his family.   He cannot speak German and has no German interests.   He has been interned."

There were many cases of close relatives of *men serving in the British Army* who were interned.   How do such men view their military service now ?   Mr. Strauss reports : " Mrs. B. came over here with her son and husband as political and racial refugees.   The son joined the Pioneer Corps the moment it was formed, and is still a member, and served with the British Army in France.   Mrs. B. is over 60, and her husband, who has no one else to care for him, is 80.   Mrs. B. has been interned in Holloway Prison."   The *Manchester Guardian* (July 17) reports from Lancashire :

" A man of 65 who has been interned has two sons in the British Army.   One of the sons volunteered from Palestine for our Middle Eastern Army ; the other was with the B.E.F.

in France, came home lately on 48 hours' leave, and spent the whole 48 in finding his father."

Finally the stupid and callous behaviour of the police in East London must be mentioned. Many "enemy alien" families fled from the pogroms in Eastern Europe and have been living in East London for 30 or 40 years. What happened to them is told in a letter to *The Times* (July 23) from Dr. J. J. Mallon, Warden of Toynbee Hall :

" It is hard to write with composure about the present treatment of friendly aliens in East London. How can one explain or excuse the internment of elderly men, many of them invalids, who have lived here blamelessly for 40 or 50 years ? Men who have not been away from London for 20 years ; men who have occupied a single residence for half a century ; men who are ailing or who have ailing wives ; obscure and helpless men about whom the synagogue and their neighbours know all that can be known ; men of whom it is not even pretended that there is any suspicion, are being interned or have been interned in scores. It does not seem to weigh with the authorities whether or not these now being interned were interned during the last War, or whether or not they have sons fighting with the Colours. Nothing seems to weigh with them except that men are alien and not over 70. Such men are taken at short notice, often inconsiderately and harshly, and apparently without leave to communicate with their families. It is hardly credible, though it is true, that innumerable families in East London do not know the whereabouts or the condition of aged and feeble fathers or grandfathers who were whisked away from them a week or a fortnight ago. I spend much of my time receiving the representatives of such families. Two who suspect that their fathers are in hospitals in Surrey have gone this (Sunday) afternoon to visit these hospitals on the offchance that they may be right and be allowed an interview, or given information. Both of these men are about to join up ; in what heart they will do so can be imagined.

" Surely in the interests of sanity and humanity and of the national cause the Government will intervene."

Dr. Mallon's letter requires no amplification. It sums up what happened not merely in East London but throughout the country to thousands of " enemy aliens " in the months of June and July.

No wonder the Home Office was too busy sorting out the " mistakes " to be able to supply " statistical information of an elaborate character " about the people it had interned. No wonder that many people (especially internees) are now doubting whether a country which cannot handle less than 100,000 " enemy aliens," almost all of whom are perfectly harmless and known to be harmless, without treating them like oxen, can seriously claim to be trusted in the colossal task of reconstructing Europe after Hitler has been smashed.

3. *Internment Conditions*

Prisoners of War Camps.—Before the *Blitzkrieg* began the only " enemy alien " internees were those on the security list—mostly Nazis or suspects—who were interned at the outbreak of war, and those placed in A Class by tribunals. The men were sent to civilian prisoners of war camps, consisting in two instances of commandeered holiday camps ; the women went to Holloway Prison. In many ways the genuine anti-Nazis who were treated as prisoners of war were lucky. For it is an undoubted fact that prisoners of war were much better treated than ordinary refugee internees in B and C Classes. There was a good reason for this. If our authorities do not treat the Nazi soldiers and civilians interned in England decently, reprisals can be applied against the British prisoners of war in Germany. Both sides have an interest in ensuring that prisoners of war are treated well. An International Convention Relative to the Treatment of Prisoners of War has been signed both by Britain and Germany, and both sides are respecting its provisions. Although the Convention does not relate to civilians, both sides do in fact apply it to civilians. The Convention prescribes standards of comfort, decency, feeding, medical treatment and recreation. The Convention is enforced by neutral protecting Powers whose representatives inspect the camps, hear grievances and report defects, and act as intermediaries for the exchange of information between the belligerents. The Swiss Government is the protecting Power for the Nazis in Britain ; the U.S. Government acts for Britons in Germany.

Compared with what was to follow, when the round-up of

B and C Classes took place, conditions in these civilian war prisoners' camps were undoubtedly good. As will be seen later, in the diary of an Austrian interned at Huyton Camp, the A Class cases who were sent to Huyton found it a change for the worse. The main fault of the war prisoners' camps was that anti-Nazis, usually in a minority, were put together with Nazi sympathisers. Mr H. N. Brailsford, who visited one camp (a converted holiday camp in Devon) to see his friend H. N., an Austrian member of the International Brigade, gives a description of conditions there (*Reynolds News*, July 14, 1940, which tallies with all other reports we have received :

" The camp was cold, damp and water-logged, but the atmosphere was kindly. The guards were obviously friendly and considerate. The prisoners were allowed to run the camp themselves, and had set up a school and a theatre. H. N. edited its wall-newspaper, and made a little pocket money by weaving fishing-nets. I found three other [International] Brigaders, two of them Germans, in this camp.

" They had one complaint, which they repeated as time went on, in letters, week after week. In this camp about half the men were Nazis, the rest decided friends of our cause. The Nazis were organised by a Gestapo man, and behaved with deliberate arrogance and brutality. They went about singing their bloodthirsty Nazi songs, and occasionally they even beat up Jewish internees.

" Our friends were equally well organised, according to the Trade Unions to which they belonged. Life in these conditions was scarcely endurable : there was daily civil war in the camp. To separate the two would have been easy ; they had already sorted themselves out."

(An internee's own account of this camp will be found in the startling appendix to Chapter III, Section 4.)

The non-Nazi women who were interned as civilian prisoners of war, because, usually for incidental reasons, they had been put in A Class, found themselves in an awkward position. They were interned in a women's prison where, not being convicted offenders, they obviously could not be subjected to the ordinary prison routine. Their greater freedom (insufficient in their own eyes) appears to have aroused the jealousy of the ordinary British prisoners who were serving terms for definite breaches of the law, and there appears to have been much friction between the internees and the prison staff, who did not sufficiently grasp the distinction between internees and convicted prisoners.

The General Plan.—For B and C Class internees, who were not regarded as prisoners of war, the authorities were under no obligation or necessity to see that camp conditions came up to the standard prescribed by the Prisoners of War Convention. Refugees have no neutral protecting Power to intervene on their behalf, but above all they have no British counterparts in Germany against whom reprisals can be applied. When general internment began the War Office, through its Prisoners of War Department, was given the task of providing and running the necessary men's camps, while the Home Office continued to handle the women. Internees were first taken by the police to " aliens' collecting stations," consisting of commandeered school buildings, barracks and the like, or to transit camps such as the one on Kempton Park Racecourse, at Sunbury-on-Thames. Here they were taken over by the military. In such places they might spend only a few hours or they might stay for several weeks. Others were temporarily put into prisons, and the prisoners of war camps were also pressed into service.

From such places internees were apparently shifted by stages in the general direction of Liverpool. As and when accommodation became available on the Isle of Man, whether through the organisation of new camps, or later through large-scale deportations overseas, internees would be shipped over to camps on the island. Since the general idea was to keep up as rapid a flow as possible into the Isle of Man and, later, overseas to the Dominions, almost all the mainland camps bore a temporary character and were plainly not suited for settled habitation. Their populations were constantly changing as fresh batches of internees arrived and others departed ; co-ordination between the military responsible for the camps and the police who filled them was so haphazard that, thanks to the internment mania of the Home Office, the camps were continually receiving fresh influxes of internees of all ages and conditions of health on such a scale as to make the camp commandants' job of providing a bare minimum of food and shelter—however great their goodwill—a practical impossibility.

On August 5, 1940, the Home Office took over the camps

from the War Office and the period of military control ended. In the following pages we attempt to give as truthful and objective a picture of the camps during the period of military control (May, June and July, 1940) as we can achieve. Once again official secrecy prevents us from giving a complete survey of camp conditions in May–July, 1940. Something amounting almost to a conspiracy of silence on these matters was organised from above. Welfare workers, liaison officers and others who had visited the camps (including Members of both Houses of Parliament) were either bound over to silence or were afraid to state the full facts of what they knew. We deplore this official secrecy. because it did not, in fact, prevent a great mass of information—possibly exaggerated—from leaking out of the camps, and as more men are released such stories will multiply. The evidence at our disposal, from reliable and carefully checked sources, is quite sufficient to show that conditions in the camps constituted an unsavoury scandal which could not be allowed to continue in a democratic community in full possession of the facts. Because we are trying to write a historical record—with the material at present available—of the results of three months of panic, muddle and lack of responsibility, we aim at being as fair and impartial as possible. If we do not entirely succeed, the fault lies with those who believe that democracy's best defence in war-time is to hush up all criticism and to ignore all unpleasant facts for fear the enemy might use them against us. After the experience of France, it is courting disaster to follow such a line in Britain.

Unnecessary Defects.—In May and June, 1940, when the big round-ups were taking place, the War Office was working harder than ever before, organising the withdrawal from Dunkirk, re-equipping the B.E.F., calling up fresh age groups and preparing at feverish speed to meet a threat of immediate invasion. On top of this it had to organise some twenty camps for internees. In the circumstances it is understandable that internment was regarded as a sideshow and farmed out to subordinate officers who knew little and cared less about the people they had in their camps. This situation *explains* most of the muddle which occurred and was used by the War Office as its standard excuse to all complaints. It does *not*, however, *excuse* (a) the continuance of this muddle for more than twelve weeks, nor (b) the cutting off of internees from news of the outside world, nor (c) the appalling muddle over communications between internees and their relatives, organisations or legal advisers, nor (*d*) the scandalous neglect of records.

Most inexcusable of all was the *cruelty* (there is no other word for it) of the officials responsible for the ban, maintained in most camps until mid-July, on all newspapers and even on camp wireless sets.   Roughly half of the internees were taken off before the French surrender, when Holland and Belgium were smashed and the *blitzkrieg* was pounding its way to Paris. They were then cut off from all outside news.   Many knew how their fellow refugees in Holland and Belgium were being hunted, tortured and shot by the Gestapo.   What was going to happen next ?   No one told them.   In the fortnight following the collapse of France new masses of internees were brought in and subjected to even worse mental agony.   For they knew how thousands of German and Austrian refugees, who had been interned all through the war in the *Stade Buffalo* near Paris, had simply been handed over for certain death to the Gestapo by the Paris police.   They knew the terrible significance of Article 19, Clause 2, of the Compiègne Armistice terms :

> " The French Government to hand over all German subjects indicated by the German Government who are in France or French overseas territory."

At this point, when all was uncertain, they were locked up and cut off from all reliable news from the outside world.   Would Britain follow France and sell out to the Nazis ?   Would they —the internees—be handed over, as in France ?   Little wonder that wild rumours circulated in all the camps.   A good example of how highly intelligent men were treated is given by a man who was transferred from Paignton Camp to Prees Heath in July :

> " Worst deprivation was no news or information of any kind whatever as to the war ;   result :   rumour and panic. When 600 were transferred to Prees Heath, near Whitchurch, *an officer was sent in advance through Paignton to tear down all hoardings, posters, newspaper headings, etc., which might give information as to news. . . .*
> " *Owing to the lack of food at Prees Heath, the prisoners believed that invasion had already occurred, that transport was disorganised and that the whole country was suffering from*

food shortage. In consequence, when food parcels arrived they were saved in case a worse shortage lay ahead."

(Later, when the camp canteen opened, they realised that their fears were unfounded.) Apprehension and nervous tension rose to breaking point when news filtered through that the *Arandora Star* had been torpedoed. Little wonder that some suicides occurred, and many succumbed to nervous breakdown.

Added to these anxieties was the general worry about relatives. In the first few weeks internees and their relatives were commonly left without any news of one another. Later, field service post cards were issued to internees to enable them to inform their families of their whereabouts and state of health. They were also issued with standard letter-paper on which they could write twenty-four lines twice a week. But communications were generally erratic and unpredictable. An ordinary letter might take anything from five days to five weeks to reach its address. In many cases letters and parcels (often with half the contents missing) would be returned from the camps marked " not known " or " gone away." Men were frequently deported before their wives received messages to this effect, or essential clothing and other necessities for the overseas journey arrived for the man after the ship had gone. A report from Huyton Camp tells the following typical episode :

" Letters which were posted here on July 13 were examined by the Censor on July 24. On July 28 the letters came back to the camp, because of remarks in these letters that no food was allowed to be sent into the camp [by relatives]. As the order had later been withdrawn by the responsible officer, who declared that it was not an order but only a suggestion, the letters were returned for that remark to be crossed out or the letters re-written. Under such circumstances it is no wonder that the internees in despair are trying to find illegal methods of forwarding their letters."

So jammed was the bottleneck of the censorship at Liverpool that, as Mr. Peake explained on August 22 :

" On August 5 the Home Office took over control. I made inquiries about the letters coming out of the internment camps. *I found at that time close upon* 100,000 *letters, written by internees, which had been held up by the postal censorship in Liverpool . . . having been held up for three or four weeks."*

Telegrams got through with less delay, but it was usually difficult to get permission to send them. Censorship organisations everywhere were desperately understaffed. On the Isle of Man, where many husbands and wives or engaged couples are interned in separate camps no more than twelve miles apart, there was no censor. All letters between men's and women's camps had to go over the sea to Liverpool, where they were censored, and back over the sea to the island. This process commonly required two or three weeks, instead of a possible twelve hours.

A third big fault common to almost all camps, at least until mid-July, was the glaring failure to keep adequate records of arrivals and departures. When the police handed over internees to the military at " aliens' collecting stations," the military usually proceeded to confiscate almost every scrap of paper and every penny in the internees' possession. An internee's documents would be put in envelopes marked with his name, and the money confiscated would be credited to him in a book. Receipts were not usually given. In many cases when the internee arrived at his final camp neither his money nor his documents could be traced—they had been " lost on the way." We know of one camp at least where the office had a great pile of cash and bank-notes and no idea of how to distribute it among its thousands of inmates. We know of another where a large proportion of the men lost part or all of their identity papers, because the envelopes containing them had been tied up in bundles and left in the rain for hours during the journey to the camp. Many of the bundles burst open, documents were trodden on, mutilated and reduced to a soggy mass. Scores of men had to rake through a dustbin (a clean one into which the damaged documents were put) to retrieve odd pages of passports or torn pieces of identity cards and visas. Few of the men released by mid-August received their papers back in full order. Many were released with no documents at all, not even identity or registration cards. When a refugee organisation inquired of the commandant of a certain camp for the passport of a released man who was due to get his American visa, the commandant replied that a trunk containing 200 passports had been dispatched somewhere, possibly to Canada. He thought the man's passport might be in the trunk! The same organisation reports that when one of its men was transferred from Sutton Coldfield Camp to Lingfield,

> "his documents, including the police registration card which had been handed over to the authorities on arrival, could not be traced anywhere. At last an emergency card had to be issued by the camp commander, in order that some document might establish the internee's identity. This strange document consisted of a piece of cardboard with a thumb-print of the man concerned, the stamp of the internment camp and the commandant's handwritten remarks."

The majority of camps appear to have had no proper records of their internees until towards the end of July. Even where difficulties were not made greater by constant changes in the camp populations, there were camps where the staff had no clear idea who their internees were. Either the documents did not arrive, or nobody bothered to organise a proper register. In some camps nothing much was done until groups of internees themselves began to organise registers. Very often the authorities themselves took weeks to trace an internee.* Some internees, usually men in key industrial positions, whose release was ordered by the Home Office, were finally discovered to have been deported overseas.

It is understandable—granted the necessity of mass internment—that it was impossible at the outset to organise mixed

---

* One anti-Fascist, who had escaped from an Italian prison, was interned for a month with a minority of anti-Fascists in a camp full of Italian supporters of Mussolini. For four weeks he was unable to let his old and sick mother know his whereabouts. He could not write letters because the special paper had not arrived. His telegrams were refused because the officer did not regard them as urgent. Finally, a wire was accepted. The next day an order for his release arrived from the Home Office. The order had been issued twenty days previously, but until his telegram to his mother arrived the Home Office had been unable to find out which camp he was in. This man believes that if he had been arrested an hour earlier he would have been put on the *Arandora Star* and probably drowned, since the men who were arrested before him suffered that fate. We know of innumerable cases of letters being held up at camps, or even sent back, because the camp staff did not know the addressee was in their camp. We know of one child, interned with its mother but separated on the journey, who took three weeks in the camp to find its mother again, because nobody knew the mother's whereabouts in the camp.

camps for married couples or families.   But was it necessary
to intern fathers and sons in different camps, or to deport sons
to Canada without a chance to see their interned fathers and
uninterned mothers ?   Was it necessary to have husbands and
wives interned in camps a few miles apart on the Isle of Man,
and yet never to allow them to meet ?   The one occasion on
which such a meeting was arranged was at the end of July,
when the wives, believing their husbands were to go to Australia,
were allowed to meet them for half an hour to discuss arrangements with them.   The men apparently had not been told of
the deportation plan, and misunderstood the purpose of the
meeting.   The dismay and confusion which followed when
these men learned that they were supposed to be going to
Australia, with no guarantee that their wives would follow,
with the possibility of never seeing them again, can hardly be
imagined.*   Finally we may venture to doubt whether all the
obstacles put in the way of non-interned wives and relatives
who—when they could afford the travelling expenses—wished
to visit internees were really necessary.   Why were visits
difficult to arrange ?   Why was it generally necessary for visits
to take place in the presence of a camp officer, which is a treatment usually reserved for convicted criminals ?

A general complaint in the early days was the herding
together of Jews and other non-Fascists with Nazis, semi-Nazis
or Italian Fascists.   Until deportation took away most of the
Nazis and Fascists this factor led to much avoidable misery.
In most men's camps by the end of July the remaining Nazis
were so few that a reminder that they were in the minority was
sufficient to keep them in order.   The position in the women's
camps does not appear to be so favourable.   Most of the Nazis
and sympathisers were, in mid-August, 1940, still there,
unsorted out ; and Jewish or anti-Nazi women who have to
share not only the same houses, but very often the *same beds*,
with them, are naturally not enthusiastic.   In the war prisoners'
camps this situation had existed for months prior to the *Blitzkrieg*, and the authorities did nothing about it.   From May
onwards they were able to plead in Parliament that the new
" intakes " of internees made separation of Nazis and non-
Nazis impossible for the time.   The same plea was used to
excuse the failure to organise regular communications, to allow

* After this meeting the men spoke of Port Erin, site of the women's
camp, as " *Port Erinnerung* "—Port Remembrance.

visiting, to arrange for mixed family camps and for almost every other shortcoming.

Apart from the haste in which wholesale internment was carried through, there was another important reason for this muddle. We have the definite impression that the War Office gentlemen in charge of internment, and far too many of the commandants they appointed to run the camps, were not only abysmally ignorant of everything connected with refugee problems, but were also not in the slightest degree interested in the men in their camps. Commandants whose whole background was the Army, many of whom had never met Germans except as enemies, men who were accustomed to ordering about physically fit young men under military discipline, or who had only dealt with prisoners who were criminals, men who were accustomed to wait for orders from above and to interpret these orders literally, found themselves in charge of internees, a very large proportion of whom were elderly, very many of whom were not, like soldiers, separated from their families for definite and understandable reasons, or, like criminals, convicted for an offence and sentenced to imprisonment for a definite period. It was a situation calling for the utmost tact, understanding, human sympathy, imagination and, above all, initiative. Although there were honourable exceptions, among the junior officers as well as among the commandants, our general impression is definitely one of lack of interest, lack of imagination and lack of initiative. The general spirit of headquarters is illustrated by the experience of one commandant who had in his camp hundreds of elderly invalids, many of them seriously ill, and neither sufficient beds nor any chairs at all. He wired the War Office for 1,500 chairs, and got the reply that chairs were not issued to soldiers. After a fortnight of patient explaining that his internees were not soldiers at all he finally had his way and got a limited supply of chairs. A number of commandants appear to have behaved in the same spirit on the spot, and some seem to have been under the impression that their internees were mostly Nazis.

It must, however, be frankly recognised that even the commandants with the best will in the world found themselves in an impossible position. Starting, in many cases, with camp sites that were almost unusable, the commandants received a steady stream of aged and infirm men, many cripples or seriously ill, whom the authorities in their mania for internment had

rounded up. Without information, without orders, without
equipment, without adequate staff, all the imagination and
initiative in the world would not have made much difference.
There were commandants who went out of their way to be
helpful, who encouraged internee self-government and community life, who promoted welfare funds for destitute internees,
who sought to break through the red tape of censorship and
delay, but we do not believe that they were the majority. The
most usual complaint of internees was not that the commandants
were brutal or unkind, but simply that they were indifferent,
uninterested and unconsciously obstructive. Some cases of gross
neglect of duties are known. We know of at least three camps
where soldiers searching the luggage of the new arrivals simply
stole internees' possessions under the noses of their officers.

The Wharf Mills Camp.—By far the worst internment camp
of which we have any knowledge was Wharf Mills, a derelict
cotton factory at Bury (Lancs). All our accounts of this
notorious " transit camp " tally : it is a disused factory falling
to pieces, rat-infested, with rotten floors, broken windows and
a broken glass roof. Here is an account of Wharf Mills from
an internee who was there in the middle of July. He arrived
there with a trainload of fellow-internees after an entire day's
travelling during which each internee had nothing to eat but
one slice of bread with jam :

" In the big hall there were 500 people. Two thousand
people were housed in the whole building. . . . The building
was surrounded by two rows of barbed wire, between which
armed guards patrolled. Already at the entrance one saw a
lot of litter lying about, the floor was slippery through oil and
grease. . . . Everywhere there were old driving belts and
in our sleeping quarters there were old shafts hanging about.
. . . We were ordered to fetch our beds—but found out
that there were only old boards. There was a row then with
the officers, We told them we wouldn't allow them to treat
us like criminals. The officers didn't say anything. We
asked for palliasses for the sick pople. Finally, an officer
led us to a store with palliasses and allowed us to take three
out. There were neither tables nor benches. We had to
eat standing. . . . The lighting of the place was through the
glass roof, but as it was partly broken, the rain came in also.
In the hall there was a stone floor, in some other rooms there

was a wooden floor, full of holes, which filled with water when it rained. . . . *There were* 18 *watertaps for* 2,000 *people to wash.* We all gave over shaving after some time. The washing provisions were absolutely inadequate. Some professors, intellectuals and Mr. Olden* tried to protest. . . . There was a fight about the lavatories. After a week there was a conference at which the doctors decided that the lavatories† were absolutely impossible. A week later we succeeded to get some lime for the lavatories. . . . The commandant refused to give any drugs for the sick without payment. There was one bath-tub for 1,800 people ! . . . Two blankets, later three blankets had to be given back, because they were full of vermin. There was no day-room, one had to stay all the time in the sleeping rooms. The few tables that were there had to be altered to sleeping boards. The laundry had to be done in an empty room of the factory, but was afterwards as dirty as before. There were some classes held in the afternoons, by professors. Prof. Eisler lectured, also Prof. Heynemann ; Dr. Glaser spoke about his experiences in Spain, Manzer about Vienna.

" There was a ' luggage control ' in Wharf Mills ; we had to go upstairs with our luggage. Behind the tables there were officers, in front of them soldiers. We had to stand behind ropes. The officers took our wallets, *the soldiers took the suit-cases and they took anything they fancied (novels, books, chocolate, pencils, paper, cigarettes) and distributed the things among themselves in front of us.* Some artists and scientists succeeded in retaining their papers, but their books were taken away. The objects were put in big wash-basins."

Race-Course Camps.—The race-course camps were better. At Kempton Park, the " collecting station " for the London region, men were billeted in the Tote buildings (large office rooms with pigeon-holes for betting transactions), in the stables (some underground) and, at one time, in tents. Conditions here appear to have been typical of a great many other camps. Men slept (often on stone floors) on thin mattresses with two thin blankets, sometimes packed a hundred to a room, with no chairs, no cupboards, nowhere to hang clothes. There was no common room—one could only lie on one's mattress, or sit in the grandstand and watch the sentries, or stroll about the

---

* Rudolf Olden is mentioned in Section 2 of this Chapter.
† These consisted of sixty buckets in the factory yard.

enclosures. A typical day's menu in mid-July (eaten standing very often) consisted of : Breakfast, large piece of bread with jam, and inky-black tea (usually without sugar or milk) ; Dinner, " Irish stew " (with hardly a trace of meat), or mixed vegetables and potatoes, with bread and more tea : Supper, bread and marge or bread and cheese, with more tea or " coffee " (" it looks like coffee, it smells like cocoa, it tastes like tea "). Kosher food was available. Medical facilities were quite inadequate, although there was a sick-bay with real beds.

At this point we insert the story of a typical journey, better than many and worse than others, from Kempton Park to the Isle of Man in mid-July. To fortify himself for the 17-hour journey each man in the Kempton Park trainload received a large piece of bread and each group of 50 was given a large chunk of cheese. When they had this " meal " they had to borrow the soldiers' bayonets to cut the cheese, since all pen-knives, razor-blades, etc., had been confiscated. Each man got a piece of cheese the size of his top thumb-joint. There were 800 men on the ship from Liverpool, and military guards barred access to the saloons. Those who were fortunate enough to possess a few unconfiscated coppers pooled them to buy chocolate on the ship. It began to rain and many had to stand in the wet without overcoats. They continued to stand in the rain for two hours on the quay at Port Douglas,* and then had to march for an hour in the rain to the camp, which they reached at 11 p.m. exhausted. On arrival at "their" houses they found that food rations had not been provided for them, but only tea. But the internees already in the houses had gone without their own dinners and saved them for the new arrivals.

In the other race-course camps of which we have knowledge conditions appear to have been in many respects similar to Kempton Park, and in some respects better. The race-course now used as a re-emigrants' camp, for instance, provided food sufficient in quantity, had a common room and a laundry, and a hospital with a bath and 16 beds. There was the usual shortage of drugs. The commandant and officers were sympathetic and took the initiative in organising a fund for destitute internees.

* Is it any wonder that, on another day, on a similar journey, a man suffering from diabetes died immediately on arriving at the harbour ? On yet another transport a man died of a fractured skull.

Tent Camps.—A typical tent-camp was the one at Prees Heath, near Whitchurch in Shropshire.   The whole community, including the hospital, was under canvas, and conditions generally were primitive.   The strain on the elderly was great and there was a big sick parade each morning.   Their clothing and the medical facilities were both inadequate for this kind of life, which even British soldiers find a strain under better conditions.   Most of the men over fifty were transferred when possible to house-camps.   The rainy weather caused much hardship, especially the roll-call which had to be held in the open (the lengthy roll-calls held in the open were complained about in many of the camps).   This camp also had a contributory fund for the destitute.   The younger men, who liked camping, bore the life more cheerfully.   A report early in August from Prees Heath states :

" Washing facilities : for the whole camp (600 people), twelve tubs of water once a day.   Until recently ill people were left without any treatment ; *only after a protest meeting of the whole camp and a threat to go on strike were those people transferred to a hospital.*   Commandant and guards were very decent, but they could not do anything for the internees. An old man who had a stroke had to be carried for weeks to and from the meals before he was taken to hospital."

A tent-camp was opened at Sutton Coldfield for about three weeks in August, 1940.   In mid-August, when 800 men were there, there were only plates and cutlery for 300.   Men slept directly on ground-sheets on the damp earth, without even straw sacks ; many of these men were over fifty.   A report on this camp says :

" The hospital is a tent only, and the entire medical equipment consists of a stethoscope and aspirins. . . . There are only six beds, and no mattresses.   Two men had heart attacks on arrival ; several sick people were brought in on stretchers.   There was one man suffering from kidney trouble, two from putrid periostitis."

But the kitchen, the laundry, the lavatories and the shower bath were in buildings, the food was good in quality, though sometimes meagre in quantity, and above all the officers were extremely kind and helpful (this was a Home Office camp).

Huyton.—The best-known house-camp (outside the Isle of Man) is at Huyton near Liverpool.   This consists of an unfinished housing estate. The houses are good and dry, but they had practically no furniture or beds right up to the end of July. During the period of maximum overcrowding the houses were supplemented with tents, in which at one time two-fifths of the men were living. We propose to describe Huyton at some length, both because a great deal of reliable information is available and because Huyton appears to have been neither of the worst nor of the best type of the mainland camp. Here are extracts from a trustworthy account of Huyton written by a released internee at the end of July, when the worst was over :

" One part of the village of Huyton was surrounded by barbed wire and converted into an internment camp. There are really three camps, which together hold 3,000 internees—Camps I, II and III. . . . In each case a camp comprise, about seven streets and is divided into five companies, As B, C, D, E.

" Each house consists of four rooms, in which 2–4 persons are accommodated, according to size. At first the rooms had no furniture except straw sacks. The few tables and chairs which there had been in some of the houses were actually removed. It was not until recently, when a new commandant was appointed, that each house was given a table, a chair, and a bench. In each house there is a bath, but coal for heating the water was issued only once. Internees were also taken to a near-by military camp for a bath. But up to the time when the writer was released only about 200 had had their turn. The young people of about 20–25 were at first in tents which on account of frequent rain were often completely water-logged. *Once when a visit of inspection by a military commission was announced, another part of the village was hastily included in the camp and the youngsters were accommodated in houses, in which they are still living. . . .* There is no protection from air-raids for the internees, as there are no shelters. There is also no first-aid apparatus. *The internees have offered to build air-raid cellars themselves. This offer was refused on the ground that it was a matter not within the discretion of the camp authorities.*

" Food is better now than at the beginning. At least one gets enough to eat. . . . For breakfast there is tea or coffee, porridge, two slices of bread, a little over $1\frac{1}{2}$ ounces of margarine, jam or honey. For lunch there is always peas,

beans, rice, or something of that kind.   Sometimes a stew
with very little meat.   In addition on Sundays stewed fruit
or dried figs.   Sometimes there are herrings with potatoes
instead of the vegetables.   Supper consists of tea, two slices
of bread, 1½ ounces of margarine and the same quantity of
cheese.   The cooking is done by the internees themselves
on a field kitchen, which stands in the open.   There is a
canteen which was set up a short time ago and is run by
internees. . . . Apart from any extra food, one has to buy
washing soap, shaving soap, razor blades, tooth paste, toilet
soap, needles and thread (since all mending things brought
with one had been taken away), shoe-cleaning materials,
newspapers, toilet paper (once nine sheets of toilet paper
were issued for six weeks). . . . Even medicines have to be
bought by the internees themselves.   There are also arrangements for pressing clothes and mending shoes, but for these
too applications take a long time. . . . It was only after a
month and a half that the internees were given a small bar
of soap and a handful of soda to clean a whole house.   In
order to give those who have no money at all a chance to
buy themselves something, the internees themselves formed
a welfare committee ; this committee distributes money sub-
scribed by more fortunate internees.

" With primitive means at their disposal internees make
their rooms more or less fit to live in.   Between meals they
can do what they like, nobody bothers about them.   They
can visit each other as much as they like, but af.er 10.15 p.m.
no one is allowed out of doors.   Musical instruments and
books which they had brought with them had been taken
away at the beginning, but they got them back after about
six weeks.   They exchange books, arrange musical evenings,
games, etc.   Once some of them were allowed to play football, under guard, outside the barbed wire. . . .

" Now writing paper is issued regularly twice a week.
However, there are difficulties if one is sent to the hospital
in Liverpool.   It may happen that one cannot write for
weeks to one's people, because no paper is sent on to the
hospital. . . . There are no towels or bed linen.   The
straw sacks are very dirty.

" Once the internees gave a concert.   They arranged themselves in an open space near the fence on the other side of
which was the military camp.   Of course the soldiers came

along and listened, joined in and clapped applause. This brought the commandant of the military camp along. He ordered the soldiers and the internees to move on. Afterwards orders were given not to sing or play near the fence. . . .

" Internees' clothes suffer a great deal. A suit is completely ruined in one or two months. Shoes generally do not last nearly so long as the roads are very dirty and the internees have no money to have them mended. Underclothes very soon become unwearable, as the same garments have to be washed each week."

This report describes Huyton after great improvements had been effected (by a new commandant), following visits by members of Parliament. In May, June and the first half of July conditions were far worse. A report on July 5 stated :

" Men of 60 have to sleep in tents with only two blankets. Some of the people are as old as 70 and more. Completely shut up from the world. Barbed wire ; watch-towers with floodlights. . . . No newspapers or wireless allowed. Wild rumours and therefore panic. . . . Sanitary conditions scandalous. No soap, no toilet paper. No proper medical attendance. High danger of epidemics. People with all sorts of infectious diseases amongst others in crowded bedrooms and tents. . . . Food is entirely insufficient and every day absolutely the same. Especially the younger people go about hungry."

A typical menu (repeated every day) of this period was : Breakfast : porridge with milk (no sugar) and two slices of bread ; Dinner : mixed vegetable stew with a good deal of potato ; High Tea (6.0 p.m.) : two slices of bread, cheese, tea, and sometimes jam. At first there was no canteen at which additional food could be bought by those who could afford it. When the canteen started it did a roaring trade . . . in bread.

Medical facilities during this period was appalling. Only one Army doctor was available for a population which seldom fell below 3,000 and was often much greater. The refugee doctors interned in the camp saved the situation by putting their services at the disposal of the medical officer and organising a camp hospital and an out-patients' department. On June 28, 1940, they drew up a memorandum for the camp authorities revealing, among other things, (1) that accommodation and nursing facilities for men suffering from acute diseases and for helpless invalids was totally inadequate. There were very few beds, no bed-linen at all, no nursing materials, no skilled nurses and no hot water. Men with infectious complaints like tonsilitis were sleeping on the floor. (2) The 300 beds (without mattresses) then available for 4,000 men were completely insufficient for the large numbers of elderly invalids suffering from heart diseases, hernia and other conditions. (3) There was a total absence of first-aid accessories, even of bandages, splints and thermometers. (4) The supply of drugs was completely in-sufficient. Insulin—a vital necessity for the numerous dia-betics in the camp—was available only for those who could pay for it. Many of the poorer men could not afford it. (5) They reported an increasing number of men suffering from psychological disturbances due to internment conditions, and numerous cases of insanity (even insane " enemy aliens " were interned, apparently). Two men had committed suicide. By July 12 another two had taken their lives and there had been two unsuccessful attempts.

Another report, sent by a group of internees to their official refugee committee on July 10, confirmed this picture of camp conditions in every detail.

Referring to the sick they stated : " It is horrifying to see seriously ill men from the incoming transports carried into the camp on stretchers." (The invalid Unity Mitford, friend of Adolf Hitler, convalesces in peace on a Scottish island.) They also complained bitterly about the ban on all newspapers, the lack of suitable rooms for lectures and other cultural activities, the ban on such lectures and activities (theatrical sketches, etc.) conducted in the German language, the con-fiscation of all political books brought in by internees,* and about the rule that no internee could write a letter to his family or friends for the first ten days after his arrival. A report of an English refugee official who visited Huyton a week later added :

" I must say that Major —— (the commandant) is as considerate as he can be, and he does not like the way things are being done ; *but he has* 4,000 *men to look after and he knows very little about them.*

" If the men fall ill they are taken to Walton Gaol Hospital.

* Major Cazalet stated in the parliamentary debate of August 22 that one internee has had his *Oxford Book of English Verse* con-fiscated as " unsuitable " !

This seems to me extraordinary, when they are more sinned against than sinning. . . . I can't believe if English people knew what was happening to innocent people who are already broken in mind and spirit and body, they would allow it to go on."

(This humane visitor did not apparently realise that it was the normal practice, during the period of War Office control, to send men who were seriously ill to military or prison hospitals. Very often men were unable to write to their families, however serious their condition, because the hospitals had no arrangements for censoring letters.) We deal with the medical treatment of seriously ill internees in an Appendix.

To conclude this harrowing description we reproduce extracts from the diary of an Austrian who was at Huyton from May 24 to July 6, 1940. This man's integrity and objectivity are above question. He became a camp official, and was released to go to the U.S.A. (with what stories to tell about England ?) His diary is the most revealing document we have so far seen :

12. V. We are interned and have to sleep on the floor in Worley Barracks.

24. V. Transported to Huyton Camp at 4.15 a.m.

15. VI. To-day there are only 750 men left at the camp, because 2,000 have been sent away yesterday and the day before yesterday to the Isle of Man. I have been asked by the Commandant to join a group of twelve men who should stay in this camp to help in the administration of the camp for the 5,000 men who are now expected.

16. VI. Sunday. There are only about 800 men left. Therefore little work. Lots of idleness and longing, longing, longing. On top of all that I live only about 100 feet off the barbed wire and so I am able to watch from the window how husbands and wives with their children enjoy their Sunday afternoon walk in full freedom. This is certainly sadism in its special kind.

17. VI. Ten days without any news. What is the matter ? It tortures my brain day and night. I cannot explain ; newspapers, etc., are prohibited and therefore we have the most terrifying rumours about the development of the war. Both telegrams which I received are from London so that I expect that my wife must have been evacuated. I have had no penny for more than a week and crave for cigarettes to-day.

18. VI. I had a terrible night. *Yesterday evening it was said that France had given in. We were completely desperate, all of us. Two attempted suicides during the night and the Commandant felt compelled to call a general meeting and to make a comforting speech. . . . .* About 300 Italians arrived to-day, fifty-eight of whom are syphilitic. My people have refused to work with them, because they are afraid of infection. I had to calm them down, but it was very difficult.

20. VI. Still no word from my wife. I do not know what to think. I hope the parents have arrived in New York all right. Sent a very energetic letter to my wife to get information about everything. . . . The people here wither away more and more from day to day. Due partly to the scarcity of food, partly to their worries. How long will all this last ? The uncertainty wears us down. In spite of all this I keep up my spirits better than all my colleagues. Many are near to suicide and I have to comfort them all, though I am almost as near to it myself. If I had only some cigarettes, but I do not dare to ask my wife for money, because I do not know whether she has got any.

22. VI. The day began with a surprise. When we woke up 200 of the Italians had been sent to the Isle of Man and also *fifty men have arrived from a camp for " A " cases which has been closed down. They began at once to protest that there were no beds, chairs or tables. I had almost forgotten that such articles existed. Furthermore they do not want to be together with Jews. They did not want to eat the food, because it was too little and not good enough.* Oh, well, we have got used to hunger long ago. When we made representations to the Commandant in the first days about the food he said to us : that he was only liable not to let us starve, but he could not give us enough that we would not be hungry. . . . They say that France has signed the armistice. Everybody is very nervous. Many say : There is nothing left worth living for. What shall become of us really ?

23. VI. It is six weeks to-day that we have been interned. At last an express letter from my wife dated from the 10th. One Pound in it. Thank goodness they are all right. And my parents landed safely. France has really signed the armistice. All are depressed. What will become of us ? *For the first time in three weeks I have been able again to buy*

cigarettes and food. It is incredible how one cigarette can change a man. Everything looks more hopeful.

25. VI. The fifty men from the " A " camp leave us to-day and we are very glad about it. To-day has been a day of tragic events and my nerves are on edge. But as I have the duty to help others I have to keep my worries to myself, and *all my fury was pressed into a letter to my wife in which I accused her about not writing to me and leaving me without news.*

27. VI. Since yesterday there are new people arriving all the time. Most of them " C " class from London. Our hopes for release are down to zero. The newly arrived say that even the women will be interned soon. . . . I am very worried about my wife. In case she will be interned as well, who is going to do all the arrangements for our re-emigration ? Our camp leader, Prof. Weissenberg*, has caught pneumonia and had to be sent to the Hospital. The doctors say that the food poor in fats and quantity has to account for it. Yesterday evening a man suffered a nervous breakdown and had to be sent to a Hospital in Liverpool. I met many friends from Kitchener Camp.

28. VI. All the time now masses of men arrive from London. . . . , *Prof. Weissenberg in spite of the fact that he is so seriously ill called a meeting of the hut leaders at which the Commandant thanked us for our active and practical assistance, and said that he would be helpless to meet the present situation without our help and that he would do everything in his power to improve our conditions.* Just now 400 new men arrived, among them 65 years old invalids and cripples whom we have to accommodate in tents on the ground which is still wet from the last rain. It is a terrible torture for me to have to tolerate all this. *Prof. Weissenberg spoke after the Commandant and said that there would be few in such a desperate position as we were. We have no idea of our future. We do not know what happens to our relatives . . . he could not continue because of a complete nervous breakdown ; we had to carry him away.*

1. VII. 780 new arrivals. Among them very old men, invalids,

* Professor Karl Weissenberg is a distinguished physicist who worked at one time with Einstein. He was formerly at Berlin University and was working at the Physics Department of University College, Southampton, before his internment.

One gentleman is 68 years old, suffers of serious heart failure and only with the greatest effort could I find him a place in one of the houses. All the others have to sleep in tents. During dinner-time, that is six o'clock, suddenly intensive anti-aircraft fire was to be heard and the men grew nervous. I shouted that it is only the wind clattering the roof of the tents, *because I was afraid of a panic which would have had unthinkable effects, because we had* 490 *men pressed into one tent, so that there was almost no space to move.* I do not know what we will do in the next air raid. It is gross carelessness to have us here where we are only four miles from Liverpool and with a big aerodrome in the neighbourhood which the Germans try to bomb all the time. Nervousness increases daily.

2. VII. The catastrophe has come. A certain Mr. Schiff has committed suicide in the cloak-room. It has gripped us all. For a minute we stood still in memory of him before sitting down for lunch. *We are now very much afraid that this will start an epidemic. Many men made some hints about it to me.* All this is worse, because of the constant rumour that our women will be interned. I feel weaker from day to day and have so many duties to carry out. I suffer under the fear of a nervous breakdown. Nevertheless I am constantly told how calm I am and how quietly I deal with all complaints and grievances. Fortunately there are some sensible men left. One shouted at me to-day that I should go to a lunatic asylum because my orders look like emanating from there. *The man who committed suicide is almost* 60 *years old and has been in a Concentration Camp for two years.* Our position is desperate : Will we fall into the hands of Hitler again ? What is happening to our wives, children and parents ? Will we never get out of this situation unworthy of a human being ?

3. VII. 690 men have been sent away with unknown destination this morning. All of them single, between 20–40 years old. Many say that they will be sent to Canada, others that they might go to the Isle of Man or to the Shetland Islands. *There are the most terrifying rumours about the methods of driving them on to the ship. I am afraid that the only effect will be new attempts at suicide. It is really a foolish idea not to tell people the destination of their voyage.* They are all completely confused.

6. VII. So much has happened until to-day that it would fill the pages of a tragic novel. *Another suicide, a man who became mad and many who turned melancholic. We are afraid now that they might attempt suicide.* Another transport with unknown destination is being arranged for. They say that all men between the ages of 20 and 50 will be deported. This caused great unrest. *A meeting was called and the married men protested against being deported and leaving their wives and children behind in uncertainty. We decided rather to be shot than to be deported.* . . . At last a telegram that I have to have my medical examination at the American Consulate. I am very worried how to get a chance to keep this appointment. I have resigned my post now which caused great protest because they have no successor. There were great rows to-day because nothing worked. I had heavy headaches all the day, but could not find one aspirin in the whole camp.

The week that followed this man's release was even worse, because the news about the *Arandora Star* had leaked into the camp, and two more suicides occurred. When a new commandant took charge later in the month a gradual improvement of conditions began. This diary shows clearly the terrible effects of suppressing news of the outside world, of the endless delays over correspondence, and of the official secrecy which prevented the authorities from telling the men who were being compulsorily deported what their destination was. It will be noted that even a man as intelligent as the diarist wrote a savage letter to his wife accusing her of neglecting to write to him. This was a common occurrence. We have seen many such angry letters to wives who were still at liberty from desperate husbands upon whom it had not dawned than an insensitive bureaucracy was capable of holding up vital letters for weeks on end and even losing them completely.

The Isle of Man Camps.—The Isle of Man Camps, which are meant to be permanent, must be now considered. As might be expected, conditions in these camps were and are a good deal better than those we have described, apart from the complaints common to all camps such as the delay over correspondence, suppression of news up to mid-July, difficulty of visits, and throwing together of Nazis and non-Nazis. The five camps which existed during the period of military control consisted of blocks of houses—mostly boarding houses—cut off from the main quarters of seaside towns by barbed-wire fences. But the men were not cared for by seaside landladies. The houses were commandeered, a minimum of furniture was left in them, and the internees were left to run things themselves. We select one of the camps at Douglas, neither the best nor the worst, for detailed description (the period is mid-July). Each house had a common room with a table, chairs, a light and blacked-out windows. The remaining rooms were used for sleeping and contained beds with mattresses, but no chairs, cupboards, tables or light. Half the men in each house would sleep on palliasses on the floor, or in some cases on couches. In theory there were two blankets per man, but the camp suffered from a chronic under-supply of blankets, and sheets of course were not available. Most houses had bathrooms, but warm baths were only available if and when—as rarely happened—coal was issued. The camp stores issued food rations for each man, and the men in each house had to do their own cooking. The kitchens mostly contained gas-stoves, but inadequate supplies of utensils and crockery. Since most of the men are naturally inexpert at cooking this arrangement caused considerable hardship and wastage of food. The food supplied was a just adequate minimum to avert hunger, but was not dietetically well balanced and tended to be monotonous. It consisted mainly of cabbage, potatoes and other vegetables, rice, plenty of kippers and fresh herrings, meat occasionally, bread and a little milk. No sugar, fruit or eggs were supplied. Invalids were able to get some extra food and milk. The camp stores also issued soap and other necessities to internees. The canteen, run by a staff of internees, sold such things as tooth-paste, razor-blades, notebooks, tobacco. It also sold—at intervals—apples, chocolate, and bread. Jam and marmalade were not available. Canteen prices were high, and although destitute internees received one shilling a week from the canteen profits and could apply for the payment of telegrams, it was not at all clear what happened to the greater part of the profits, since proper accounts were not kept. It is believed that they go to the Manx Government. Recreation facilities were good. There was a football ground and a stretch of grass-covered open space. Footballs were available, but little used ; medicine-balls were more popular. Internee gym-instructors organised classes which were attended mostly by the young. Sea-bathing under armed guard was permitted. It was also permitted to leave the camp for turf-cutting, paid at the rate of 1s. a day. This was a holiday rather than hard work. There was an ample supply of interned medical practitioners working under a competent English doctor, but there was the usual shortage of medical equipment (though not nearly as bad as Huyton in June). The most seriously ill were sent out to hospital, where accommodation was severely limited. The camp was run in the usual way by house-leaders, under group leaders and camp supervisors who worked with the military staff, most of whom were intelligent and helpful, although the commandant appeared uninterested and difficult to approach. But the internee staff—as in many camps—was a bureaucracy rather than an elected self-government, and tended to make things unpleasant in many petty ways for men who asked awkward questions. The commandant produced a type-written news-bulletin which was pinned up on a notice-board. This bulletin was generally regarded as an insult to the intelligence of the internees and greatly resented by them. Towards the end of July the *Daily Telegraph* and the *Times* and two Sunday papers were allowed to circulate, and the rumours from which every one suffered began to die down.

Life in most of the men's camps on the island followed the same general lines, with considerable variation in details, particularly with regard to facilities for recreation and cultural pursuits. One camp lacks adequate open space for exercise. Another recently opened camp at Douglas consists of comfortable little houses grouped in a square around large and pleasant grounds. Rooms were equipped for cultural pursuits, and exchanges with other camps were being organised in order to bring fathers, sons and brothers together. In yet another camp 900 of the 1,300 men in mid-July were former members of the Kitchener Camp at Richborough. This made the organising of community life a simpler matter than in some of the camps where all the men were strangers.

The Manx Government, which has wide powers over the camps, appears to have behaved in a rather obstructive fashion. Suspicions that it has been seeking to make a profit out of the internees have been voiced in many quarters. Whatever the truth in these allegations, it is known that the Manx Government caused unnecessary difficulties by forbidding camp canteens to sell anything but fruit, chocolates and personal requirements, in spite of the general clamour in the men's camps for the sale of ordinary *bread*, and in spite of the fact that the canteens get the bulk of the supplies over the sea from Liverpool, and not from the island at all.

One grave problem which the Home Office has only a few weeks left to solve is the serious medical situation. Most of the mainland camps are plainly not inhabitable in winter at all, and only tolerable in summer for young and healthy men. It is clear that the authorities will not dare and do not intend to keep internees in tents, stables, Tote buildings, derelict factories and the like for very much longer. But the Isle of Man camps are apparently intended to be permanent. In mid-July there were 11,000 men interned on the island, and these included between one and two thousand cases of tuberculosis, heart disease, diabetes and other serious conditions. Except for the new camp at Peel, all the men's camps are on the east coast, which experiences very bad weather from September onwards, when winter conditions set in. It was authoritatively expected that there would be 1,000 cases of illness among the 11,000 men by the beginning of October, 1940. The island just does not possess the accommodation necessary for proper hospital treatment of so many sick men, over and above its ordinary population. We know for a fact that *discussions were proceeding in July with a view to forming a Jewish cemetery at Douglas, because, even if boat communications with the mainland were regular, the large number of deaths to be expected would make it impracticable to ship the bodies over to Liverpool for burial in the Jewish cemetery there.* If the release of all non-suspect invalids is not accomplished by the end of September at the latest, the Home Office runs the risk of being directly responsible for the killing of scores of innocent victims and opponents of Nazi tyranny, many of them men whose health, ruined in Nazi prisons and torture chambers, cannot stand up to the " humane " conditions in the British internment camps. A few deaths have already occurred both on the journey to camps and in hospitals to which sick men were transferred from the camps. If further deaths are to be avoided the Home Office will have to get very busy.

Finally, there are the women at Port Erin and Port St. Mary. They, too, are billeted in boarding houses, but the landladies remain in possession, and receive payment for their charges in the same general way as landladies of evacuated mothers or civil servants are paid under the Government's evacuation scheme. Although most of the women probably know how to cook, cooking is done by the landladies, and the internees help. In the first few weeks there were few complaints about living conditions, except that extras had to be paid for at exorbitant prices, which was a hardship since so many of the women are domestics and factory workers or dependent wives who had not been in a position to save money. Later, when over-crowding began, there was a general complaint about having to share beds. Since the women are mostly in A and B Classes the proportion of Nazis and sympathisers was higher than in the men's camps. Apart from the usual complaints about communications and information, the main difficulties in the women's camps seem to be due to lack of organisation,* understaffing and the lack of sympathy and understanding shown by the commandant appointed by the Home Office. Right down to the end of July the women in the Isle of Man camps were definitely discouraged from participating in the administration of the camp, let alone electing leaders and organising a community life of their own. It is reported that even the women doctors interned on the island found it difficult to get their professional services accepted, in spite of the usual inadequacy of medical facilities provided. It was still apparently true in early August that the crying need of the women's camps was for organised community life, welfare, recreation and information services, not only for the women, but for the numerous children interned with them. A school for the children was badly needed. The suppression of news of the world outside seems to have been more complete than in almost all the men's camps and, although the proportion of women of Nazi sympathies cannot be more than 10 to 15 per cent., there would seem to have been a marked tendency for all the internees to be treated literally as " enemy aliens."

Centres of Free German Culture.—Such, in general, appear

* A letter from the wife of a well-known Socialist writer (also interned) on July 19, says : " Every day there are new excitements and new regulations. You have to queue for hours in the rain to get the five shillings which you are allowed to take from your own money once a week. Queuing for your mail, queuing for this and queuing for that. Always among a crowd of hysterical women, and sometimes among Nazi women. . . . Organisation ! People who are sent food parcels get only the string and the carton."

to have been the living conditions of " Anderson's prisoners " in May, June and July, 1940. The brunt of making such circumstances tolerable fell upon the internees themselves, in some cases actively assisted and encouraged by sympathetic camp officers, but more often left to rely on their own initiative by uninterested or occasionally obstructive commandants. The degree to which they took the initiative in self-government and administration of camp life depended not only on what the commandant would permit or encourage, but also on the morale of the internees. In camps which contained a leaven of " politicals " or of men actively associated with organisations like the Austrian Centre, informal groups or committees were often formed which played a big part—if the commandant was agreeable—in organising feeding arrangements, medical services, welfare funds, records, news bulletins and a hundred and one other activities. In other camps, however, internee self-government was nothing but a democratic cloak for a camp bureaucracy appointed by the commandant from among the first arrivals, who were often men of Nazi sympathies. The unwillingness of the commandant or the indifference of the internees in such cases prevented self-government from becoming a reality. But the camps in which morale was highest were precisely those in which self-government was most developed and in which co-operation between elected officers or committees and the commandant's staff was usually most harmonious. In many camps the ban on newspapers was overcome by smuggling, and in one camp at least a " black exchange " developed. A newspaper could be hired for ninepence for a quarter of an hour. In another camp a houseful of men would gather each evening to discuss and analyse the day's rumours, and decide which were preposterous and which might be tentatively accepted as possibly truthful. In yet another camp —when rumours of the outbreak of a highly infectious disease were causing great anxiety—the interned doctors went round holding meetings at which they described the symptoms of the disease in detail in order to combat unfounded fears.

For the organisation of cultural life the camps were so full of men of learning and artistic merit that most of the camps by the end of July were developing into centres of free German culture. In many of the camps the scientists and university teachers, usually without the necessary books or paper, began to organise " People's Universities." In one Isle of Man camp the " University " offered language classes (English, French and Spanish) in the mornings, and lectures and seminars on a wide range of subjects in the afternoons. The " University " provided weekly courses or single lectures on Darwinism, psychology, climate and human life, biology, music, mathematics, mechanics, economics, heredity and race theory. There was even an advanced seminar on mediæval economic history conducted by an interned Cambridge University extension lecturer ! Discussions were also organised on Federal Union and on the economic future of Europe, but the camp bureaucracy stopped them out of fear that the commandant might object to " politics " !

In another Isle of Man camp, which contained over 200 youngsters under twenty-five, there was in addition to the " University " for adults a " Youth University " which provided the following curriculum :

1. Languages : English and French (Spanish if possible).
2. Mathematics and Physics.
3. Technical courses :
    Introduction to Electro-mechanics,
    Introduction to Wireless and Television Telegraphy.
4. Economics.
5. History.
6. Philosophy.

In addition a school was organised for boys who had been interned while preparing to take Matriculation or Higher Schools' Certificate examinations, so as to ensure that internment would not spoil their educational careers.

At the end of July, when newspapers were allowed and conditions were beginning to become a little human, a number of Isle of Man camps began to produce duplicated camp " newspapers," while others made use of " wall newspapers." The Mooragh Camp reads the *Mooragh Times*, contributors to which include Robert Neumann and Bruno Heilig. The *Onchan Pioneer* is conducted in a lively journalistic fashion, with a " Camp Reporter," " advertisements " (" Café Bauer, Caterers for His Obscurity, the Internee of Onchan "), extracts from the press about internment policy and all kinds of announcements. No 2 (August 9) reports an art show by Herr Nunnenmacher, the well-known sculptor, in House No. 9

and announces a forthcoming exhibition by all the painters in
the camp, organised by the artist-adventurer Jack Bilbo.
No. 3 (August 14) announces that the " Popular University "
has provided 600 class-hours and 300 individual lectures and
that its total attendance reaches the figure of 16,250 !

Similar cultural activities sprang up in most of the men's
camps. Even in a camp like Kempton Park the youth group
was able to organise concerts, cabarets and similar social
events. In almost all the camps concerts, poetry, recitals,
theatrical sketches were organised as a matter of course, as
soon as the acquiescence, if not the encouragement, of commandants could be obtained. In one Isle of Man camp a
number of the boarding houses, although practically denuded
of furniture, were found to contain pianos. Some men had
brought instruments with them, and concerts and solo performances would be held in the common-room of the largest
house. Well-known actors would perform sketches or declaim
poetry from memory, or give readings from Shakespeare.
Many informal cabaret shows and sing-songs were also organised. Such were the ways in which these " enemy aliens "
kept up their courage and used their time profitably to learn
something.

The Standards of the Prisoners of War Convention.—The
Prisoners of War Convention lays down standards for the
internment, under military discipline, of young and healthy
men belonging to the enemy's armed forces. The Convention's
standards are clearly a bare minimum for interned refugees
from Nazi oppression who do not need to be under strict
military discipline, and half at least of whom are either not
healthy enough or are too old to be soldiers. If it is necessary
to keep such men locked up, it is evident that they are entitled
to a much higher standard of comfort and personal freedom
than genuine prisoners of war. And yet during the whole
period of War Office control there can be no doubt that
in all the most important respects the conditions of interned
refugees were well below the Prisoners of War Convention
standards. Article 10 requires that " the premises must be
entirely free from damp, and adequately heated and lighted ";
they must consist of " buildings or huts which afford
all possible safeguards as regards hygiene and salubrity."
Article 12 required that clothing, underwear and footwear
shall be provided and regularly replaced, and that canteens

shall sell food and personal requirements " at the local market price." Article 15 requires that " medical inspections of prisoners of war shall be arranged *at least* once a month." We know of no camp where this held good. Article 20 requires that regulations, orders, announcements, questions, etc., " shall be communicated to prisoners of war in a language which they understand." This rule was frequently neglected, especially at the " collecting stations." The provisions for communications are revealing. " Not later than one week after his arrival in camp, and similarly in case of sickness, each prisoner shall be entitled to send a post card to his family informing them of his capture and the state of his health " (Article 36). It was only in July that this post card system began to operate efficiently, and we doubt whether, all through the period of military control, sick men in hospital were able to send such post cards to their families. " Letters and remittances of money or valuables, as well as postal parcels addressed to prisoners of war, or despatched by them, *shall be exempt from all postal charges.* . . . Presents and relief in kind intended for prisoners of war shall also be exempt from . . . any charges for carriage on railways operated by the State " (Article 38). Such benevolence is unknown to interned refugees and their families. The Government has no interest in enforcing this particular article of the Convention, since, in the case of refugees, it derives no reciprocal advantage for British internees in another country. " Prisoners of war shall be permitted to receive *individually* consignments of books, which may be subject to censorship " (Article 39). For interned refugees the authorities amended this provision so as to forbid any books to be sent to individuals except *new* books sent direct by the publisher or by a bookseller of repute. " The censoring of correspondence shall be accomplished as quickly as possible " (Article 40) ! ! !

Article 42 ensures a right of petition both to the camp authorities and to the neutral protecting power, and forbids punishment of any kind even if complaints are groundless. Who is the protecting power for interned refugees ? The Huyton men sent telegrams to Miss Eleanor Rathbone, Secretary of the Parliamentary Committee on Refugees, and to the Trades Union Congress in the second week of July. A German trade unionist described the effects (in a letter to Transport House) as follows : " This brought us some rest, but also new officers, who have threatened to deprive us of all privileges, and to take all foodstuffs and fruits out of the parcels sent to us. In this case we would refuse any kind of work." Although complaints must be transmitted immediately to the neutral protecting power, we know of telegrams to official bodies to which internees look for protection which were delayed for weeks or never arrived at all. Article 77 requires the authorities to set up an Information Bureau which must keep detailed records about each prisoner and *has the duty of notifying his next-of-kin of his whereabouts as quickly as possible.* It must also furnish a weekly list of new prisoners to the protecting power, must answer all inquiries, and is responsible for collecting the personal effects of prisoners who are released or die.* Throughout the whole period of military control no such Bureau was established, and relatives were never officially notified of an internee's whereabouts. The authorities never issued any lists of interned refugees to bodies like the High Commissioner's Office for Refugees or the Joint Consultative Committee on Refugees which might be described as the refugees' protecting powers. An Information Bureau was finally opened at Westminster on August 12, 1940.

One general defect of the camps is not covered by the Prisoners of War Convention. Hardly a single camp has any lighting or black-out facilities, and, as far as we know, no camp has any air-raid shelter, and all first-aid arrangements are grossly inadequate. In one camp the men were told to stay in their quarters during air raids. Any who came out would be shot. These defects may lead to serious consequences in the coming months.

After this lengthy review of the internment scandal, what are we to say of a Minister like Mr. Eden, who was asked on July 9 if he could assure the House that camp conditions were in no way below the standard of the Prisoners of War Convention, and who replied :

" I am very anxious that there should be no doubts that we are doing all we can and should in this matter. I have asked my hon. friend (the Under-Secretary) to make especial investigations, and I am confident that I can give the Hon. Member that assurance."

* A common complaint of released internees was that their luggage was not given to them on release, but was sent on separately and was frequently lost on the way and never seen again.

What are we to say of Sir Edward Grigg's statement on July 18, which continued this confusion between civilian Nazis and genuine refugees :

> " It has been agreed with the German Government that the terms of the Prisoners of War Convention will be applied, so far as possible, to civilians interned as enemy aliens. This agreement has been scrupulously observed in all established camps. In other camps formed at very short notice to accommodate the recent intake of aliens, it was impossible to ensure from the first an equally high standard, but shortcomings are being rapidly remedied so that the same standard will be observed in all camps."

We leave the reader to answer these questions for himself, and in particular to decide why the official mind persistently refuses to admit any distinction between Nazi subjects of the Third Reich and refugees, many of whom have spent their lives and ruined their health fighting oppression . . . except in the case of refugees who happen to be " useful."

4. *Deportation*

The Arandora Star.—On the evening of July 3 came the news over the wireless that on the preceding Tuesday (July 2) at 6 a.m. the 15,500-ton Blue Star liner *Arandora Star*, on its way to Canada with 1,500 German and Italian internees on board, had been torpedoed and sunk by a Nazi U-boat off the west coast of Ireland. Many who heard that news bulletin were sickened by the apparent gloating manner of the announcer who spoke of " great hulking brutes " of Nazis on the ship who swept everyone aside in their rush for the life-boats, and of how the " poor Italians " stood no chance against this mad scramble and were drowned by the score. In the same news bulletin was reported the arrival of the first shipload of real Nazi prisoners of war at Quebec and Montreal. Reference was made to the arrogant behaviour of Nazi officers and pilots, and the ship's crew's description of the young Nazis as " skulking, swaggering louts " was quoted. The same two official stories were reproduced at greater length the following morning in the press, and the more sensational newspapers presented the story of the *Arandora Star* in a lurid and revolting manner. Everything was done to give the impression that the ship had contained only Nazis and Italian Fascists. But all over the country the relatives of thousands of interned " enemy aliens " spent sleepless nights wondering if their husbands, brothers, fathers and sons had been on that ship.   For they no longer trusted official assurances, after seven weeks of unexplained internment ;   and *this was the first news they, or the British public, had that internees were being sent overseas.*   Rumours had been circulating around the refugee organisations but the secret had been well guarded.   If the *Arandora Star* had not been sunk the news might not have leaked out for a good deal longer.   At any rate this ghastly tragedy dragged out of secrecy the most startling revelations of official stupidity and incapacity, and taught every intelligent " enemy alien " in the country one lesson :   never to believe the promises of the British authorities again.

Consider the Parliamentary history of the *Arandora Star*. On July 9 Mr. Cross (Minister of Shipping), who was not responsible in any sense for deportation, made the following statement on the basis of material provided by Mr. Eden, who was one of the Ministers responsible :

" I am informed by my right hon. Friend the Secretary of State for War that all the Germans on board were Nazi sympathisers and that none came to this country as refugees. *None had category B or C certificates or were recognised as friendly aliens.   The Protecting Powers have been given lists of the missing passengers in order that the next of kin may be informed.* . . . Every endeavour will be made to separate enemy aliens of Nazi or Fascist sympathies from those of anti-Nazi and anti-Fascist sympathies."

The fat was in the fire.   *Only* A Class men had been on the ship, and everyone, except apparently Mr. Eden, knew that many A class men were staunch and proven anti-Nazi fighters, some of whom had fought in Spain or worked illegally against the Nazis in Germany.   And Mr. Eden was passing on the names of the missing, via the Protecting Power, to the Nazi Government.

The question was hotly pressed by M.P.'s the following day, during the debate on refugees.   Mr. Graham White stated that he had heard from survivors that at least 200 German refugees had been on the ship.   Mr. John Parker mentioned the names of Louis Weber and Valentin Wittke* (*see* Section 2

* His widow mourned him in internment on the Isle of Man.

for details). Col. Wedgwood spoke of three Italians he knew of who had been on the ship, men " who had fought Mussolini throughout their lives. . . . I do not know whether or not they lost their lives. They were old men, and I think they are dead." Mr. Peake's reply was classic :

> " All the War Office, who have custody of these men, have is a nominal roll of the names of those on board. They have to check against that the names of those saved before they can arrive at the names of the missing. *Having arrived at the names of the missing, they transmit those names to the Home Office—I am not sure whether they have been received yet— who transmit them to the refugee organisations because it is only the refugee organisations who will be able to get in touch with the relatives.*"

Thus " all the Germans on board were Nazi sympathisers . . . none came to this country as refugees . . . none were *recognised* as friendly aliens " but—" only the refugee organisations will be able to get in touch with the relatives " ! *Why* was there *only* a " nominal roll of the names of those on board " ? Why were the names and addresses of relatives not taken before the men were put on the ship ? We do not know.

Neither Mr. Peake for the Home Office, nor Sir Edward Grigg for the War Office was anxious to admit any responsibility for the deporting of " enemy aliens." After some pressure Mr. Peake had previously revealed that

> " the question of sending refugees and internees overseas is a decision that is not taken either by the Secretary of State for War or the Home Secretary. It is a decision taken by a Committee of the Cabinet, presided over by the Lord President of the Council " [Mr. Neville Chamberlain].

Whereupon there were angry protests about Mr. Chamberlain's absence from the debate. Sir Percy Harris described it as an " insult to the House."

Who *was* on the *Arandora Star* ? Even to-day the matter is not finally settled. In the debate Mr. Graham White read out a letter he had received from a young man :

> " My mother and I are British born, and my sentiments are all with this country. My father, an Italian, came to this country as a young man, and fought for the Allies in the

last war, when he was badly wounded in the head. . . . He had no political ideas and he did not belong to any association. . . . On June 11 he was taken away to be interned. On hearing of the *Arandora Star* being torpedoed we were rather worried. We found that he was on the *Arandora Star* and posted missing. Up to the present we have not had any news from the authorities at all. I am an only son and will soon be twenty. I applied to join the L.D.V. but was turned down because my father was Italian. I managed to join the A.F.S. ; you can imagine the state of mind of my mother, who has long been in delicate health. . . ."

We can also imagine the state of mind of this young man who was to be called up in a month or two to serve under the War Minister who had put his father on the *Arandora Star*.

It was discovered that the former Reichstag Deputy, Karl Olbrisch, had been drowned (*see* Section 2 for details. His widow was still on the Isle of Man in August. On July 9 the Council of Austrians in Great Britain received a telegram from Mr. Kurt Regner, Secretary of the Liverpool Branch of the Austrian Centre prior to internment : " Twenty Austrian *Arandora Star* survivors penniless, wire money to me at once c/o Commandant ——, Lea Camp, Miltonbridge." Money was immediately wired to Regner, but the Commandant replied with a letter :

" We enclose for your information a telegram from Internee Regner. We would add, however, that these internees have now left for an unknown destination, and you could not therefore send any assistance to this address."

Regner vanished. Finally on August 8 Mr. Eden told the House :

" Kurt Regner is on the way to Australia. Twenty-two other Austrians were saved, of whom 14 are on the way to Australia and 8 are in this country. *In the case of those who have been sent to Australia, there was no time to arrange interviews* [with their families], *but there was nothing to prevent their writing letters, subject to censorship.*"*

* At that time an internee was not allowed to write a letter for the first ten days following his arrival at a camp. If this rule applied at Miltonbridge, Regner cannot have had an opportunity of writing before he was sent to Australia.

" Enemy alien " Regner, who was thus rushed out of the country without a chance to see his mother and his sister (who were half-crazy with distraction) after his rescue from the *Arandora Star*, is a well-known Austrian *Socialist* lawyer. He had been a leader of the Austrian Socialist Student Movement and had defended many working-class people in trials. He was one of the leaders of an anti-Nazi demonstration at Baden, near Vienna, on March 11, 1938, was beaten up and escaped by night to Czechoslovakia, whence the Czech Trust Fund later brought him to England. His tribunal put him in A Class and he was interned—with Nazi seamen and others— at Seaton Camp, Devon. Other Austrian survivors include Karl Mayerhoefler, a Social-Democratic refugee ; Ernst Seemann (19), a member of the Austrian Socialist Youth Movement, who worked as an agricultural labourer until the Dorchester tribunal ordered his internment ; Michael Glass, Deutsch, Schoenmann, Kurt, Franz, Moser, Stephan, Schiessl, Spruch, Weger, Frankl, Gutmann, Schramml, Lanziger, Weiss, Reich, Ehrlich and T. Pulitzer, all anti-Nazis identified by the Council of Austrians. Pulitzer was in hospital paralysed in both legs in early August, and Sir John Anderson was being pressed for his release.

Anti-Nazi Austrians who are known to be missing include M. Baum, Ernst Spitzer, A. Neumann, H. E. Beck, L. Beck, A. Glaser, F. Holdengraeber, R. Kubak, Fritz Neufeld, Erich Dangl and Rudolf Schenk. Fritz Neufeld (a Jew) had been brought over to England by an Agricultural Committee to train for land work. Erich Dangl, for whose release the Council of Austrians had applied, had managed to get out of Nazi territory *legally*, and refused to go back as he was a strong anti-Nazi. He was only able to marry his wife in this country because he was a non-Jew and she was Jewish. His tribunal apparently found this story suspicious and ordered his internment. Rudolf Schenk was a determined opponent of the Nazis who was assisted to come over to England with his fiancée (whom he subsequently married here) with the help of the Society of Friends. They sent him and his wife to Cornwall where he was being trained for agricultural work prior to emigrating to South Africa. The local tribunal ordered his internment, against which, with the backing of the Council of Austrians, he appealed. *Three weeks after he was drowned on the " Arandora Star " the Council of Austrians received a letter from*

*the Home Office stating that the Home Secretary " has recon-
sidered the case, and regrets that in the existing circumstances he
is not prepared to authorise the release of Mr. Schenk."* The
right hand knew not what the left hand did !

On August 6 Lord Faringdon told the House of Lords :

> " I consider that whoever was responsible for these men
> and, after their internment, for their transportation, is
> answerable for their deaths."

The reader can decide for himself whether he agrees.*

Out of the 717 Italians on the *Arandora Star*, 470 were
drowned.   Less is known about them ; the majority probably
were Fascists or sympathisers, but a considerable proportion
were not.   Here are two representative cases that have leaked
out.   Mr. Silvestro D'Ambrosio (68), confectioner and restaur-
ateur of Hamilton, Scotland, " had been 42 years in this
country, had applied for naturalisation as a British subject a
few days before Italy entered the war.   *Two of his sons are
serving in the British Army, and one is in the Canadian Expedi-
tionary Force.*   In addition, two other sons have registered for
service " (*Glasgow   Forward*, July 13).   D'Ambrosio was
interned ; had he been two years older he would have been
spared, and would not have been drowned on the *Arandora
Star*.   Mr. D. Anzani was also drowned.   He was Secretary
of the Italian Section of the League of the Rights of Man in
London, an organisation whose anti-Fascist and anti-authori-
tarian integrity is known all over the world and is beyond
dispute.   (Before war broke out the French section of the
League was trusted by the French Government with the task
of compiling lists of genuine Italian anti-Fascist refugees who
should be exempted from the normal restrictions placed on
foreign residents.)   Mr. Anzani had lived in this country for
31 years, modestly working as a tailor.   He was one of the
best-known anti-Fascists in Britain, and his whole life was
devoted to assisting refugees from Mussolini's terror and
organising anti-Fascist activities.   There was never a shadow
of suspicion against him (unless the police dislike anti-Fascists).
His widow is left destitute.

As facts of this kind were leaking out in July, the responsible

---

* As this book goes to press we have received the first full account
from an *Arandora Star* survivor still in this country.   His tragic
story has been added as an appendix to this section.

authorities were not idle. On July 16 Mr. Eden repeated that all the men on the *Arandora Star* were Italian Fascists and A Class Germans or Austrians :

> " It was understood by my Department that none of these Germans were refugees, but I am making further inquiries on this point. . . . I can give the House the assurance that it is not the intention to send abroad anti-Nazis in contact with Nazis."

On the following day Sir Edward Grigg " hoped " that a complete list of the survivors and the missing would be available " in the course of the next two or three days." The list —still not complete—was apparently finally issued early in August. There was a good reason for this delay. Not only had no proper records been kept by the authorities, but men chosen for deportation had in many cases persuaded or paid other men to take their places on the ships. A memorandum issued on July 10 by internees at Huyton made the following allegations :

> " Again to-day another transport has been assembled. It leaves to-day. In spite of the most express promises to maintain above all the principle of voluntary departure, the majority were forcibly pressed into the group under threat of the use of arms. Some were taken from their beds in the night ; in a few cases where the commandant permitted exchange, sums up to £15 and in one case over £100 were offered to people who volunteered to exchange."

Rumours of substitutions on the *Arandora Star* reached M.P.'s, and on July 23 Mr. Eden stated that :

> " in view of the allegations that have reached me, instructions have been issued that immediate inquiries should be made into all the circumstances of this case."

He also promised to find out who was responsible for the selection of the individuals put on the ship. On July 30 he made a further statement :

> " The selection of internees to be transferred to Canada in the *Arandora Star* was ordered by my Department *from Germans and Austrians who were in category A, and from Italians who were members of the Fascist party*.* There were

* Like Mr. Anzani !

on board 473 Germans and Austrians, and it has been verified that all of these had been individually ordered to be interned on grounds of national security, and accordingly came within category A. *Fifty-three of these persons were or claimed to be refugees,* but had nevertheless been placed in category A.* There were also on board 717 Italians, and it has been verified that all but 26, regarding whom inquiries are still proceeding, were listed as members of the Fascist Party."

(A similar statement was made in the House of Lords on August 6 by the Duke of Devonshire. He added that deportation of internees was " decided on when . . . the risk of invasion was imminent, and it seemed desirable both to husband our resources of food and get rid of useless mouths and so forth " !).

The following day Mr. Peake at last threw some light on the difficulties of tracing internees :

" There has been some confusion in the internment camps, largely due to the large number of people interned and partly due to the fact that accurate records at the moment are not available, because there was considerable confusion owing to the amount of impersonation in regard to those sent to the Dominions. We are endeavouring at the present moment to secure an accurate list of the internees in each of the camps."

Finally on August 6 all pretence was dropped. Mr. Attlee explained that, apart from the defective lists supplied to the Swiss and Brazilian legations,

" any information available will be supplied to any next of kin who apply to the special Information Bureau which will be opened next Monday at St. Stephen's House, Westminster."

Mr. Graham White retorted to this :

" Does not the right hon. Gentleman agree that it is the responsibility of those who were responsible for the shipments to notify the next of kin, and further, is he seized of the fact that in their anxiety and anguish to know what has

* Like Karl Olbrisch !

happened to relatives, people are now writing to Members of Parliament and asking them to look at the list in the Library ? "

Mr. Attlee replied that " every endeavour is being made to inform the next of kin, but in some cases it is very difficult to find out who are the next of kin."

This sorry story is not over. On August 22 Mr. Attlee told the House that Lord Snell had been " asked to undertake an inquiry into the selection of aliens to be sent overseas in the *Arandora Star*." M.P.s who know the facts doubt very much whether the matter will ever be entirely cleared up. So do we.

How Deportation was Organised.—The *Arandora Star* was only one of several ships which in the first half of July carried nearly 7,700 internees to Canada and Australia. Some time in June Mr. Chamberlain's Committee of Ministers took the decision to deport prisoners of war and internees, and this policy was continued until mounting protests from all sides forced a suspension of the shipments. No one objects to the shipping overseas of genuine prisoners of war and Nazi civilians, who are enemies of the British people, and of people who really wish to go, but in addition to these thousands of internees (most of whom were refugees) were herded on to boats like cattle and shipped away in the greatest secrecy, usually without a chance to see their relatives and friends before departure, often without a chance even to write to them, and in most cases without their wishes being considered. The revelations produced by the *Arandora Star* episode showed clearly—out of the mouths of the Ministers themselves—that the War Office, the Home Office and Mr. Chamberlain between them made a complete mess of the job of selecting people for deportation in a sensible and democratic way and of organising the overseas transport of less than 8,000 men. People who remember how smoothly the local authorities and the school teachers in September, 1939, organised the transport, not of a few thousands, but of over a million children out of the towns into the country, will be aghast at this exposure of official inefficiency. What the authorities *thought* they were doing was described by Mr. Peake on July 10 :

" Canada has agreed to take 6,000 to 7,000 prisoners of war and internees. They have all now arrived there, and the categories sent have been, in priority, prisoners of war,

Nazi seamen who have been interned and rank as civilian internees, internees who have been interned for security purposes, single men in category B, and particularly those who took no objection to going. *So far as possible, therefore, we have sent to Canada the most dangerous classes of internees, and where we have had to make up the number we have selected single men under the age of fifty and in preference those who expressed a wish to go.* The Italians who were included for sending to Canada were those who had been interned for security reasons."

What they *actually* did and the effects that were produced can best be described from the numerous letters and reports that came out of the camps all through July. A report from Huyton on July 10 stated :

" This camp is a clearing camp ; up to now internees removed from here have been grouped together compulsorily. Information as to destination is either refused or false destinations given. These facts increase the unrest among the internees. The information of the torpedoing of the *Arandora Star* with 1,500 refugees compulsorily shipped on board has created a feeling of panic among many of the internees which the provocative elements, mostly Nazi, seek to exploit and to drive the internees to open resistance against the camp administration. These elements, who are clever enough to remain in the background, are even advocating the burning of the tents and houses. A calmer majority of the internees succeeded in frustrating this provocation and in restoring some degree of quiet."

A report from a British refugee official who visited a certain men's camp a few days later states :

" The Commandant told me that he has to produce 1,000 men at a time to fill a ship ; the men do not know to which country they are to go. If only 700 put their names down for going, he has to make the list up at random and their relations know nothing."

At the beginning—until the *Arandora Star* disaster became known—considerable numbers of men did volunteer for deportation. One reason why they did so was explained by Mr. Peake in the debate of August 22 :

" They were receiving no letters and no newspapers, and they were hearing rumours that Holland and Belgium had been overrun, that France was conquered, that parachutists had landed in this country, that Hitler might arrive here at any moment. It is not, in my view, very surprising that considerable numbers of these people, who thought they would be the first victims of persecution if the Germans were to arrive here, were anxious to go overseas."

(It should be understood that there were no volunteers on the *Arandora Star*.) Many of the men selected to make up the quota were also " persuaded " to volunteer by powerful moral pressure. They were told that if they did not agree to go, other men, old and unsuited for the journey, would have to be sent. In many cases they were given promises of all kinds about conditions in the Dominions, about reunion with their families and so on. After the sinking of the *Arandora Star* became known few men believed such promises. Mr. Zinnemann, an internee on the Isle of Man, explained in a letter to *The Times* (August 6) how one group of men was persuaded to volunteer :

" On July 10, twenty-two married men left this camp voluntarily for oversea under a guarantee given to them in the name of the Command that their interned wives in Port Erin would accompany them in the same convoy. A week later it was admitted that the guarantee had not been kept. Furthermore, letters from Port Erin, dated July 10, say that all women there had been told on exactly the same day that their husbands would leave for oversea and it was hoped to reunite them there at a later date. Apparently not even an attempt was made to fulfil the given guarantee. The twenty-two men left, trusting the word of the Command, as they had no possibility to communicate with their wives."*

Little wonder that this method of getting rid of the " useless mouths " of the " most dangerous classes of internees " produced panic, nervous collapses and a few suicides in the camps. Little wonder that the official records were muddled up even more than they would have been otherwise by the big scale

* On August 13 Mr. Peake explained that "completion of the arrangements which were being made for sending these wives, and other married internees with their wives and children to Australia, had had to be deferred pending further communication with the Australian Government."

on which substitutions appear to have taken place, so that the authorities are not quite certain whom they have deported. Did they know, for example, that they shipped off to Canada " a man of the utmost scientific distinction who was doing work in connection with war wounds, which nobody else in the world can do ? " (Mr. Pickthorn told the House on August 22 that the Home Office ordered this man's release three days after the War Office had deported him.)

Under the age of 16, children are not held in English law to be responsible for their actions. Scores of boys of 16 and 17 were deported because they " volunteered." They were at the " age of consent," but we do not know what pressure was applied or what fairy tales were told them to extract their consent. Here is one story out of many of a lad who " volunteered " (*Hansard*, Aug. 1):

> " Mr. J. P. Morris asked the Home Secretary whether he is aware that Horst Giesener, 16 years of age, son of a domestic servant, Kate Giesener, a German refugee residing at 70, Cavendish Road, Kersal, Salford, was interned on 16th May ; that the Home Office in a communication, dated 17th July, stated that if the boy's employers notified their willingness to employ him he would be released ; that the employers did signify such intention, but the boy has not yet been released ; that letters and parcels sent to him at Huyton Camp have been returned ; that prepaid telegrams sent to the camp have not had a reply ; that a telephone message to the camp elicited the reply that his name was not on the list of internees, and that he probably had been sent overseas ; and will he, in order to ease the sorrow of the boy's mother, have inquiries made to ascertain the whereabouts of her son ? "

> Sir J. Anderson : " I am now informed that this boy volunteered to go to Australia, and embarked on 10th July."

Mr. D. Baruch (56), a German Jew, of Liverpool, has lived in England for twelve years. He was a member of the St. John Ambulance Brigade and volunteered for service in France. Because he was not technically a refugee, a tribunal ordered his internment in October, 1939. He had a heart attack, and was cared for by fellow-prisoners as the police would not let him see a doctor. He was interned, together with his eldest son, for five months, four of which he spent in various hospitals. He was then released on health grounds. His illness probably saved him from the *Arandora Star*. Two months later (in May, 1940) his wife and two younger sons were taken. He believes his boys have been sent to Australia. Mr. Baruch, left alone, clamoured to be re-interned, either with his wife or with his boys ; but the police told him : " We are not going to intern you, because we do not want you to die in the camp."

These are only two typical stories. We could fill a dozen Penguins with similar ones. There were even a few cases of families being split up between Canada and Australia. So great was the scandal about deportation that for the last shipments genuine efforts appear to have been made to encourage volunteering and to discourage compulsory deportations, at least of men in C Class. But on July 25, Sir John Anderson was asked if he would not deport any internees without first giving them a chance to apply for release, at least in the case of C Class men. He replied : " I should hesitate to give the specific undertakings " for which M.P.'s were asking, but promised to deport none but volunteers or men whose families would be able to accompany or follow them.

Treatment in the Dominions.—What happens to the 7,700 German, Austrian and Italian internees who have been deported, once they arrive in Canada or Australia ? Mr. Peake made the following statement on July 10 :—

" They will be interned in the Dominions when they arrive. . . . It would obviously be within the power of the Dominion Government to order release in suitable cases, but the Home Secretary will retain the overriding power here of ordering release in any case where he is convinced that release will be in the national interest, or in the interest of our war effort."

On August 6, he added :—

" Arrangements will be made to bring back to this country any person whose release is authorised unless the Dominion Government concerned is prepared to allow him to be at large in the Dominion, and he himself desires to stay there. . . . Exactly the same conditions (for release) will apply in the Dominions as are applicable here."

If, as in England, release is the exception and not the rule, most deportees will presumably remain locked up. How will they be treated? Mr. Shakespeare (Under-Secretary for Dominion Affairs) explained on July 23 that " the Dominions . . . intend to apply that Convention [on the Treatment of Prisoners of War] generally to civilian internees." On July 30, Mr. Peake added the information that there was no risk of confusion between A and B and C Class internees in the Dominions because they had been sent on different ships, and that information was being sent " as to the distinctions to be drawn, both as regards A, B and C, and as to the privileges to be afforded to the different categories." When Mr. Wedgwood asked whether the Home Office realised that many A Class deportees might just as easily have been put in C Class, and that they were " interned marked ' A ' because of their Socialist actions, which are no longer a bar ? " Mr. Peake replied (at long last !) : " I am aware of the fact stated by my right hon. Friend," and explained that the Home Office was sending to Canada " detailed information about each individual internee." Yet when asked on August 20 if he had made sure that the Canadian Government would not intern anti-Nazi refugees and Nazi prisoners of war together, he stated : " The Canadian Government have been asked to separate B and C from A internees." Evidently Mr. Peake was *not* " aware of the fact " at all ; plainly he still believed that Olbrisch, Wittke, Weber and Regner *were* Nazis because they had been put in A Class. He also explained that the Government from London would " review the cases of Category B and C internees who have been sent to Canada with a view to authorising their release in proper cases." He did not say how this review would be carried out. Two days later the Home Secretary explained that the Regional Advisory Committees were now to visit the camps in Britain to resume their review of B cases, but he expressly stated that such a review would not be possible for deportees (" obviously, that will be difficult if the tribunal is in this country and the alien is away "). For the refugee in Canada or Australia the British policeman thousands of miles away will evidently be the sole judge deciding whether to release him. On August 7, Mr. Peake explained that the Home Office would " get into touch with the Canadian and Australian authorities " about providing clothing for the deportees, and that he was inquiring into the question of sending on articles confiscated from internees before deportation and postal orders sent to them. On August 14, he stated that the Home Office would not send a representative to Canada to watch over the treatment of deportees. He added :

> " The War Office have sent a liaison officer to Canada, who will, *it is hoped*, be able *to some extent* to act in this capacity, both as regards prisoners of war and internees, but, having regard to the comparatively small numbers sent to Australia, I do not think there is any necessity, at present at all events, for a liaison officer there."

Thus the treatment of internees was still being left to the War Office, with the " hope " that " to some extent " the War Office, after its gross mismanagement of internment camps, can be relied upon to do the job properly. On August 20, he saw no need to grant an exit permit for a qualified British welfare worker to visit the Canadian camps : " *I have no doubt* that the Canadian Government will make arrangements for welfare workers in Canada to visit the internment camps."

These vague assurances are not at all encouraging. As we write near the end of September we have evidence that there is still the utmost confusion about the fate of the men shipped to the Dominions. Up to the time of writing deportees had not been allowed to cable to their relatives in Britain, as was done as a matter of course when English children arrived in Canada about the same time, to give them news of their safe arrival. Scarcely any letters had yet arrived, since the deportees were apparently not allowed to write until they reach their final internment camp in the Dominions. The friends and relatives of these thousands of men spent weeks of anxious waiting for news that did not come. The news that the Dominions will apply the Prisoners of War Convention standards to deported internees is disquieting, (*a*) because as we have argued it is too low a standard to apply to most interned refugees, (*b*) because it implies that the official mind still believes that the mass of internees somehow " belong " to Hitler and are therefore dangerous men who must be kept under restraint, which is an unwarranted insult.

APPENDIX : A SURVIVOR'S ACCOUNT OF THE TORPEDOING OF
THE " ARANDORA STAR "

The majority of *Arandora Star* survivors were shipped away
again as soon as possible, as we have seen. But Sir John
Anderson told Parliament on August 22, 1940, that seventy-
one survivors were still in Britain (presumably men who had
been too ill to be sent off when deportation was proceeding).
A man of international repute, released in August from Prees
Heath Camp, reports to us the following :

" The survivors of the *Arandora Star* were brought to
a camp next door, separated from the ' C ' aliens by a
barbed wire fence. The majority of the *Arandora Star*
survivors were Nazis and amused themselves by hurling
abuse through the wire with such phrases as ' Dirty Jewish
swine ! ' etc. *It was well-known to the Class ' C ' aliens
that among their neighbours from the ' Arandora Star,' and
in the same camp, there were and still are thirty Jews.* Severe
punitive measures are enforced upon any Class ' C ' aliens
attempting to pass a letter out of the camp, and so avoiding
the censor. One young man, caught doing this, was told
by the Commandant that, as punishment, he would be sent
to join the *Arandora Star* survivors. He fell on his knees
and wept, and the Commandant, relenting, knocked him off
all communication to and from the outside world for a
fortnight."

Thus still in August, 1940, nearly eleven months since they
were first sent to a prisoners of war camp, and after all the
terrible experiences they had gone through, anti-Nazi survivors
of the *Arandora Star* were still inhumanly locked up together
with Nazis of the most violent and brutal character, because
some tribunal put them in A Class.

What this has meant in the way of mental torment and
physical suffering will be evident to anyone who reads the
poignant and horrifying story which a resourceful anti-Nazi
survivor from the *Arandora Star* has at last succeeded, nearly
two months after the disaster, in making public.

Let this " useless mouth," this " person who claimed to be
a refugee," but was not recognised as such by Mr. Eden's
Department, speak for himself (the following report is abridged
and the headings are our own) :

The Prisoners of War Camp

.In Warner's Camp, Seaton, Devonshire, there were about 600 to 700 internees. About 240 Nazis, seamen brought to England on the *Adolf Woerman* (Captain Burfend), a representative of the *I. G. Farben* (the German Dye Trust), Germans who owned factories in England, etc. Among them were Gestapo men and Nazi assassins (Kittel and Gülchert, who boasted to have been amongst the murderers of Rosa Luxemburg).

About 200 Jews who had been interned by Tribunals or by the police, some being there since war began. Among them some who came to England without visas, had quarrels with refugee organisations, have been punished before, did not please the judge of the Tribunals, some who had the same names as politically suspected persons. I did not meet a single one whom I could suppose to be a Nazi agent.

One hundred and forty anti-Fascists were grouped as following: fighters of the International Brigade in Spain: Nass, Schütt, Frick; Czech anti-Fascists: Wenk, Wallrath, Seeman, Kirste, Schmidt G.; progressive political refugees: Olbrich, Weiss. Progressive people living in England for a long time: Baruch. Austrian refugees: Dr. Regner, Moser, Dangl, Meyerhöfler, Schönmann Franz and Willi; Jewish seamen from the British ship *Lucy Borchard*; trade-unionists: Kleeblatt, Frey, Neuberger, Lindenberg, Kohn. German seamen: Polly, Senona, Lorenz Weber. Seamen of neutral ships: Apel, Artelt and many more. Until June, in spite of many protests, we remained interned together with the Nazis. Most of the appeals to come before an Advisory Council were ignored, not let through (by the commandant) or refused.

In June, all of a sudden, the internees were asked, who was pro and anti the Nazis. The Nazis lived on the right side of the camp, the anti-Nazis, Jews and refugees on the left. We shared meals as well as sitting-rooms and sport. At this time newspapers were forbidden. The anti-Fascists asked for complete separation from the Nazis and pointed out the danger that parachutists could co-operate with the splendidly organised Nazis. The answer to this was: machine-guns were directed against all on the corners of the camp. The Nazis had a wireless in spite of the prohibition, which never could be found, and even a short wave transmitter, it was said. . . . In June, half of the internees, Nazis, anti-Nazis, Jews went away.

Many feared that the war was over and they were to be extradited. Later on we, who stayed behind, learned that this transport *I.* had gone to Canada (so we learned unofficially from the guards). Nazis and anti-Nazis were together in this transport in spite of the promises.

Sent Off Without Information

On June 30, 1940, we (the rest) left Seaton by train. Most of us had had no letters or news of our families for a month. We were not told the destination of the journey. Only one piece of luggage was allowed. The rest was to be sent after. Matches and lighters were taken from us.

In the afternoon we arrived in Liverpool, on the pier. We were brought on board a ship with two guns. Certain exits were closed with barbed wire and so were the wireless cabin and conning bridge. A medical officer examined our eyes for trachoma. We were allotted to cabins before entering the ship without regard to old age or weakness.

Our Seaton transport consisted of 182 persons, among them 12 Nazis. In the cabins were palliasses beside the beds laid out on the floor. Cabins meant for two had to serve for four, cabins for one, for two persons. But, as the majority were supposed to stay in a kind of magazine which was without air and light, we arranged that six persons slept in cabins for two and sometimes four in cabins for one. When we went to fetch cutlery and plates we noticed (*a*) that a number of Italians were on board, who thought we were going to the Isle of Man, (*b*) that the Nazis, who were sent away from Seaton from time to time before us, though separated from us, were on board too (under the leadership of Captain Burfend of the *Adolf Woerman*). The food was excellent and more than sufficient. We left Liverpool at night. Many had relatives and wives in Liverpool, but could not see them. We were not allowed to walk on the promenade deck, where armed guards were on patrol all the time. We had lifebelts in our cabins. But I noticed that there was no boat drill. There were 12 lifeboats with a capacity of 60 each; they were worn out. One of them was a motor-boat. There were approximately about 1,700 to 1,900 persons on board. There were very few sailors and officers on board, but many soldiers. It was said that our destination was Canada.

The Torpedo Strikes the Ship

On July 2, at 7 in the morning (most of us were still asleep) a hollow explosion was heard in the engine-room. I tried to switch the light on—in vain. I thought we had run upon a mine. Cries, steps and running started in the corridors. I dressed scantily and went on with a lifebelt. I wanted to go to the lifeboats. The armed guard prevented me from doing so. I went to the other side to a small half-open deck. There many men were already busy throwing pieces of wood into the water. I could not see any officer nor any sailor; nobody could give any advice. *Most of the rafts were left on board and were tied down with wire, which could not be loosened in the hurry and without implements.* Many could not believe that the ship was sinking. Some became hysterical. I saw lifeboats and wanted to go on the deck again, where the boats were. Suddenly two shots were fired. Later on I heard that internees were shot at, who wanted to go to the lifeboats, which were reserved for English soldiers only. But as the soldiers were no seamen, they cut the ropes with an axe when the boat was only half-way down to the water and were drowned.

The Struggle for Life

The Nazis went at once on deck in files of two under the leadership of Captain Burfend; they had access to the lifeboats. They had many seamen and brought down about seven lifeboats. Captain Burfend stayed on board (eight lifeboats were in the water altogether) and was drowned. I came to the upper deck; no lifeboats were left. Scenes of distress. A man hanged himself; a 62-year-old Jew sat in despair on his suitcase and could not be persuaded to put on his lifebelt. The old and ill people in the decks below had no chance. Among them there was the 75-year-old Julius Weiss who had been in England for fifty years.

I advised two soldiers who were still standing guard with drawn bayonets to throw away their bayonets and to spring into the water. They said they were not allowed to because they had not had an order, but I persuaded them. I did not see an officer, military officer or sailor, who would have helped us or the privates. As the boat heeled over I climbed down a rope ladder with a plank in my hand into the water. The decision to do so was very difficult for me. I swam away from the ship and saw it sink.

In the Water

It took thirty-five minutes from the explosion to the sinking of the ship.   The water was full of oil ; hundreds of planks and pieces of wood with barbed wire threatened us.   The first hours in the Atlantic Ocean were dreadful.   The water was terribly cold, with fog and slight rain.   Cries, praying, shouts of " Mother ! " by old and young in every language (Italian, German, English, Hebrew) depressed us terribly.   Old people got heart attacks and died.   Bodies swollen by water floated beside me.

After about three hours a coastal aeroplane sighted us.   It cruised about for hours over our heads, as if it wanted to tell us that rescue was coming.   We took fresh heart.   After six-and-a-half hours I sighted one of our lifeboats.   I swam to it. An English sailor (first mate) was at the helm.   I spoke to him in English, told him that I was quite exhausted, and asked him to take me into the boat.   He said, " Full up."   I held on the helm and implored the others in the boat, who drew me, quite exhausted as I was, into the boat.

Rescued by Destroyers.

After an hour the destroyer H 83 *St. Laurent* from Canada came.   Behind her was a British one.   On board the Canadian destroyer rum, hot chocolate, food were awaiting us.   The sailors gave us their raincoats, trousers, etc., to dress those of us who were almost naked.   We sailed shortly after 4 o'clock in the afternoon with about 600 survivors.   Of our Seaton group of 182 persons, about 101 were drowned, among them Olbrich and Kirste.

We learned on the destroyer that we had been torpedoed, that the *Arandora Star* had sent out no S O S, that the destroyer at the time of the torpedoing was only one and a half hours' distance from our position, and that many could have been rescued if an S O S had been sent out.   Only at 11 o'clock in the morning did the destroyer get the order from London to sail to our rescue (after a report by the coastal aeroplane). In Greenock (Glasgow) an escort awaited us, which led the healthy ones of us half naked and barefoot through the piers. We who were destined for the hospital waited half naked, barefoot on the pier over four hours, standing in the streets for the ambulances.   We arrived at the Mearnskirk Hospital.

In Hospital.

The nurses were very kind to us. Although we were promised that our families would be told of our rescue, nothing happened. Our letters were not posted. Not before July 11 did we get clothes and were brought to Donaldson Camp, Edinburgh, where we were kept imprisoned in schoolrooms over night. The food was quite insufficient. The Swiss Consul, on behalf of the German Government, put one pound at the disposal of every German or Austrian survivor, which was only rejected by F. Weiss, F. Schoenmann and Ehrlich. The refugees did accept it (with exception of four stateless persons, who were not entitled to it). On the 6th August we arrived at Prees Heath, where we were interned with the Nazis.

We hope Lord Snell, in the course of his inquiry into those responsible for picking the men to be put on the *Arandora Star*, will visit Prees Heath and find out what this man and his anti-Nazi comrades locked up there have to tell him.

5. *The Effects of Wholesale Internment*

Sir John Anderson has a standard formula for silencing criticism of internment conditions :

" I am afraid that hardship is inseparable from the conditions in which we live at the moment."—(June 6, 1940.)

We ask the reader to judge for himself whether the hardships we have described *are* inseparable from the " conditions in which we live at the moment." The plain fact is that thousands of innocent refugees have been treated like cattle in the name of national security. The interned and deported refugees are neither soldiers nor criminals. Even if they accept internment as inevitable, as soldiers accept military service, they do *not* see the necessity of the ghastly treatment that has been meted out to them. Nor do they accept internment as inevitable because they have been " found out," as criminals would. They have no sense of having done wrong, and yet they have been denied the right of every criminal caught in the act ; to hear the evidence against them and to prepare their defence ; to go free if acquitted, or to be detained for a definite period in a definite place if they are found guilty. They have been treated worse than soldiers, because they do not accept their hardships as inevitable, and worse than criminals, because they have been deprived of the civil rights that even criminals enjoy. Sir John Anderson has ignored *Habeas Corpus* with a vengeance, and the great majority of his victims have been not the hundreds of Blackshirts he has detained without trial, but the non-Nazi and anti-Nazi refugees.

For these reasons we cannot accept Sir John's stock excuse for every unpleasant action he takes. We wholeheartedly support the view expressed by Lord Cecil in the House of Lords on August 6 :

> " I feel most strongly that the history of what has taken place with regard to these unhappy aliens is one of the most discreditable incidents in the whole history of this country. . . . The grossest injustice has been committed under the influence of an unreasonable and unreasoning terror, aroused not by this kind of people at all but people who were called the Fifth Column. People forget that the original Fifth Column consisted of the nationals of the country concerned, who were traitors. . . . Unhappily there came one of those waves of panic which do occur in war-time, and it was said, ' Oh, we cannot wait for any of these elaborate measures for inquiring into the guilt or innocence of individuals ; we must intern the lot ' ; and that became what I believe is called a slogan. Well, that was the most ridiculous nonsense ever devised to take in a people in a moment of great excitement."

Effects on British Public Opinion.—The effects upon the British public of this officially organised hunt for " aliens " were very damaging. In the first place it encouraged a widespread feeling of uncertainty and suspicion of all foreigners. Following the official lead in the wholesale dismissal of " enemy aliens " from public service and from many key industries, private employers in May and June, 1940, began in many parts of the country to discharge all foreigners in their employ—not merely " enemy alien " refugees, but even Irishmen and other citizens of neutral countries. Some local authorities held inquiries into the ancestry of their *British* employees, and dismissed all whose parents were not both British-born. The Nazis classify as Jewish any person who has one Jewish grandparent. In some parts of Britain a similar hunt for " alien " grandparents among public employees was undertaken. The British Red Cross Society has purged itself of all persons of "alien" ancestry, and some local authorities have proudly published figures of the "aliens" they have turned out of Council Houses. Many men—including a Manchester man who fought in the British Army in the last war and won the V.C.—have been refused membership of the Home Guard because they or their fathers are technically of "alien" origin. Men whose "alien" fathers were rich enough to afford to pay for British naturalisation were not so treated. Official policy and the shameful anti-"alien" press campaign produced in June a widespread spy-mania, and, as Mr. Tom Harrisson pointed out, a section of the public became almost pogrom-minded. Happily these feelings had dwindled again by August almost right down to their former low level in the subconscious of the most ignorant and prejudiced section of the public. It was a passing phase.

The hunt for "aliens" affected the thinking and intelligent section of the public in a different way, especially that section which had some personal knowledge of refugees and their problems. After an initial phase of acceptance of internment as a necessary—though temporary—emergency measure, as news leaked out about who was being interned and deported and how it was being done, there followed a growing wave of indignation which began in July and continued all through August. Among this section of the public the new "aliens" policy has caused widespread confusion, dismay and even disillusionment. It sowed strong doubts not only about the efficiency of our political and military leaders, but even about the honesty of their intentions. For behind the confusion and dismay lurks an unpleasant, though insufficiently appreciated dilemma : either (a) internment was mainly due to panic on the part of generals and politicians who, having "missed the bus" all over Europe, were going berserk ; or (b) if such an explanation seems absurd, internment was due to more sinister and truly undemocratic motives. If panic and frustration were the main causes of wholesale internment, people might begin to ask themselves : "Can we trust such men, after what has happened in France, to lead us anywhere but to defeat?" If the motives behind internment were the more sinister intentions of certain men in power to lock up anti-Fascists and progressively to restrict civil rights and liberties under plea of military necessity, then people might begin to think : "What is the war about anyway? Are our rulers not putting their feet on the path that led France to betrayal?" This dilemma has not been clearly and explicitly formulated, but the present confusion of the thinking section of the public is likely to crystallise into consciousness of just such a dilemma if the whole attitude of the Government to " enemy aliens " does not undergo a big change in the near future.

Effects on Refugee Morale.—However, the intelligent section of the public who have personal knowledge of refugee problems is a small minority. The effect upon the refugees has been similar but much more powerful. We have already given ample evidence of the acute mental anguish internment and deportation caused among the refugees. It must be remembered that the majority of refugees have never felt themselves fully at home in Britain. When they fled from Germany and Austria they were not welcomed with that warm human democratic solidarity which they had expected would be afforded by a free country to the victims and opponents of tyranny. They had great difficulties in entering Britain at all, because the Government, bankrupt of constructive ideas about employment policy, was concerned only with preventing people from becoming a burden on public funds, and such ideals as democratic solidarity were quite outside the range of vision of " practical " politicians. On the contrary the refugees were obliged to conclude that it was far easier for a Nazi with money, no matter how base and sordid his ambitions, to enter this country than it was for a penniless refugee, no matter how noble his character or how distinguished his record in the struggle against oppression. For years they had to endure the sight of their hosts officially kow-towing and making concessions to Nazi reaction, if not actively assisting it, without daring to criticise or make suggestions because they were here on sufferance and were expected to be grateful (as indeed they were). The majority of refugees were compelled to live in an atmosphere of charity and pity rather than one of sympathy and solidarity. They could never completely suppress the feeling that they were outsiders rather than members of the British community. All the splendid work of the refugee organisations inevitably bore the stamp of charity, because official policy limited them to this role. It is not surprising therefore that refugees should be extremely sensitive to changes in the official atmosphere, and should react violently to them. The outbreak of war, which suspended many plans for re-emigration, and the general common sense and sympathy of the British public, knit the refugees far more closely to the British community since they were now actively involved with it in a common fate. The reversal of policy in May struck them all the more violent a blow because it was so unexpected. Internment, deportation and general muddle has brought all those latent doubts and fears once again to the surface, with serious and not easily reparable effects. Internment has not demoralised the majority of refugees, but it has taught them never again to trust the word of an English official. This theme of mistrust and suspicion runs like a *Leitmotiv* through almost all the hundreds of letters, memoranda and conversations of refugees which we have examined. Whether they believe that " the English are mad " (the majority view) or that Britain is going the same way as France, or whether they have no clearly thought out explanation of the reasons for internment, the dominant note is mistrust. The Home Secretary is now allowing internees to proceed to the U.S.A. when their re-emigration plans are completed. Every one of these men who goes to America in the next few months will have tales to tell which will reflect no credit upon Great Britain. Especially among the important Jewish community in America such stories will not encourage those who are pressing for American assistance to the British war effort.

A minority of refugees were driven to demoralisation and despair. We have already mentioned the numerous cases of nervous collapse among internees, and the suicides which occurred in at least one camp at the period when deportation began. The aftermath of one of these suicides reveals just how far the British police, when stupidity and prejudice gives them a free hand, can come to resemble the Gestapo in the eyes of refugees. A report from an English refugee official in a provincial town contains the following passage :

" The police came to our local refugee committee to ask for £12 for the funeral expenses of G.B., a man of 68 who had committed suicide. His daughter eventually paid. I believe the Jews in Germany were often presented with the corpses to dispose of."

We believe this incident to be unique ; but that even one such case could occur is a terrible reflection upon the humanity and intelligence of our authorities.

It is impossible to put down in writing an account of the state of crazy terror and distraction to which some (not the majority) of the relatives of internees were reduced by the incarceration of their loved ones and their breadwinners. Women reduced to destitution, living on small doles from refugee committees or the Assistance Board, wondering when their own turn would come, spent days trapesing from one Government Department to another, from one refugee office to another, in search of information about interned relatives which it was nobody's business to know or which nobody could find out. One typical letter to a refugee committee from the wife of a German internee tells the whole story. After describing her frantic efforts to get herself deported to Australia with her husband, she concludes :

" . . . Dear Madam, since 1933 they are chasing us. My husband had to emigrate to Czechoslovakia to save his life in 1935. I had to stay in Germany of course ; and to do my duty like thousands of other brave men and women did. Until 1936 I worked alone and separated from him. I could escape in 1936 in the last minute only to Prague, and lived together with my husband in Czechoslovakia. In February, 1939, my husband came to England. I was once more alone, being in Prague when Hitler marched in. I suffered the most horrible time of all my life alone, illegal, until I was able to cross the frontier to Poland, and came to England without any belongings. I am 36 years old, and hope I shall never lose my optimism. But I assure you frankly, I can't stand it through a third time. *In Germany and in Czechoslovakia it was necessary, and therefore one became even more tough. But there is no necessity at all now to separate husband and wife.* What shall I do, what can I do to prevent this ? Please, dear Madam, be kind enough and send me your advice at once. Perhaps you might be able to bring our case to the knowledge of the War Office."

Some non-interned refugees committed suicide. Many such suicides were not reported in the press, and most unsuccessful attempts are not known. A brief survey of local London papers alone down to mid-July, 1940, shows two suicides reported in March, one in April, two in May, nine in June, and nine in the first nineteen days of July alone. Only one of these refugees (Dr. Wilhelm Stekel, the authority on sex) committed suicide for reasons clearly not connected with the outcry against " enemy aliens " and the fear of internment. There is some doubt also about the two suicides in March, but no doubt about any of the later ones. Typical are the C Class Austrian married couple (over 50) who poisoned themselves in Richmond Park because they feared they would be interned and separated ; the German (aged 46) who poisoned himself the night before he was to have been interned (" His wife said they had been here five years and had no money troubles," but he had been " worried about the possibility of being interned and of late had threatened to take his life ") ; the widow (aged 64) of a German professor of psychology who poisoned herself after receiving notice to quit her Council house ; the German-Jewish school-teacher (aged 50) whose life was broken up when the police ordered her to remove from a " protected " area. She drowned herself in the Thames and left a note thanking England for its kindness and concluding " May England be victorious."

Dr. Emil Krasny, an Austrian Jewish Doctor of Laws, was interned in July. His wife (aged 51) left alone, took a fatal dose of sleeping draught. A few days later Dr. Krasny was released from the Isle of Man and attended the inquest on his wife at Paddington on July 31. " He looked a broken man." On July 10 Miss Eleanor Rathbone told the House of Commons the story of a German refugee professor of Chemistry (aged 62), an international authority on dye-stuffs, who had been kept in Germany for fear other countries should profit by his knowledge. He had been tortured for seventeen days in a concentration camp before he got away to England. In England he had been working for a year on a process for utilising sisal waste in submarines. When the police came for him he warned them he could not stand another internment. They gave him a few hours to get ready, and he poisoned himself.

On July 25 Sir John Anderson told Commander Locker-Lampson :

" Much as I sympathise with the widow, I regret that it is not possible to make any grant to her out of public funds."

Effects on Refugees' Conditions.—The effect on the material situation of refugees was disastrous. Wholesale dismissals and internment of breadwinners have reduced large numbers of refugees to penury, very often after they had begun to get on their feet through finding work.   No material for a survey of the employment position of " enemy aliens " is at present available.   But there are many isolated facts which point to what was going on.   The 1,000 refugee girls working in nursing and midwifery services at the outbreak of war lost their jobs (a) through forced removals from " protected " areas and (b) through the Ministry of Health order on June 10, 1940, to dismiss all " alien " nurses from hospitals under the Minis-try's Emergency Department.   Six hundred nurses were dis-charged under this order.   Forced removals and private dismissals of domestic servants resulted in the London Metro-politan Area alone in a rise of Jewish refugee domestics re-ceiving financial support from 1,225 in June to 2,700 in July. Non-Jewish cases rose from 58 to 230 and Czech cases from 35 to 75.   The Assistance Board was responsible for those who had had at least half a year's work, the Domestic Bureau of Bloomsbury House maintained the rest.   The cost was roughly shared half and half between the two bodies.   The Domestic Bureau's placings fell to nil.   The numbers placed in jobs by the Employment Department of Bloomsbury House fell from an average of 60 in each of the first three weeks of May to an average of 22 each week in June, and then fell right down to six in the week ending July 20.   The Jewish Refugees Committee estimates that the direct additional expense involved in main-taining the nurses thrown out of work, persons evacuated from " protected " areas and the wives and other relatives of in-ternees, excluding cases maintained by the Assistance Board, was at least £2,000 in June.   This was offset by the internment of men maintained by the Committee.   In July the figure must have been higher, since there was a big increase in the number of destitute relatives of internees, following the general round up of the last part of June and the first part of July.

Commenting in July, 1940, on the general employment situation, the head of Bloomsbury House Employment Depart-ment points out that the Auxiliary War Service Department began by prohibiting the employment of " aliens " only on really important industrial work, but gradually appears to have decided that the Order in Council of November 17 permitted them to ban all employment of aliens except in purely private undertakings which were not in any way concerned with " work of national importance."

" This has, of course, had the effect of severely restricting the opportunities for placing, and during the last half of May, June and the present month the number of placings have steadily fallen each week until they have reached a negligible quantity. The fall in placings is not wholly due to the activities of the Auxiliary War Service Department. The policy of indiscriminate internment has frightened employers from having anything to do with an Austrian or German by birth. They have felt that it was hardly worth while going through the trouble of obtaining a permit when the man might be interned after having been employed for a few days. The attitude taken up by the A.W.S. Department has restricted the work of local Employment Exchange managers until they have refused to issue permits to anyone who was likely to be employed on Government work. No danger to the country would have been incurred could' the managers of the local Employment Exchanges have been permitted to exercise some discretion. They are at least familiar with the local conditions and are much more competent to judge on the question whether a particular job is one upon which an alien should or should not be employed."

Effects on Production.—Turning to production and commerce, considerable dislocation—including dislocation of essential war production—was caused by internment, but it is impossible to make any estimate of the total extent. It is certainly known that key-men in all kinds of industrial jobs were interned by the hundreds, and in Section 2 of this Chapter we have mentioned a few typical instances. Quite apart from what may have happened in the general field of ordinary industry, the refugee enterprises on the Treforest and Team Valley Trading Estates were hard hit. In July, according to the Committee for the Development of Refugee Industries, forced removals and internments had deprived one firm employing 150 British workers of all its seven refugee key-workers. They had been put in B Class because they did not require to travel. One man was completing a process which would eliminate all the wastage of raw material (amounting to 80 per cent.) involved in the manufacture of zipp fasteners. He was shipped off to Canada before they could get him released. The four directors or key-men of another firm (thirty-eight British workers) which supplied neighbouring factories working on Government contracts with paper boxes, were interned or evacuated. This firm had a year's outstanding orders to fulfil and export contracts for cigarette papers amounting to £2,500 a month. A firm (seventy-four British workers) manufacturing hand-screen printed silk for export was brought to a standstill by the internment of its key-man, upon whose technical skill the whole business depended. A firm employing 320 British workers and manufacturing imitation jewellery and Gablonz ware was crippled by the loss of its directors, who included an expert in the making of artificial pearls. The firm was building up an important export trade with America (which presumably the Government wishes to encourage), but the factory was finally commandeered by the authorities and converted into a canteen. And so we could go on.

In agriculture a similar process took place. Ninety agricultural workers on the register of the German Emergency Committee, mostly fully trained, were interned. The Committee's plans for a new refugee farm colony in South Wales had to be abandoned. The farm had twenty-six and a half acres of fruit trees, all planted and ready to yield, and 1,500 square feet of glass for salads and vegetables. Two other of the Committee's centres had to be closed down in June. One in Cornwall (fourteen acres) had 400 head of poultry, twenty-four pigs and seven goats as well as a market garden. It was closed at thirty minutes' notice, and the British wardens were left stranded without labour. Other farm colonies under the G.E.C. suffered in July. The Y.M.C.A. reported at the beginning of July that work on fifteen farms was held up because refugees they had placed on them, and in whom they had the utmost confidence, had been interned. The 120-acre farm under the Central Council for Jewish Refugees at Tingrith, Beds, was threatened when neighbouring districts ·were declared " protected." But the Council succeeded in persuading the authorities to appoint a retired police inspector to live on the farm as resident British supervisor and to impose such restrictions on the " aliens " as he thought fit. The farm could be turned into an internment centre without interrupting essential food production by surrounding it with barbed wire and allowing a Home Guard detachment to assist the police inspector to keep control. This did not prevent the internment of men on this farm in July, the David Eder

Farm had to be dissolved, and 50 young men with a year's training at Apsley Town, East Grinstead (big poultry farm, orchard, market garden, etc.) were taken away. Four farm colonies for children under the Young Pioneer Movement for Palestine had been shut down owing to forced removals or internment of the adult staff and many of the elder boys. Sixteen " enemy alien " refugees under the Czech Trust Fund who were doing agricultural work and forty-three who were working under the Forestry Commission were interned, as well as another seventy-eight who were about to start training for forestry under the Commission. Although a number of other agricultural centres controlled by the refugee organisations were not closed down, they all suffered to a greater or less extent by the internments in July.

Much of this damage to production is being or will be repaired, because many of the men engaged on these types of work will probably be released in due course. Since the end of July the employment situation showed slight signs of improving again. On July 4 the Ministry of Health removed the ban on " enemy alien " nurses in non-military wards and on Czech nurses in all wards, and by the end of the month about 250 had been taken back into employment. The Domestic Bureau of Bloomsbury House also reported a slight revival in placings. But in general the economic situation of refugees was decidedly worse in early August than at any time since the outbreak of war. The shallow roots which they had developed prior to May were largely torn out again in the following months, and the process of rehabilitation will be quasi-impossible if thousands of breadwinners are kept in internment.

Cultural Damage.—In the cultural sphere the damage was also great, but is even more difficult to assess. We know of cases of research interrupted or ruined, of half-finished books that may never be completed, of painstaking intellectual or artistic endeavour that may never come to fruition.* Some

* By chance a friend of the well-known elderly German artist, Ludwig Meidner, discovered that many of his paintings and most of his drawings and sketches had been left behind in his room when he was interned. He found that Meidner's landlady had rented the room to a new lodger, who had crammed all the canvasses and folios anyhow under the bed ! He was able to take away this valuable material in two taxi loads. It represented half the artist's lifework ; a few pieces were damaged.

indication of the situation is afforded by the Secretary of the Society for the Protection of Science and Learning, who wrote to us early in August : " We are at present not quite managing to cope with the enormous amount of work the applications for the release of interned scholars and scientists are giving us." The lack of imagination of heavy-handed policemen and of the bureaucratic civil servants above them is best illustrated by the story of the Department of Arts at Dartington Hall, which has been crippled by official policy.   The Dartington Trustees encouraged Kurt Jooss (referred to in Section 2) to bring over his School of Dance from Essen.   He came with fifteen students and two members of his staff early in 1934. His school quickly attracted students to Dartington from all over the world.   In 1935 Jooss re-formed his ballet company and undertook his first international tour.   Artists in many other fields were attracted to Dartington, and by the outbreak of war there were, in addition to the Ballets Jooss and the Jooss-Leeder School of Dance, a Studio of Art, a Studio of Music and a Chamber Music Group at Dartington.   Each of these enterprises was a teaching unit, with English, Continental and American pupils and a mixed English and German staff.   In all the Dartington arts centre had some sixty-five " enemy aliens " working in it, almost all of whom were personally known to and liked by the local police officials.   During the first six months of the war the Department continued its work. Amongst other activities the Arts Studio designed posters for National Savings Week ; the Chamber Music Group and a Dance Group performed for war charities ; while the Ballets Jooss undertook an English tour from October to December, 1939, and then went on tour in the U.S.A. and South America. In May, 1940, the whole area was declared " protected."   The entire German staff of the Arts Department had to leave the district, and most of them were interned, in the areas to which they had scattered, because they were " unemployed."   Kurt Jooss had not sailed with his Ballet on the grounds that he wished to remain in and with England in its struggle against the Nazis and in the belief that the time would come when his services in one form or another might be made use of.

Meanwhile the Ballets Jooss were enjoying a tremendous success in South America.   They were playing every night to crowded audiences.   In some towns the ballet *Chronica,* exposing the principle of dictatorship and showing how it is ultimately disastrous to all who come in contact with it, was received with such enthusiasm as to provoke spontaneous anti-Nazi demonstrations after the performance. In addition the Ballets Jooss gave complete performances the entire proceeds of which were given to the British Red Cross. But Jooss, who was planning to join his company in Rio de Janeiro, was interned, as were Leeder, Oppenheim and Heckroth (who was compulsorily deported), his principal colleagues. As we go to press we are informed that *Sir John Anderson will only release Kurt Jooss if he undertakes to emigrate to Brazil and not to return to Britain.* Gross stupidity, or doing Goebbels' work ?

Effects on Opinion Abroad.—When we began writing this book we imagined that the policy of wholesale internment of refugees from the Nazis would be widely used, both by Dr. Goebbels and in the American Press, to demonstrate that Britain is not a democracy fighting for noble principles, but simply a country which is jealous of its German rival whom it is seeking to destroy for purely sordid reasons. We expected that every anti-Nazi refugee who was interned would be used, both in Germany and in neutral countries, by the opponents of the British war effort as one more proof that Britain has forsworn democratic principles. Inspection of the American Press and Nazi broadcasts shows that this is not exactly what has happened. The Nazi news bulletins have treated internment of refugees in Britain without undue emphasis, and with little comment, though with a certain amount of condescending sarcasm. No doubt the Nazis are pleased to learn that many of their bitterest enemies are now locked up in Britain. Perhaps they refrain from making full propaganda use of these facts because they do not want to encourage the British Government to release the internees again. Whatever the reason, the Government has no cause to congratulate itself on providing Dr. Goebbels with such excellent material, if he cares to use it, for damaging Britain's good name and casting doubts upon the honesty of the Government's war purposes.

Although the Nazis have made little use of this propaganda material in their own country, there is some evidence that they are " putting over " such arguments through various channels (especially the smaller newspapers) in the U.S.A.

The biggest American papers, however, all through July, 1940, carried very little news, limited mostly to strictly factual reports, on the internments in Britain.   We have the impression that this is mainly due to the fact that the big American papers (and their London correspondents), which are not unsympathetic to the British war effort, were deliberately " clamping down " on such news, in order to avoid creating unfriendly feeling towards the British Government.   In this respect they are behaving exactly like a large section of the British Press prior to the collapse of France, when many of our newspapers deliberately suppressed news tending to show the French Government in a bad light, often news about internment measures and arrests similar in character to those we have described.   This impression is strengthened by the way in which several of the big American papers gave pride of place to stories about the internment of Fascists in England.   Thus the *New York Post* gave front-page space on June 28 to the arrest of Lady Mosley, and put the arrest of Captain Pitt-Rivers on page two ; and on July 9 reported the arrest of Sir Barry Domvile and his wife on page three, complete with a photo of the couple.   On page eight of the same issue it reported that " War Secretary Anthony Eden " had promised an investigation into the conditions of interned refugees, following a wave of public criticism.   The *Chicago Daily News* published on July 11 details of arrests of British Fascists under the headline " Britain Finally Cracks Down on Pro-Nazi Group," but in the third paragraph under the same title added a note on the House of Commons debate on refugees of the previous day.   In no big papers have we found any reference to anti-Nazis or anti-Fascists on the *Arandora Star*, and practically no material on internment conditions has been published.   The whole question was largely ignored.   Once again our Ministers have no cause to congratulate themselves. They have been lucky, because the big American papers do not wish to make things awkward for them.   But there is evidence that information has been leaking through and has been used in America against the British war effort by many anti-war, pacifist or isolationist groups.

An indication of what may be happening in neutral countries is given by an outspoken letter, published in *The Times* of August 16, 1940, from nine London correspondents of leading newspapers in four neutral European countries :

"Foreign correspondents of the neutral Press have watched with great anxiety the discussion in the House of Commons regarding the measures promised in order to repair the harm done to the traditional reputation of British fairness by the indiscriminate internment of refugee aliens. Our expectations, however, have not been fulfilled.

"We now raise our voices just because we are guided by feelings of deepest sympathy towards Britain. In our journalistic work we endeavour to establish a favourable picture of Britain's spiritual and moral strength. For this reason *we deem it our duty to emphasise the damaging impression created abroad by the spirit and methods of the refugee internments. Millions of sympathisers with Britain's case begin to doubt whether the British ideals of humanity and justice still prevail.*"

They then severely criticise Sir John Anderson's " utilitarian " policy of only releasing the minority of internees who can be " used," and conclude :

"We feel entitled to express our deep concern because we realise better than anybody else *what tremendous harm has been done to Britain's case in foreign countries by adopting a principle which is entirely contrary to the traditional British ideals. All efforts to promote good will for Britain's case abroad are bound to suffer by such shortsighted and inhuman methods.*"

Effects on the Refugee Organisations.—The main effect of wholesale internment upon the refugee organisations was to produce a state of complete dislocation lasting for weeks on end and to throw all their work into utter confusion. Although the Information Bureau at Bloomsbury House normally deals with 1,000 to 1,500 callers every day, and makes it unnecessary for half of them to be interviewed by refugee committee officials, the Bureau was not able to prevent interviews given by the Jewish Refugees Committee from increasing by 50 per cent. in June and even more in July. The Statistical Department of the Jewish Refugees Committee estimated that out of 12,500 German and Austrian men interned in Britain possibly as many as 10,000 were registered with the Committee, that 2,500 out of 7,500 men deported were registered with the Committee, and 2,000 out of 3,800 women interned. If this

estimate is correct it means that the Jewish Refugees Committee had to deal with anything up to three-fifths of all cases
of internment, and that letters, telephone calls, or visitors
about some 14,000 different individuals came pouring into the
Committee's London and provincial offices in an overwhelming
flood that did not begin to dwindle until the Government
opened an Information Bureau of its own on August 12.
Neither the Jewish Refugees Committee nor any of the other
bodies handling refugees had the machinery or the staff available to cope with such a deluge of complaints, appeals and
inquiries.   Government Departments also were deluged with
problems and inquiries ; yet it apparently never occurred to
them that they might co-operate with the voluntary organisations, instead of ignoring all the experience and knowledge
those organisations had accumulated, and might assist them
in giving the information about individuals for which the
relatives of internees were clamouring.

All other work, except inquiring about internees and interviewing and assisting their relatives and those thrown out of
work, practically came to a standstill in consequence.   Much
fine work was thrown out of gear, and constructive plans had
to be abandoned.   In the middle of June the refugee organisations · set up at Bloomsbury House a new Department for the
Welfare of Interned Refugees, to work in collaboration with
the existing Joint Committee for the Welfare of Prisoners of
War and Internees.   The Department appointed two liaison
officers (a quite inadequate number) who were given permission
by the War Office to visit the internment camps, to make
representations about the welfare of internees, and to assist
them with their emigration plans and personal affairs.   The
Department appears to have done what it could, during the
period of War Office control, to assist in improving conditions
in the camps, but the haste in which the camps were established
apparently made it impossible for the authorities to tackle the
problems which arose, especially since they habitually dis-
regarded the expert knowledge and experience of the long-
established refugee organisations.   Parliamentary deputations
to the Government Departments concerned were also arranged,
as well as a debate in Parliament, but little impression appears
to have been made upon the authorities until late in July,
when they began to yield quite as much to public opinion
generally as to pressure from the refugee organisations.   In

fact one of the defects of the Bloomsbury House type of organisation is its disinclination to resort to publicity, to seek actively to rally public common sense behind it in support of an intelligent policy. When a major crisis occurs the Bloomsbury House organisations show a marked preference for relying solely upon private representations to the appropriate authorities, coupled perhaps with questions in Parliament and a few letters in the Press. When they are up against a scandal they hesitate to make the facts public for fear it would jeopardise their relations with the authorities. When they have to fight the authorities—as they have had to over the internment scandal—their fight tends to be less effective because they have not paid adequate attention to informing and arousing public opinion to back them up.

Smaller organisations such as the German Emergency Committee suffered little less severely from the dislocation that arose than the Jewish Refugees Committee; 700 refugees under the Czech Trust Fund were interned by the third week of July, including sixty-four " friendly aliens " wrongly registered by the police. Among the interned were many metal-workers, turners, fitters and weavers, as well as forestry and agricultural workers. Internment has simply wasted considerable sums of money spent by the Fund on training men as welders and forestry workers. What happened on a small scale with them happened on a far greater scale with other bodies. The International Student Service, a large proportion of whose students were interned, in addition to trying to get them out again, gave what help it could to build up the " People's Universities " in the camps, many of which were promoted by the students. The I.S.S. is seeking to send in supplies of books and to arrange for courses of lectures to be given in the camps.

The work of the Council of Austrians in Great Britain was seriously hampered by internment. The evacuation resulted in the shutting down of ten provincial branches, including Bristol and Liverpool. General internment robbed the Austrian centres in Manchester and Glasgow of their best male workers, and the women, with less money than the men, and with the police in many provincial areas objecting to " meetings of aliens," had a hard job to carry on. At the London centre the repair workshop was deprived by internment of its workers and of many of its customers who owed it money

and had to close down at the end of June.   The highly popular
Laterndl theatre had to close down soon after its first anniversary
as one after another of its leading actors were taken.   Then
the Austrian Studio for Arts and Crafts had to be liquidated.
By hard work it had gradually gathered together the best
Viennese artists available and had built up a small market ;
the first big order for 10,000 felt flowers for export had just
been completed when internment made it impossible to continue.   Many orders had to be abandoned.   The Centre as a
whole suffered a more than 50 per cent. reduction in income.
Half its members were men ;   many of its women members
are now on assistance allowances, living on twelve to seventeen
shillings a week and unable to pay membership dues.   Average
expenditure per head in the café fell from elevenpence to
sevenpence each day in July, 1940, in spite of the dearer price
of food.   Higher costs of postage and most other services on
top of all these blows are endangering the Centre's future
existence.   The Austrian Centre, in spite of these difficulties,
organised a fund to assist its interned members, and in two and
a half months raised £110, which was distributed in cash or
in kind among those most in need.   Newspapers and several
hundred books were also sent to the camps.   The value of
the Austrian Centre as an agency for binding refugees together
and keeping up their feeling of solidarity is shown by the
hundreds of letters it receives from internees, which it does
not hesitate to publish or pass on to Members of Parliament.
The Free German League of Culture had a similar experience.
The overhwelming majority of its male members were taken,
its officials were not spared, its finances severely damaged.
Its theatre club lost amongst others Gerhard Hintze and John
Heartfield (both mentioned in Section 2), actors such as Erich
Freund, Manfred Fürst, Josef Almas and Margarete Rubi,
the musician Alan Gray, the writer Jan Petersen (author of the
anti-Nazi novel, *Our Street*, deported overseas) and many
others.   But the League, now largely run by women, has kept
its theatre going.   As their German actors went, Austrians
and German-speaking Czechs took their places.   Every sphere
of the League's work had been expanding right down to the
end of May, after which internment hampered further progress.
Like the Austrian Centre, the League has been active in collecting funds and despatching parcels to its interned members.

CHAPTER IV

1. *Official Explanations of the New Policy*

IN the twenty-one days on which Parliament sat prior to the debate of July 10 there were only three on which some aspect of the " enemy aliens " problem was not discussed, and in the eighteen sittings which intervened before the debate of August 22 only one was free from any reference to " enemy aliens." In the debate itself Mr. Osbert Peake for the Home Office and Sir Edward Grigg for the War Office had the uncomfortable task of explaining and defending the Government's policy. On no less than six occasions prior to the debate the Home Secretary had explained that internment had been necessary for " paramount reasons of military security," the " exigencies of the military situation " and the like. No other reason was mentioned at all.

But Mr. Peake, in the debate, produced a whole lot of other reasons. According to him, the initial internment measures were necessary for two reasons : the change in public opinion and the demands of the military authorities. Of public opinion he said :

" The invasion and overrunning of Holland and Belgium, which was attributed in the public mind so largely to Fifth Column activities, made a radical change in the situation. The people of this country were not able to realise the great distinction between our position and the position of Holland and Belgium. *Holland, for instance, had a treaty with Germany, whereby they could not refuse the admission of any German, and I am told that something like* 300,000 *Germans had come into Holland shortly before the act of aggression.* Moreover, the public did not realise that those countries were at peace with Germany, and were only too anxious to appease Germany at the time that these disasters took place."

The military reasons he described as follows :

" For the first time, we were faced with an enemy in possession of ports very close to this country.   It was represented to us by the military authorities, on military grounds, that the whole of the coastal belt on the East and South-East coasts of England must be made into a protected area.   Not only did they press upon us that enemy aliens, about whom we know so much, should be turned out, but they pressed upon us also that neutral aliens, about whom we knew much less, should be removed.   It was, in my view, quite impossible when a policy of this kind was put forward by those responsible for the defence of this country against invasion to refuse to accept it under those circumstances."

The Army said : " Turn them out."   Why did the Home Office decide to intern the men ?   The decision to clear the coastal belt was undoubtedly sensible and cannot be questioned. But why internment ?   Mr. Peake explained :

" The result of declaring the whole of the eastern and south-eastern coastal belts a protected area was that large numbers of aliens were torn up from the shallow roots which they had been able to acquire since they came here and had to remove.   They had no jobs, and had to proceed, with public feeling what it was at that time, in the face of suspicion and mistrust. . . . *The only practical method of dealing with the situation was, in fact, to intern the males.* It really would have been impossible to have forced a flood of many thousands of aliens into places where they were not known and where they would have no jobs.   In my view, the most humane thing to do with those aliens at that time, and with public feeling what it was, was to put them into temporary internment."

Why was the decision later taken to extend internment ? Mr. Peake gave a number of reasons :

(*a*) " There was, in the first place, greatly increased un-employment amongst aliens of all kinds.   It became in-creasingly hard for these refugees to find jobs.   If they fell out of jobs they could not get others.   The burden on the refugee organisations was greatly increased—and indirectly, of course, to some extent, the prospective burden on the Government, which now makes a contribution to the funds of those organisations, was increased also."

(b) " It was further felt that in the event of serious air raids on this country many of these people would be in personal danger. . . . I was assured that, in the event of serious air raids in that district [the Team Valley Trading Estate, where ' enemy alien ' business men had been officially encouraged to start enterprises], there would be serious danger to those refugees . . . from our own people."

(c) " Many of these refugees were at that time in a state of such alarm, on account of the hostility and suspicion which was shown towards them, that they themselves came to us and asked us to pursue a policy of internment for their own personal safety."

(d) " The last, and the most urgent, of all the considerations which weighed with us was that *this policy was strongly advocated by the military authorities.*"

What is to be said of these explanations ?

(a) The " flood of many thousands of aliens into places where they were not known and where they would have no jobs " was *not*, in fact, prevented by the " humane " and " practical " method of temporarily interning " enemy alien " men. If the Home Office feared this " flood " from the coastal belt, why did they only intern *men* who were " enemy aliens " ? A " flood " of women, children, invalids and men over sixty, constituting the great majority of " enemy aliens " in the coastal belt, did occur. Internment of the men made it certain that their dependants, deprived of their breadwinners and required to remove at short notice, should be left penniless. Nor did it prevent a large number of harmless women, employed as domestics in the coastal belt, from being stranded without jobs or money. They, however, were not interned. Hundreds of them had to be accommodated temporarily in the workhouses of London and other large towns outside the coastal belt, until their approriate relief committees could hunt them out and provide them with shelter and assistance.

Internment only reduced the " flood " to a small extent, since only 2,000 men were taken from the coastal belt. They were only a fraction of the " flood," which included the great bulk of *all* foreigners in the coastal belt. Foreigners of other nationalities also, in many cases, lost their jobs, and they had no relief committees to assist them. But there was no question of interning any men except " enemy aliens."

(b) Unemployment was " greatly increased . . . amongst aliens of all kinds," and the financial burden on the Government-subsidised refugee relief agencies was growing. This is quite true. The policy of declaring large areas " protected " (the military necessity of which we do not question) and later of officially ordering the dismissal from work of large numbers of " enemy aliens," in itself inevitably created unemployment. Indirectly, too, the Government's whole policy assisted in fostering that anti-foreign feeling which led all over the country to the throwing out of work of thousands of foreigners of *all* nationalities, because employers preferred to be " on the safe side." By extending internment the Government did nothing to relieve this situation—psychologically it made it worse. Further internment merely turned the Government's (" indirectly " and " to some extent ") " prospective " financial burden into an actual and unavoidable burden. Internees have to be maintained at the Government's expense.

(c) The danger of our own people " attacking enemy aliens " if large-scale air-raids began : There is no doubt that this was a danger in certain areas, and that it will remain a danger as long as the public is not educated above the level of irrational xenophobia. The Government cannot shirk its responsibilities of leadership in this respect, as we explain in the following section. There is no doubt too that some refugees themselves wished for internment for their own safety. But they did not ask for the wholesale round-ups which were organised, they did not ask to be treated as " potential enemies " (as Sir John Anderson admitted they were being treated, Hansard, June 6), they did not ask for the disgraceful internment conditions to which they were subjected, and they did not ask for indiscriminate (and in many cases compulsory) deportation overseas. The situation—if there was any serious danger of disturbances—could have been met by the voluntary internment of those who preferred to be out of the way, with adequate time given for personal affairs to be wound up and arrangements for families to be interned as units, and under conditions which would not prevent them from working. The refugee committees could easily have organised hostels or colonies for voluntary internment under some kind of military guard.

In any case, if the danger of anti-" alien " attacks was so great, why intern only the men ? Everyone knows that women played their part in Holland in assisting parachutists. Will the internment of the men spare the women from molestation ? And why intern only German and Austrian refugees ("about whom we knew so much ") ? Everyone knows that there may be Fifth Columnists among the recent arrivals from Holland, Belgium and France and among neutral foreigners ("about whom we knew much less "). If anti-foreign disturbances occur, it is doubtful whether people will be in a mood to discriminate between Dutchmen, Flemings and " enemy aliens."

2. " The Public Clamoured for Internment "

The True State of Public Opinion.—The next argument for " interning the lot " was that public opinion demanded it. This argument came strangely from a Government which persisted in ignoring such undoubted expressions of public opinion as the British Institute of Public Opinion survey early in July, 1940, which showed that 77 per cent. of the people wanted Mr. Chamberlain dropped from the Cabinet, 63 per cent. wanted Lord Simon to go, and 57 per cent. wanted Lord Halifax to resign. Very similar results were produced by a Mass-Observation survey of opinion about Mr. Chamberlain at about the same time.* The Ministry of Information very sensibly makes use of Mass-Observation and other opinion-analysing agencies to keep the Government in touch with trends in public attitudes. Did it occur to the Government— to Mr. Eden, or Sir John Anderson, or Mr. Chamberlain, or General So-and-So—to use these agencies to find out the *real* state of public opinion concerning " enemy aliens " ? We doubt it.

This is the story that Mass-Observation tells. In the second half of April, 1940, Mass-Observation reports showed the following state of affairs :

" April has been marked by a campaign against ' the enemy in our midst,' the sinister, invisible enemy ; the Fifth Column. A campaign against the Fifth Column, led with restraint by M.P.s, *has been whipped up into something rather different in the Press ; a campaign to intern all refugees. The*

* Yielding to ill-health Mr. Chamberlain resigned at the beginning of October, 1940.

*Sunday Press has been particularly active on this subject ;
several papers have ignored the point made by M.P.s and the
serious weeklies, namely that the Fifth Column may be mainly
composed of persons in high positions, British born and bred.*
We made a small investigation on public feeling about the
Fifth Column in the last days of April, after the Press campaign had been raging. We found that the majority of
people hardly realised what the phrase meant. We also
found that the level of ordinary people's feeling about
refugees was much less intense than that expressed in some
papers. Detailed interviewing in several areas in London
and Western Scotland produced less than one person in a
hundred who spontaneously suggested that refugees ought
to be interned *en masse*. The majority expressed some dis-
approval, or only qualified approval of refugees, predomin-
antly for economic and financial reasons. People feel that
an influx of refugees threatens their jobs, and even the whole
internal economy of the country. Many people over-
estimate the number of refugees, putting the figures in
millions.

" *This antagonism against the refugee from above, which has
not yet (early May) percolated right through to the mass,
is a logical part of the general increase of antagonism towards
the German people from above. The mass of Britishers are now
in a borderline phase between the initial, Premier-inspired idea
of the war to end Hitler, and the growing leadership trend of
blaming the German people for Hitler. As all Germans
everywhere become the enemy, tolerance to refugees is likely to
decline further.*"

Commenting on these results, Mr. Tom Harrisson, Mass-
Observation leader, wrote in the *New Statesman* (July 13,
1940) :

" Until various newspapers and other leaders of public
opinion began a clamour for internment, there was little
feeling on the subject in the Press, among the ' ignorant.'
For ignorant, ordinary people are, on the whole, ready to be
tolerant of their neighbours—that is one reason why politics
based on anti-Semitism have failed so miserably in this
country.

" It needed several weeks of intensive campaigning, from
powerful upper class and *responsible* quarters, before ordinary

people decided that aliens ought to be interned. Events in Holland and Belgium naturally accelerated the process, but if the main influence of opinion leadership had been towards a reasonable policy for aliens, and if responsible editors and ministers had openly taken up this line, public opinion would have followed. As it was, *we never had a word from any responsible person explaining over the radio or in the mass papers the distinctions that could be made between different sorts of aliens. Little was done to prevent the phrase ' Fifth Column ' becoming a stunt. So, when we repeated our survey in the middle of May the whole atmosphere had changed ; many people who a month before were inclined to be tolerant of aliens were now almost pogrom minded.*

" Ordinary people are not ignorant in any absolute sense. They are only ignorant on matters in which they have not been instructed. *If our leaders want to carry the country with them on any subject, it is their job to put the facts clearly before the public, and thus extend the area of ' informed opinion.' That is democracy. It isn't true that there are certain people called leaders who know the facts and who are ' wise,' who are trying to get decent things done, but are forced to do the wrong thing by ' public hysteria.' Yet this theory of democracy has become extremely common in recent years.*"

This survey of how anti-" alien " public opinion was in fact largely *created* by responsible individuals who should have known better may be contrasted with Mr. Peake's weak plea that

" The invasion and overrunning of Holland and Belgium which was attributed in the public mind so largely to Fifth Column activities, made a radical change in the situation. The people of this country were not able to realise the great distinction between our position and the position of Holland and Belgium."

It was not primarily the invasion of Holland and Belgium that " made a radical change in the situation," but (*a*) an anti-foreign campaign conducted in the Press and elsewhere by so-called " responsible " people, and (*b*) the total failure of any Minister of the Government publicly to counteract this campaign by an appeal to common sense.

Guilty Consciences.—Looking through the newspaper files

we find that not all papers took part in the anti-" alien " campaign. There were many honourable exceptions. The worst offenders by far were the papers of the Rothermere group, closely followed by some of the Kemsley papers. One is struck by the fact that *the newspapers which were loudest in the agitation against refugees were those which, before the war, were the most assiduous in their advocacy of appeasement and of kowtowing to dictators.* Many of the signed articles in these papers were written by publicists who in peace-time had become generally regarded, not as British journalists, but almost as English mouthpieces of Goering and Goebbels.

In demanding general internment the motives of such gentlemen and of their Press Lords were hardly motives of unalloyed patriotism. Written all over their articles is the Guilty Conscience. By taking this " super-patriotic " line it is pretty evident that they were making of the anti-Nazi German and Austrian refugees a convenient scapegoat for their own sins— their pro-Nazi past. Perhaps too they were doing something more sinister. Doing Goebbels's work ? Possibly, since Dr. Goébbels's controlled papers could, if they chose, argue that even the British had realised that the eternal danger is the Jew ; that the British had been obliged to borrow the concentration camp method from the Nazis ; and that the whole thing proved the falsity of the British Government's claim to be fighting a war for freedom. *In effect*, they were doing Goebbels's work ; but they were doing something else. By insinuation, by denunciation, by downright and unashamed lying in some cases, they were creating the impression that the British Quislings are, not like the Quislings of all other countries, " true-blue " natives of their own country, hidden influences in high positions in our own political and economic structure, but an " alien " Fifth Column of refugees from Nazi oppression. The one per cent. of truth in the statement that some refugees may be Nazi agents was magnified into a 99 per cent. lie : that all " enemy aliens " must be locked up, because they are not to be trusted. Were they not thus helping to divert attention from the real Fifth Column danger in this country, the Fifth Column that speaks English with a public-school accent ? Was not the anti-refugee agitation to some extent a method of strengthening our native British Fifth Column whom the Nazis are trying to use ? May not this agitation, to some extent, have been actually inspired by British " Nazis of the Soul " ?

We cannot answer these questions with certainty, but there is an unpleasant flavour about some of the Press material we have examined that is not adequately accounted for by the possible brainlessness of its writers.

In many cases the " Guilty Conscience " motive went hand in hand with a much simpler commercial motive. It was a good " stunt " to play the super-patriotic game along the lines of least resistance. After the Norwegian, Dutch, Belgian and French tragedies, when " Quisling " and " Fifth Column " became words on everybody's lips, and there began to grow amongst the public a genuine fear of Fifth Columnism in Britain, it was obviously a " good line " for certain popular newspapers, with large circulations, to exploit this condition of mind by starting heresy hunts, and by posing as being more energetic in the public interests than the Government itself. This kind of thing was calculated to be good for circulation.

The Rothermere Press.—Consider the *Daily Mail*, the paper which long ago wanted to " Hang the Kaiser " and warned us that " They will cheat you yet, those Junkers." This paper for years conducted a " Hats off to Hungary " campaign, the object of which was to revise the Versailles settlement at the expense of a democratic country like Czechoslovakia for the advantage of Hungarian reaction. It passed later to a wider campaign in favour of Hitler's claims in Central Europe. Especially through the pen of its special correspondent, Mr. Ward Price, the *Daily Mail* consistently stated the Nazi case against Austria and Czechoslovakia. Shortly before the Nazi seizure of Austria Lord Rothermere himself published an article on the theme " Races not Places " justifying the Nazi absorption of Austria with the Nazi argument that in the long run " race " is the paramount consideration. At one period, too, Lord Rothermere " took up " Mosley's Blackshirts and gave them publicity in his Press. Mr. Ward Price published two books shortly before the war, one (*I Know These Dictators*) praising Hitler and Mussolini, the other pushing accommodation with the Nazis. More than any other paper the *Daily Mail* trailed the Nazi propagandist red herring of the " Bolshevist " menace and depicted Germany as the defender of Western civilisation.

On April 20, 1940, the *Daily Mail* was limiting itself to demanding that " the police must round up every doubtful alien in this country." On May 24 Mr. Ward Price was going

full blast.   Under the title "Act! Act! Act!—Do it now"
he wrote :

> " The rounding-up of enemy agents must be taken out of
> the fumbling hands of local tribunals.   All refugees from
> Austria, Germany and Czechoslovakia, men and women
> alike, should be drafted without delay to a remote part of the
> country and kept under strict supervision. . . . As the head
> of a Balkan State said to me last month : ' In Britain you fail
> to realise that *every* German is an agent.   All of them have
> both the duty and the means to communicate information to
> Berlin.'   Certain ' diplomatic bags ' leaving this country are
> at the disposition both of such people and also of disaffected
> Britons."

This is but one of many recent diatribes from the pen of the
man who " knows these Dictators."

On July 12 the *Daily Mail* published an innocent-looking
article by Miss Alice Hemming, called " Canada is all out to
Win."   It contained the following far from innocent passage :

> " In Montreal a shopkeeper told me that he is convinced
> that Hitler drove out the Jews and political opponents with
> the express purpose of sending Gestapo agents among them
> to the Christian countries that took them in.   ' Where did
> so many of them get so much money to live on ? ' he said.
> ' Poor refugees—huh !   All they have to do is to say Hitler
> was mean to them and we take them in and feed them, and
> half of them are spies ! '   Enemy aliens here in Canada and
> any who did not seem able to behave themselves and appre-
> ciate the advantages of life in the New World have been
> clamped behind barbed wire with the vigour and thorough-
> ness that is typical of this Dominion."

And so we could go on.

The Kemsley Press.—Following the crescendo of the *Daily
Mail* came the strident but less consistently maintained clamour
of the Kemsley papers.   Before war broke out the *Daily Sketch*
supported through thick and thin the policy of appeasing the
dictators.   The *Sunday Chronicle* had been more independent,
and had published a number of anti-Nazi articles.   But Mr.

Beverley Nichols was allowed to publish a long stream of pro-Nazi drivel (no other word fits) in his feature " *Page Two*." For example, he had a long controversy with a Rabbi who objected to his excusing Nazi anti-Semitism. After war broke out, putting aside the memories of his controversy with the Rabbi, he rushed into print with denunciations, not only of the Nazis, but of *all* Germans, and lectured the young men at Oxford University (who *will* have to fight) for not being as intensely patriotic as himself. He later, when it was " fashionable," proceeded to attack the refugees, without mincing his words. Beginning with an article demanding internment of all Germans and Austrians, which was decorated with a picture of a prison van, with a caption to the effect that we interned them all in the last war, he worked himself up to the following frenzy in the *Sunday Chronicle* on May 26, 1940 :

" ' The Fifth Column.' And what about the spies here ? Don't skip this, because you have read before that we ought to have interned the lot. We have not interned anything like the lot. I hate writing this. I have German friends, but I would very willingly indeed see them all, yes all, behind bars, and I have told them so to their faces. Why should we be blown up as we are walking over a bridge, unless it is strictly necessary ? Or poisoned by contaminated water, or hit on the head by the local gasworks, as it descends to earth ? No, sir. The letters readers send about Germans who are going free in their own district would make your hair stand on end. Particularly the women. There is no dirty trick that Hitler would not do, and there is a very considerable amount of evidence to suggest that some of the women— who are very pretty—are not above offering their charms to any young man who may care to take them, particularly if he works in a munition factory or the Public Works."

Mr. Nichols carried on in this strain in the following months. On August 4 he wrote in the *Sunday Chronicle*, addressing Lady Oxford :

" Are you not aware that the present position of Britain as a highly industrialised nation, a tragically trustful nation, and a nation that is swarming with foreign refugees, is an ideal *terrain* for the employment of the Quisling weapon ? . . . Even if some aliens have been unjustly interned, can anybody honestly say that we have been harsh in this matter ?"

It is disgraceful that this ex-Bright-Young-Thing, ex-flower-fan, ex-Pacifist, ex-Buchmanite, ex-supporter of Mosley, ex-pro-Nazi, should not feel a sufficient sense of shame to refrain (*a*) from telling us that the " Quisling weapon " is wielded by "aliens," when the whole point about Quisling and his friends is that they are *natives* of their country, and not "aliens " at all, (*b*) from finding a cheap and easy way to stifle his own uneasy conscience by blood-and-thunder outbursts against refugees who cannot answer back.

Other Papers.—These were the worst offenders, but many other newspapers succumbed to the temporary panic or to the temptation of lurid sensationalism at the expense of refugees, during May and June. Even the sober *Times* for a period (e.g. leader on May 18) urged that no chances should be taken with "aliens." The general atmosphere which was thus worked up, deliberately by some papers, unwittingly by others, was well described by Wenzel Jaksch (*New Statesman*, June 22) :

> "You can hardly imagine what discouragement and depression all that alien-baiting, in which part of the Press has indulged lately, produces in men who have always believed in something like democratic solidarity. This is not a question of the personal well-being of a few thousand refugees. It is a question of honour and of common sense. It is deeply regrettable that even the *Daily Herald* thought fit to encourage the suspicion that sees a Fifth Columnist in every alien and to extend it to men who have risked their lives and their freedom in illegal work against the Nazi régime. On May 17 the paper triumphantly informed its readers of a ' Secret Swoop on 30,000 Germans.' On the same day it announced a ' hunt ' of aliens working in the A.R.P. The result of the ' hunt ' has never been published. If it had, the public would have learnt that a few dozen Jewish refugees, in patriotic zeal and obeying directions from their Relief Committees, had enlisted for A.R.P. work. On May 31, the *Daily Herald* quoted Sir Neville Bland's notorious broadcast under the commendatory heading ' Don't trust a German.' "

The Bland Broadcast.—The anti-refugee agitation was not confined to the Press. One incident that caused tremendous damage and confusion was the wholly deplorable talk broadcast on May 30 by Sir Neville Bland, British Minister in Holland, who alarmed the nation by his description of the Fifth Column at work in Holland :

> " It is not the German or Austrian who is found out who is the danger.   It is the one, whether man or woman, who is too clever to be found out.   That was apparent in Holland —where, as I have already said, many of the obvious Fifth Columnists were interned at the outbreak of war—but where there still remained a dreadful number at large to carry out the instructions they had from Germany.
> " I have had German friends in the past, and I hope that I may live to have a German friend or two again one day ; and I hate to have to say this to you ; but I find it my duty to say it, and say it I will : Be careful at this moment how you put complete trust in any person of German or Austrian connections.   If you know people of this kind who are still at large, keep your eye on them ; they may be perfectly all right—but they may not, and to-day we can't afford to take risks. . . .
> " Be watchful and vigilant of all that goes on around you, whether it be in your factory, in your office, in your regiment, or even in the house next door.   Holland learned many lessons from Norway.   We have many lessons to learn from Holland.   And for all we can tell, there may still be some devilish surprise in store for us. . . ."

More than any other single speech, article or distorted news item, this broadcast was responsible for much of the panic which captured a large section of the public in the following weeks.

Are Refugees Dangerous ?—We are not criticising the authorities for taking any *necessary* security measures which the prospect of immediate invasion required.   But we do emphatically believe that the wholesale and indiscriminate round-up which we have described, and the present policy of making release the exception even for non-suspects, are both mistaken and harmful.   The main lesson of Holland was, after all, not that you cannot trust genuine refugees, but that—as Mr. Peake stated on July 10—a country that sought to appease the Nazis to the extent of admitting hundreds of thousands of Nazi *citizens*, as and when the Nazi Government demanded, was plainly asking for trouble.   As Mr. Peake explained, the position in Holland was quite different from that of Britain. Britain has admitted only a small number of German and Austrian refugees, who were carefully checked before they were even granted entry permits, and sifted and resifted after their arrival. *Holland had a treaty by which she could not refuse admittance to any single Nazi citizen who wanted to enter Holland. That is the price of appeasement.* These exported Nazis were the main Fifth Column force in Holland. *Hardly any* cases of Nazi agents posing as refugees were discovered either in the Low Countries, in Scandinavia, or in France. We should be surprised if there were not a single traitor among the refugees ; we should be still more surprised if there are not ten times as many traitors to be found in the City of London and the Mayfair drawing-rooms where Ribbentrop was once welcomed.

That is the main lesson of Holland : that appeasement does not pay. The second lesson, especially the lesson of Norway and of France, is that the most dangerous traitors may be some of our countrymen. Norway and France did *not* succumb, like Holland, to exported Nazis, but to internal treachery largely organised by influential men—officers, politicians, industrialists, financiers—belonging very often to the " best " families in the land. Why did not Sir Neville Bland, Ward Price and Beverley Nichols mention that ? Why did they keep off this delicate subject ?

Refugee-baiting.—There were many in Parliament, in provincial upper circles, and privately in the background who, out of stupidity, ignorance or for less honest reasons, joined in the baiting of refugees, and directly or indirectly fostered this ' public clamour ' to which Sir John Anderson felt obliged to yield. There was Sir Annesley Somerville, M.P. for Windsor, who complained in Parliament on June 6 that the internees were being kept in " luxurious idleness," and drew from Miss Eleanor Rathbone the retort that this was a " cruel insult " to the internees. He was the man who said in the debate following Hitler's seizure of Czechoslovakia, " Let Herr Hitler expand as fast as he can in South-East Europe ; we shall still have our share of the trade." Sir John Wardlaw-Milne, M.P. for Kidderminster, joined in with a similar complaint about the treatment of " alien women interned in the Isle of Man." At the end of 1938 he was supporting appeasement in the *Anglo-German Review*, official organ of the notorious pro-Nazi " Link." There was Mr. Higgs, M.P. for Birmingham West, who on the same day asked the Home Secretary whether he was aware that " small batches of foreigners are meeting together in order to advance their common interests, and will he give instructions to prohibit all assemblies of aliens ? " There was armament-magnate Sir Patrick Hannon, M.P. for Moseley, who on June 11 wanted to prevent " aliens and undesirable persons " from travelling in trains " with members of His Majesty's Forces to and from the provinces."

Lieut.-Colonel Sir Thomas Moore, M.P. for Ayr Burghs and Trustee of the R.S.P.C.A., on July 4 warned the House that " servants' registry offices are still sending alien, including German, servants to all parts of the country," and on July 18 was worried about " aliens " working in the Civil Service. He was the man who, on April 25, 1934, published in the *Daily Mail* an article with the title " The Blackshirts have what the Conservatives Need," in which he asked : " What is there in a black shirt which gives apparent dignity and intelligence to its wearer ? . . . As I listened to the vibrant tones of Sir Oswald Mosley . . . I got my answer. There was little if any of the policy which could not be accepted by the most loyal follower of our present Conservative·leaders." Latterly he became a member of the Council of the Anglo-German Fellowship. In the House of Lords there was Viscount Elibank, who on May 23 drew attention to the " inadequacy of the steps that were being taken to control the large numbers of aliens, both male and female, who might be utilised by Nazi Germany for nefarious purposes. The country was ridden with domestic servants of alien origin, many of whom were not trustworthy." In July this same noble Lord was worried about arming the workers in the factories (" It makes a great many of us in this country very nervous and very anxious as to what may happen "), and sought to excuse the treachery of Pétain, Weygand and Laval with the remark :

" When they found Communism to the extent that I have described, they went over to the other side [i.e. the Nazis] to save from the Communists what possessions they happened to possess."

This view of treason in France has been described by Mr. H. G. Wells as " sympathetic consternation."

Leaders Must Lead.—Such was the genesis of the anti-refugee opinion, which was not public, but was *made* public by deliberate agitation organised by responsible people, either out of sheer panic, unreasonable prejudice, desire to exploit the sensational, or for the more sinister reason that they had something to hide.   There is no doubt of the strength of this opinion at one time, although to-day the tide is running strongly the other way.   We may express a doubt, however, whether such opinion may rightly be called " public " rather than " manufactured."   At any rate it reflects little credit on the judgment of the Ministers responsible, if it is true that they yielded to such a clamour ; although, no doubt, this opinion was strongly pressed upon them, not in public at all, but behind the scenes in Government departments, in police and Army " representations," in lobbies and clubs, over dinners and at week-end parties, by people " who matter."

It is all the less creditable, since, as Mr. Harrisson remarks : " We never had a word from any responsible person explaining over the radio or in the mass papers the distinctions that could be made between different sorts of aliens."   That is the most lamentable aspect of the whole matter.   As Mr. Wilfrid Roberts, M.P., said in the debate of July 10 :

" If the Home Office and the Government were anxious to prevent public opinion being ' panicked,' why did we not have that information [about Holland] long ago ?   What has the Government done to try to correct the impression created by the stories which have appeared in the Press ? I feel that the Home Office and the Government were very willing to accept newspaper propaganda and a public atmosphere of nervousness as an excuse for carrying out a policy which they thought would not be altogether popular with the whole country."

No answer to these questions was given, because none could be given.   On May 29, in answer to a question by Mr. Sorensen, Mr. Peake had told Parliament :

" I cannot recall any case since the beginning of the war of anything which could be described as a hostile act having been proved in a court of law to be attributable to either of the classes of aliens [i.e. German and Austrian refugees from Nazi oppression] mentioned in the hon. Gentleman's question."

Pressed by Mr. Sorensen to " make that as publicly known as possible to counteract extravagant anti-refugee agitation," Mr. Peake replied that this matter was " at present under consideration." A further question by Mr. Sorensen to Mr. Law (Joint Under-Secretary of State for War) on June 12 *received no answer at all*.

In the debate of July 10 Mr. Graham White remarked that " it would be well for the Government to make a plain statement that they do not regard every alien as hostile and as an enemy." No answer was made. And so this statesmanlike failure to lead public opinion, this bold shirking of the responsibilities of educating the public went on, until, at the end of July, when the damage had been done and public opinion was at last realising it, Ministers of the Government began to agree —and to say so in public—that the mass of the internees are genuine refugees against whom there are no grounds for suspicion. But there was hardly any recognition of this fact in modifications of internment policy.

Must we not agree with Mr. Harrisson that " if the main influence of opinion leadership had been towards a reasonable policy for aliens, and if responsible editors and Ministers had openly taken up this line, public opinion would have followed " ? The business of responsible leaders is to inform and educate, in order to win popular support for wise measures. If they do not do this can they escape the suspicion that, by appearing to yield to an outburst of uninformed and manufactured opinion, they are in fact using " public opinion " as an excuse for something they want to do anyway, but which might not be popular (as Mr. Wilfrid Roberts suggested) until the right atmosphere has been created ?

3. *The " Opinion of the Army "*

The final reason given for " interning the lot " was the " opinion of the Army." This means of course the opinion of commanding officers like Field-Marshal Ironside, until recently Commander-in-Chief of Home Forces, and his colleagues, an opinion which of necessity weighs very heavily with the War Office and the Cabinet. Why did the " Army " (thus defined) conclude that for security reasons the majority of male Germans and Austrians had better be locked up or sent overseas ? We do not know. During the debate of July 10 Members repeatedly pressed for explanation of the military grounds for general internment. Mr. Silverman asked explicitly :

" On what grounds did the War Office persuade the Home Office or the Government, that it was necessary, in the interest of national security, to intern large numbers of people about whom the War Office, *ex hypothesi*, knew nothing, and about whom the Home Office knew everything ? "

He drew from Sir Edward Grigg the bellicose remark :

" I make absolutely no apology for the fact that one of the factors which has had to be weighed in deciding the policy which we are now following is the opinion of the Army, an opinion in which I believe the Army represents the great majority of the people in this country."

That was all.

It is, however, clear that the " Army " had no grounds for believing that any but a small minority of refugees from Nazi oppression were in any way suspect. Apart from statements on three different occasions by Mr. Peake that there is nothing against the general mass of internees except their nationality, Sir John Anderson has stated that they were interned " for reasons for which they are not responsible " (Hansard, July 23). The Government has full powers, which it uses freely, to detain foreigners of any nationality and British subjects about whose reliability there is any serious doubt. " Interning the lot " in the case of " enemy aliens " might be understandable if it were a *temporary* emergency measure, so that " enemy aliens " could once again be sifted and those in any way suspect of harbouring hostile intentions retained in internment. But the policy of mass deportation and of keeping all but the " useful " locked up is something quite different.

We are not entirely persuaded by the repeated statements of Sir John Anderson, Mr. Peake and the Duke of Devonshire that the " Army " pressed so strongly for wholesale internment that the Government was forced to adopt this policy. There is no doubt a large measure of truth in these statements, but we are not convinced that the Home Office in particular put up a very stubborn resistance when pressed by the military chiefs. We have the impression that it yielded with a good, rather than a bad grace. At any rate, whilst the Duke of Devonshire told the Lords on August 6 : " I do not think I am betraying any secret when I say the decision the Government came to was, in effect, forced upon it by the military authorities," Sir John Anderson told the Commons with commendable bluntness on August 22 : " I am not going to say that I allowed my judgment to be overborne. I acted as I thought right in the circumstances. I would not have done otherwise. I would have resigned without hesitation if I thought I was being pressed to something which was not justified." Clearly Sir John has no need of the Noble Lord's excuses. He knows his own mind. There need not, however, be any doubt that the " Army " did insist on internment too. The reasons it advanced we cannot pretend to know, since Sir Edward Grigg's lips are sealed. But we can make a reasonable surmise at the motives behind this military pressure.

It seems probable that some of our Army Chiefs themselves succumbed to a panic unworthy of soldiers, and found the Home Office not unwilling to yield to a pressure inspired by a " public opinion " largely created (as we have shown) by papers like the *Daily Mail*. Partly, no doubt, this was due to the subconscious belief lurking in their minds that " once a German, always a German." Too many of our Generals simply believe that this is a war of England against Germany (and Austria), so that all " Huns " are enemies. Too many of our military chiefs appear to be so saturated with undemocratic traditions of discipline and obedience to established governments (*however* established) that they inevitably regard as the " enemy " all those who speak the language of the enemy government, and cannot see the necessity of appealing to *peoples* over the heads of *governments*, or conceive of the possibility of positive action to encourage revolts in enemy territory against dictatorial régimes.

But partly, too, it is possible to detect in this " opinion of the Army " a desire on the part of certain brasshats and politicians to justify their usefulness. Consider the following sequence of events. In a broadcast speech on April 3, 1940, Marshal Goering stated :

" The German armed forces in one firm block are facing Britain and France in the west. It is here that the decisive blow must be struck, and for his decisive blow the Führer has mobilised all our resources."

On April 4, Mr. Chamberlain made his reply to these threats :

" Why was it that Hitler, despite all his long preparation for war, did not at the outset try to strike a knock-out blow at Britain and France ?   Whatever the reason—one thing is certain—Hitler missed the bus."

On the following day the Chief of the Imperial General Staff, General Sir Edmund Ironside, added his word.   In a, by now, sensational interview with the *Daily Express*, he said :

" Time is against Germany.   She cannot forever keep her armies in the battle area, poised for action, and then make no move.   Her morale is certain to suffer.   *Frankly we would welcome an attack*.   We are sure of ourselves. We have no fears. . . .   It's too late now.   *We are ready for anything they may start.   As a matter if fact we'd welcome a go at them*."

Fifty-three days later Denmark, Norway, Holland and Belgium had succumbed to *Blitzkrieg*, and General Ironside had been " promoted " (on May 27) from being Chief of the Imperial General Staff to the chief command of Home Forces. Another three weeks of *Blitzkrieg* and internal treachery achieved the surrender of France on June 17.   On July 20, General Ironside was again promoted, this time to the rank of Field-Marshal . . . and retired on half-pay.

Looking back on those seventy-four days in which five countries succumbed to *Blitzkrieg* and treachery, we can understand why it was that many of our political leaders and military commanders—who had been warned for years about " indirect aggression " and had seen the *Blitzkrieg* in action in Poland and had failed to recognise it—were taken by surprise.   They had " missed the bus " with a vengeance.   Is it astonishing that, having made up their minds not to be " caught napping " again, they demonstrated their preparedness by " interning the lot " ?   If it is true that the " opinion of the Army " weighed very heavily with the authorities when they decided on general internment, must we conclude that Field-Marshal Ironside, during those eight weeks when he held the key position of Commander-in-Chief of Home Forces, was one of the men responsible for forming that " opinion of the Army " ?   We cannot say.   Military chiefs do not have to answer questions in Parliament.   Whoever the generals responsible, it is tragic that our refugees from Nazi oppression should have been made into the scapegoats of commanders and politicians who have shown themselves incapable of waging that revolutionary and democratic warfare which is the only way of defeating Nazism and Fascism.

4. *A Reason that was Not Given*

The final reason for " interning the lot " is one that has not been explained by Government spokesmen. Since the war began to go against Britain, official policy in home affairs has shown an alarming authoritarian trend, not merely in the treatment of " enemy aliens," but also in a distinct tendency to whittle away the traditional civil rights of British citizens. The majority of British citizens believe they are fighting Hitler precisely to preserve those rights from destruction. They are therefore willing to accept such restrictions of personal freedom as are obviously necessary for military reasons, but not encroachments on their liberties which do not appear to be militarily necessary or in accordance with their democratic faith.

Precisely because the spirit of the British people remains firmly democratic there has occurred a vigorous and altogether healthy public reaction against recent proposed encroachments on civil liberties. Public common sense was also quick to realise that the privilege of asylum afforded to foreign refugees cannot be dissociated from our own civil liberties. We recognise fully that in a situation of great military urgency there must be no hesitation in taking whatever measures are needed for national security. Public alarm has, however, been aroused by a large number of incidents, and by the shoal of new Defence Regulations which appear to have little connexion with security properly understood, and which reveal an unmistakably bureaucratic and undemocratic frame of mind. A few episodes must suffice to illustrate this argument.

(1) *Press Censorship :* There occurred a definite attempt to extend censorship from its legitimate sphere of preventing publication of military information of value to the enemy, to a blue-pencilling of news and views that are politically unwelcome to certain people. Three incidents out of many may be quoted. On July 12, 1940, Mr. Duff Cooper justified suppression of views with the remark that :

" Criticism of the efforts that we are making in the war at the present time which is likely to encourage our opponents and discourage our friends should, *in my opinion*, be censored."

In June, political censorship was definitely in the offing when the Press Censor held up an article on Spain which was to appear in the *Tribune* and suggested to the editor that it be rewritten.   In July, 1940, Sir John Anderson made it clear that he had power to suppress *any* newspaper (under Defence Regulation 2D), and to seize its printing press (under D.R. 94B), which, *in his personal opinion*, he believes to be systematically fomenting opposition to the successful prosecution of the war. Such powers are wide enough to justify the suppression of almost any newspaper which adopts a consistent critical attitude of our war effort.   D.R. 2C obliged the Home Secretary to give a preliminary warning and stated that he must be satisfied that " serious mischief may be caused by subsequent publications of a similar character " ; but D.R. 2D removed these obligations.   The Home Secretary has these enormous discretionary powers invested in him personally, and is not obliged to consult any legal opinion, to frame any charges, or to present any evidence before a court of law. The matter came to a head at the end of July, when Mr. Duff Cooper was planning a wide extension of his powers of censorship.   A conference organised by the National Council for Civil Liberties on July 21, and addressed by Mr. Henry Nevinson, Lord Strabolgi, Mr. Frank Owen, editor of the *Evening Standard*, and other prominent men, clearly showed the trend of public feeling, and in the following week Mr. Duff Cooper dropped his plans.

(2) *Other Threats to Freedom of Speech and Opinion :* Under this head we may mention the outbreak of silly prosecutions for " spreading alarm and despondency," " insulting words and behaviour " and the like.   There was the famous and significant episode of the " Silent Column," by means of which the Ministry of Information was busy turning ignorant people into petty informers against their neighbours, until Mr. Churchill consigned it to " innocuous desuetude." Finally, there is the mysterious Swinton Committee.   Maurice Webb stated in the *Daily Herald* of July 23, 1940, that this Committee

had been set up to advise the Government on action to be taken against " dangerous and subversive persons." Its members include Lord Swinton (Chairman), Sir Joseph Ball, former head of the Conservative Party Research Department, and Mr. Crocker, the lawyer who unmasked the " fire-raisers."

Mr. Webb added :

> "They have played a big part, I am told, in getting a number of dangerous Fifth Columnists under lock and key. . . . But there are certain names on the committee which make me raise my eyebrows. These names suggest that the search for dangerous and subversive persons will not be as discriminating as it ought to be."

Many newspapers expressed suspicions that this body had something to do with the numerous raids by the police on the homes of harmless and respectable members of the trade union and Labour Movement, and possibly with a secret circular sent to headmasters asking them to report on any members of their staff whose political opinions may be considered (by whom ?) to be " subversive." Nobody wants to find out about secret measures necessary for defence, but Mr. Churchill refused, on July 23, to make any statement about the membership of the Committee or the character of its activities. Early in August it was revealed that Mr. A. M. Wall, the trade union leader, had been added to the Committee. On August 15, in the midst of a very angry scene in Parliament, Mr. Churchill refused to state the salaries paid to Sir J. Ball and Mr. Crocker, and explained :

> "About ten weeks ago, after the dark, vile conspiracy which in a few days laid the trustful Dutch people at the mercy of Nazi aggression, a wave of alarm passed over this country, and especially in responsible circles, lest the same kind of undermining tactics and treacherous agents of the enemy were at work in our Island. . . . I felt in that hour of anxiety that this side of the business of National Defence wanted pulling together. I therefore asked Lord Swinton to undertake this task . . . because he was the best man to do it."

And so three undistinguished Conservatives and one prominent trade union leader got to work.

(3) *Detention Without Trial :* Another disturbing symptom
was the detention without trial of more than 1,200 British
citizens who, *in the Home Secretary's opinion,* are persons of
" hostile origin or associations." Their cases are examined in
secret by an Advisory Committee (Chairman, Mr. Norman
Birkett), before which they may or may not appear, and which
may or may not allow them legal representation. The Committee informs any internee of the grounds for his detention
if he wishes to know. It advises the Home Secretary, who is
not obliged to follow its advice, whether to release internees or
not.* It is vitally necessary to get our British " Nazis of the
soul " under lock and key, but a large section of the House of
Commons believes that Sir John Anderson's method is wrong
and dangerous. If there is evidence against them, charges
should be laid before properly constituted courts of law, or
special tribunals if necessary. Public proceedings by due
process of law would provide a splendid method of exposing
and routing the British Fifth Column. Matters involving
military and other official secrets could be discussed *in camera,*
as is the established practice. The courts themselves should
have the power, which is at present the personal prerogative
of the Home Secretary and the Regional Commissioners, of
ordering a suspect's detention. This point of view is being
strongly pressed by members of Parliament who are poles
apart from Captain Ramsay or Sir Oswald Mosley in their
political opinions and have no sympathy whatever for them as
individuals, because it involves a vital principle of British
civil rights.

The Home Secretary has the same powers of " preventive
detention " over all foreigners, but they have no Advisory
Committee which may consider an appeal from them. " Enemy
aliens " may be simply detained on grounds of their nationality,
or under the Prerogative on individual grounds (117 were so
detained in July, 1940). " Non-enemy aliens " can be detained
in custody under deportation orders, since deportation cannot
be enforced in war-time. These deportation orders do not
have to be issued by a magistrate after hearing a formal charge
against the " non-enemy alien " present in court to defend
himself. In July, 355 " non-enemy aliens " were so detained.

* The Home Secretary stated (July 28, 1940) that he had accepted
the recommendations of the Committee in all the seventy-four cases
he had so far received reports on.

As Sir John Anderson explained to the House on August 22, these were persons

> "about whose record and conduct *I* have full information which has satisfied *me* that they ought to be deported, if deportation were practicable, and that they cannot safely be left at large under present conditions. *In such cases no useful purpose would be served by further investigation by a tribunal.*"

(Why not ? Is there to be no check on the Home Secretary's discretionary powers ?) Similarly for British subjects, the Home Secretary made it clear at the same time that :

> "All orders for detention under Regulation 18B are made, or in some cases confirmed, by *me* ; and it is *my* duty to satisfy *myself* in every case that the detention of the person concerned is necessary on one or other of the grounds specified in the Regulations."

The Home Secretary's powers of preventive detention of foreigners and British subjects alike—so reminiscent of the Gestapo—raises the whole question whether *Habeas Corpus* is still to be respected in this country, or whether one man shall have the power henceforth to lock up whomsoever he pleases. It is a big issue.*

(4) *War-Zone Courts :* On July 16, 1940, Sir John Anderson tried to rush the Emergency Powers (Defence) (No. 2) Bill through Parliament in one day. The Bill empowered the Government to issue Defence Regulations setting up " special courts " to operate in places " where, owing to military developments, the ordinary machinery of justice can no longer meet, or fully meet, the requirements of the case " (e.g. in the case of invasion or devastating air raids). The courts would be set up " if and when an area is declared to be a war-zone

---

* When Mr. Aubrey Lees, imprisoned on suspicion of Fascist activities, appealed to the Court of Criminal Appeal for release under a writ of *Habeas Corpus*, he was set free before the Court considered his case and no judicial decision on the principle involved was taken. The Solicitor-General, Sir William Jowitt, explained to the Court on October 2, 1940 : " The Advisory Committee has made the recommendation for release and the Home Secretary, *feeling inclined to act upon it,* has suspended the order under which Mr. Lees was detained." The order was not cancelled, but its operation was suspended.

area," and would dispense with juries and any right of appeal, even against death sentences. The precise circumstances in which an area was to be declared a war-zone, and *even the offences punishable by death*, were to be defined in a Defence Regulation and not in the Act. The general feeling of the House was voiced by Mr. Kingsley Griffith :

> " There is to be no appeal . . . but the rules of evidence are to be preserved and legal representation is to be afforded. But there is nothing about that in the Bill. What are we passing to-day ? Are we dealing with this Bill or with the right hon. Gentleman's speech ? It is all very well for anybody to come before this House and say, ' I have a Bill which entitles me to cut off your head, but I can assure you that I am only going to cut your toe nails.' "

The House of Commons was thoroughly alarmed ; for the first time under Mr. Churchill's Government a vote was taken and the Bill had to be redrafted. After a second battle in the House of Lords on July 30, appeal against death sentences was included in the Act, and it was promised that appeal against long terms of imprisonment would be provided for in the Defence Regulation.

This survey of trends in Home Affairs shows clearly that the treatment of " enemy aliens " is not a problem that can be dealt with in isolation from the general issue of civil liberties in war time. We cannot escape the feeling that both the Home Office and the Ministry of Information have been tending to adopt an unwelcome autocratic attitude towards the man in the street. Some of the measures we have mentioned are more appropriate to Ireland during the " troubles " or Bengal under Ordinance rule than to a civilised democratic community, even if we have got our backs to the wall. On all these issues—including the treatment of " enemy aliens "—the reaction both of Members of Parliament, of the still free press and of the public generally, has been vigorous and sensible. The abandoning of censorship plans and modifications of policy in other directions were forced through by the determination of back-bench M.P.s of all parties, with the support of the majority of newspapers. Britain owes a genuine debt of gratitude to those who, in Parliament and in the Press, waged a real battle for freedom on the Home Front in the second half of July, 1940. The battle still continues.

There is an unpleasant flavour about the following incident. Mr. Fred Uhlman was a distinguished barrister in Stuttgart, specialising in the defence of political opponents of the Nazis in Republican days. In 1933 he fled to Paris where he soon acquired a reputation as a painter, exhibiting regularly in important galleries. Later he came to England, where he became Chairman of the Artists' Section of the Free German League of Culture. He married a daughter of Lord Croft, at present Joint Under-Secretary of State for War. He was put in C Class by a tribunal, and became an unpaid air-raid warden in Hampstead, later being forced to resign on account of his nationality to the regret of his fellow wardens. A week before his wife gave birth to a daughter he was rounded-up and interned in the Isle of Man. Lady (Edward) Pearson, who is Lord Croft's sister, is a well-known Blackshirt. In 1934, she founded a branch of the British Union of Fascists in Sandwich (Kent), and in 1936 was announced as Blackshirt candidate for Canterbury. On June 4, 1940, she was detained by the police, but by an order under D.R. 18A on June 8, she was released subject to the condition that she enter no " protected " area and notify her address to the police. On July 11, Sir John Anderson told Parliament that

> " the decision taken in this matter was taken by me personally after consideration of the facts reported by the local police . . . no extraneous consideration or argument whatsoever was taken into account."

It is episodes of this character, whatever the truth behind them, that lend some colour to the grave view voiced by Mr. H. G. Wells, in an article in *Reynolds News* of July 28 :

> " In this country, as in France before reaction threw aside all pretence, a deliberate and systematic intimidation of liberal-minded foreigners is going on.
> " So that even while we are at war with the Axis Powers and their subjugated ' allies,' people in positions of authority and advantage in this country are allowing the collection, internment and ill-treatment of all those disaffected subjects of our enemies who would be most willing and able to organise internal resistance in their own countries on our behalf. . . .
> " Everything these people do is calculated to convince their victims who have sought our aid and protection that

the fate that has overtaken their fellow refugees in France may come to them in turn, that Britain is willing to betray them and will betray them, as France has betrayed its Spanish and German refugees, and that the best prospect of safety for them is to make their peace with our enemies quickly now, and do whatever is required of them here against us. This is not a case of administrative stupidity ; that is my point ; it is a case of ' doing Goebbels's work,' of enemy activity entrenched in our midst. . . .

" The hard necessity of our present situation is to identify, punish and repudiate that nest of traitors immediately, and to replace them as promptly by men and women who are prepared to encourage, organise and arm to the utmost the forces of revolt in France, Germany, Spain, Holland, Belgium, Scandinavia, and all the subjugated countries generally, in one vigorous common fight against repression.   That is not only the path of righteousness and human service, but the clear common sense of any clean patriotism in us."

Possibly Mr. Wells overstates his case, although he is prepared to place his evidence for these accusations before " any responsible public body."   There is nevertheless, we believe, a point at which ignorance and panic join hands in this matter with pigheaded reaction of the most dangerous character.   A *British* Fifth Column, consisting of " non-political " (that is anti-progressive) men of the type who before war broke out were outspoken in their support for the " anti-Bolshevik " Hitler and the " robust attitude " towards " Communism " of the Axis Powers, has, mainly behind the scenes, welcomed, applauded, egged on, pressed for, assisted in, every step in the wrong direction taken by the authorities in dealing with " enemy aliens " and other matters of home defence.   We are not suggesting an organised conspiracy ; we are not accusing Ministers of being in the pay of Hitler.   But our impression is that, in the background, " advising," " suggesting," pressing our authorities, there exists a well-hidden and intangible " body of influential opinion," emanating from Colonel Blimps, bureaucratic and autocratic civil servants, narrow-minded aristocrats, selfish business men and discredited, fourth-rate politicians who should be reduced to political impotence without delay.   Such men are not Blackshirts or members of any Fascist movement.   They are the types who correspond to

Laval, Pétain, Weygand, Tardieu, Baudouin, Ybarnegaray, Chiappe and their like in France—the men who try to use Fascist movements for their own ends, but prefer boiled shirts and a " non-political " attitude. The Home Secretary will find his real, true-blue, British Fifth Column in such circles—not among the thousands of harmless Jewish men Sir John Anderson has interned, men whose very pronunciation of the English language debars them from being " enemy agents." It is unfortunately true that in all the eight countries Hitler has conquered since 1938 there has been a more than adequate supply of native Quislings, speaking their own mother tongues to perfection, to ensure his success.

5. *Conclusions*

Internment and deportation of " enemy aliens " and the locking up of hundreds of " friendly aliens " and British citizens without the making of any charges or the presenting of any evidence before a court of law are unfortunately well within the emergency powers the Government has taken unto itself in the name of national security. The Home Secretary in particular has more power concentrated in his own hands than it is safe to entrust to any one man in a democratic country. He can if he chooses abolish almost every one of the fundamental liberties which Englishmen believe they are fighting to preserve. Mr. Churchill promised the House of Commons on August 15 that the Government would not consciously use its immense powers over the life and freedom of British citizens " in any unfair, oppressive, or un-British spirit " ; but promises are no substitute for guarantees. We have described in the course of this book many ways in which thousands of harmless individuals have already suffered from the conscious use of those powers in an " unfair, oppressive and un-British spirit." What guarantee is there that similar treatment will not gradually be extended to all British citizens who try to think for themselves and are not willing to become " silent soldiers " in a " silent column " blindly following the Government and its military commanders without a word of criticism ?

Internment and deportation of refugees are a sordid and disgraceful scandal, but in spite of our lengthy analysis of the reasons why this policy was adopted, we find it impossible conclusively to apportion the blame between Mr. Eden, Sir John Anderson, Mr. Chamberlain's Committee, the Army chiefs, and the subordinate officials (Chief Constables, Home Office officials, Prisoners of War Department of the War Office, etc.) under these Ministers. It is probable that certain military chiefs and the War Office did clamour for general internment. On the other hand the Home Secretary has himself said (Hansard, July 23, 1940), that he regards general internment as " necessary and indeed inevitable." Sir John Anderson has in any case shown a remarkable capacity for ignoring public opinion when he chooses to. But we also know from Sir Edward Grigg's statement on July 10 that " many points have been put up to the deciding body—the War Cabinet—about major questions of policy of this kind." Through what channels were those issues " put up " to it ? We may hazard a guess. We know that the decision to deport " the most dangerous classes " was taken by a Cabinet Committee presided over by Mr. Chamberlain, a member of the War Cabinet. Has the Committee taken any other major decisions on " enemy aliens " ? Since Committees of the Cabinet are not set up simply to decide whether or not to deport interned " aliens," it is reasonable to surmise that Mr. Chamberlain's Committee did have a share in other major decisions concerning the fate of " enemy aliens." Can we identify the Committee ? Many Members of Parliament believe that it is the Cabinet Committee on Home Defence. This view is quite probably correct. We may also ask whether the literally unmentionable Swinton Committee, which also apparently deals with " home defence," has had anything to do with pressing general internment of " enemy aliens " upon our authorities.

Decisions to intern individuals are taken by the Home Office, but it is not so certain who decided that categories of " enemy aliens " should be interned. The Home Office has the responsibility for carrying out those decisions, but again it is not clear exactly how precise were the Home Secretary's instructions to chief constables, how much discretion was left to them, either deliberately or through vaguely worded instructions, and to what extent the chief constables left their subordinate officers free to use their own judgment in individual cases. We have grounds for suspecting that the Home Office's instructions to chief constables were not at all clear and that individual chief constables could interpret them very widely or very narrowly. It is also not at all clear what kind of " special information " or " doubts " the police acted upon in deciding to intern individuals who were supposed to be exempted, especially the thousands of men suffering from serious illnesses who were carried off. We suspect that 90 per cent. of this " special information " consisted of distorted fragments of gossip and tittle-tattle reported to the police by suspicious neighbours, and that most of it would not be accepted as evidence in a court of law.

Although the War Office ran the men's camps and the Home Office merely put men into them and took them out again, responsibility for many of the worst features of internment is still shrouded in mystery. Who was to blame for the ban on all forms of news ? Who was behind the incredible muddle over correspondence ? Whose job was it to keep adequate records of internees ? Who decided how many men there should be in any given camp ? The decision to deport the " most dangerous classes " of internees was taken by Mr. Chamberlain's Committee, but who carried it out ? In September, 1940, Lord Snell was still trying to find out who picked the men who were put on the *Arandora Star* and who were responsible for the failure to keep proper records of them and their next of kin. We have evidence that in certain camps C.I.D. men chose some men (not Nazis) for deportation from a secret black list. But it is not clear whether the majority of deportees were selected by Home Office officials, War Office officials, or by the Camp Commandants.

Clear answers to most of these questions have never been given in Parliament. Now that the whole responsibility for internment and deportation has been vested in the Home Office it is becoming fashionable for Home Office spokesmen to answer questions relating to events in May, June or July with the statement that they were not responsible because they were not in charge.

During the whole period of War Office control of the camps the confusion of responsibility was so great that " passing the buck " from one Department to another became a major feature of Ministerial answers to awkward questions. During those agonising weeks the responsible authorities more and more assumed the guise of Peer Gynt's Boyg, an intangible, invisible presence, elastically yet irresistibly blocking the way, speaking in riddles which might portend good or ill, and tirelessly repeating the slogan : " Go round about ! "

CHAPTER V

WHAT NEXT ?

1. *What Is and what Must be Done*

The " New " Policy.—As one ghastly story after another
leaked out of the camps opinion in Parliament and the press
grew increasingly indignant throughout July and August, 1940.
Many tragedies that could never be put right had occurred ; but
a general demand grew up for a remedying of all the damage
that could be repaired. After the debate of July 10, Sir John
Anderson began to show signs of yielding a little. He
announced on July 23 that he would consider releasing C Class
men falling into the exempted categories whom he had never
intended to intern at all (except if they were individually
suspect), and later published a White Paper giving a list of
these exempted categories—the same categories that the police
had been required not to intern in the first place. Sir John's
" new " policy was not new at all : *he merely proposed to correct
the mistakes the police had made in carrying out his original
policy, but showed no signs of modifying that policy.* As he
put it :

> " There can be no question at the present time of revert-
> ing to a position in which the internment of aliens of enemy
> nationality shall be the exception rather than the rule."

In addition he set up an Advisory Committee and an Advisory
Council. The Committee consists of Justice Sir Cyril Asquith
(Chairman), Sir Herbert Emerson (High Commissioner for
Refugees) and Major-General Sir Neill Malcolm (former High
Commissioner for Refugees from Germany), and its object,
according to Sir. John Anderson, is to " assist me in dealing
with this problem of the control of aliens of enemy nationality."
Its terms of reference are :

> " (1) to keep under review the *application* of the principles
> laid down in regard to the internment of enemy aliens
> and to make to the Home Secretary such suggestions
> and recommendations thereon as they think fit ;

" (2) to advise the Home Secretary on such proposals for modifying the internment policy *as he may refer to them from time to time* ; and,

" (3) to examine, and make recommendations upon, such individual cases or groups of cases *as may be referred to them from time to time by the Home Secretary.*"

The Advisory Council is attached to the Refugee Department of the Foreign Office, and consists of Lord Lytton (Chairman), Sir Herbert Emerson (Vice-Chairman), Sir Neill Malcolm, Miss Eleanor Rathbone, M.P., the Marchioness of Reading, Mr. E. Edwards, and nine other Members of Parliament (including Mr. Graham White, Mr. Noel-Baker, Viscount Cranborne and Earl Winterton), several of whom are connected with the Parliamentary Committee on Refugees. Its terms of reference are :

" (*a*) To suggest measures for maintaining the morale of aliens in this country so as to bind them more closely to our common cause.

" (*b*) To review and if necessary to suggest measures for the co-ordination, to the end described in (*a*) above, of the work of the various refugee committees and other voluntary organisations concerned with aliens in this country.

" (*c*) To maintain contact with the various Government Departments having responsibilities in connection with refugees and other classes of aliens and with foreign Governments or National Committees established in this country.

" (*d*) To advise and assist the Home Office in the arrangements made for the welfare of enemy aliens in internment camps.

" (*e*) To study, and make recommendations upon, the problem of finding occupations for enemy aliens in internment camps."

The terms of reference of the Asquith Committee, it will be noted, are very carefully worded. It keeps " under review *the application of the principles laid down in regard to the internment of enemy aliens* " and makes recommendations on this point. But who " lays down " those principles whose application the Asquith Committee has to watch ? Apparently the

British Government itself decides the *principles* of internment, and the Committee is limited to telling Sir John Anderson the best way of carrying out his internment policy.

The functions of Lord Lytton's Advisory Council are much wider and the Council is clearly in a position to achieve a great deal if it works intelligently and energetically.   The fact that its membership overlaps considerably with that of the Parliamentary Committee on Refugees and that the High Commissioner is vice-chairman gives some grounds for confidence. The fourth point of its terms of reference, " to advise and assist the Home Office in the arrangements made for the welfare of enemy aliens in internment camps," suggests that the Government is at last willing to listen to informed opinion about internment conditions.   The fifth point, making recommendations about work schemes for internees, is necessary, but it is surely a matter on which the interned refugees themselves have every right to be consulted.   The first three of the Council's points of reference relate to " aliens " generally and are not restricted specifically to " enemy aliens."   But one big point is missing from the terms of reference both of the Committee and of the Council : neither body is competent to discuss and advise on questions of general internment policy unless the Home Secretary chooses to refer such questions to it.   General questions about the whole nature of internment are excluded from their scope, unless the Lytton Council cares to recommend that the most obvious method of " maintaining the morale of aliens in this country so as to bind them more closely to our common cause " is to release all who are not suspect and make some attempt to redress the harm done to them.   Probably it is all to the good that the League High Commissioner sits in this Council, but it is a pity that he is not, as a member either of the Council or of the Committee, in a clear position to discuss the whole basis of the Government's internment policy, but is limited to welfare and employment problems of internees, advice on *applying* the Government's principles of internment, and general questions of morale, refugee assistance and co-ordination of Government Departments.

The exempted categories embodied in the July White Paper were conceived in a very niggardly and narrow-minded spirit. With one or two exceptions the whole attitude to internees which inspired it is the attitude of a farmer to his horses or cows—" use them or lock them up."   Unless an internee was ill or had certain other narrowly restricted grounds for release on compassionate grounds, the White Paper only made it possible for the " useful " to be released. In fact on August 22 Sir John Anderson was only able to announce that the release of 805 men had actually been authorised.

The snail's pace of release and the narrow-minded utilitarianism of the " new " policy soon aroused such a storm of protest, that on August 22 the Home Secretary announced some further concessions which were embodied in a revised version of the White Paper issued on August 26. Whilst sticking to a policy of general internment, Sir John Anderson had adopted the Asquith Committee's recommendations to extend certain exempted categories and to add a new one, and hoped more relaxations would follow from further recommendations by the Committee. In addition, men in B Class (unreviewed) who came under one of the exempted categories would be sent before a new special review tribunal, and, if placed in C Class, released. All other B cases would be reviewed by tribunals who would probably visit the camps. For Italian internees the same general conditions of release would apply. Applicants for release would have to appear before a special Advisory Committee (Chairman, Sir Percy Loraine, former Ambassador in Rome), consisting of " persons with special knowledge of Italian politics and life."

The August White Paper contained 19 categories for release. These include three age groups : under 16, over 65 (July White Paper : over 70) and young persons under 18, if living with a British family, or at school, or living with " a parent, step-parent or guardian to whose care the Secretary of State is prepared to allow them to return " ; and the " invalid or infirm." (" Internees receive medical attention in the internment camps " ! and the camp's medical officer will certify that a man should be released. No provision is made for an internee to call in his own doctor to examine him). Internees who have been discharged from the British Army " on grounds not reflecting on their loyalty to this country or their personal character," and " persons who have, or have had, a British-born or naturalised son in His Majesty's Forces " are eligible for release. (If your son is a *refugee* in the Pioneer Corps you remain locked up.) " Persons about to embark for emigration overseas " are " released " in the following way. The re-emigrant is interned at Lingfield Race-course Camp and only allowed out to attend interviews at the U.S. Consulate. On the day his ship sails " the alien is taken to the port of departure " where, presumably, he meets his wife and children, and becomes a free man when he sets foot on the American " soil " of the ship.   Another category, not apparently included in the Home Secretary's original instructions, but thought out a month later and put into the July White Paper, consists of " cases of special hardship."

Eleven of the remaining twelve categories are all of the utilitarian variety.   One group consists of men holding certificates from the Aliens War Service Department, key workers in industries engaged on work of national importance, skilled workers in agriculture, commercial food-growing or forestry, and men with permits to live and work in " protected " areas. Employers of twelve or more British workers " in works or factories engaged in work certified by a Government Department to be of value to the community " will be released.   This is an improvement on the July White Paper, which specified that such men would only be released if the business would close down without them, thereby throwing British workers out of work.   There is also a professional group of exempted persons : doctors and dentists authorised either to practice or to qualify for practising (other doctors, the majority, will remain locked up, their abilities wasted until the Home Secretary decides to " use " them) ; ministers of religion if holding a spiritual charge (except in German churches.   The dozens of refugee pastors and theological students preparing for ordination in Britain will have to conduct their studies behind barbed wire) ; and finally " scientists, research workers and persons of academic distinction for whom work of importance in their special field is available."   In the July White Paper the work available had to be " work of *national* importance," but the Asquith Committee advised dropping the word " national," since the " benefits of science and learning are often indirect rather than direct."   If this category is interpreted literally, there are many eminent men in this group (especially musicians, actors, artists, architects, lawyers, historians, economists, etc.) who will be kept under lock and key, no matter how useful or how genuinely anti-Nazi they may be, because " work of importance " is *not* available.   Much depends in the case of this group on the functioning of the special committees set up by the Vice-Chancellors of Universities, the Royal Society and the British Academy, to make recommendations to the Home Secretary. There were indications in August, 1940, that these committees were taking a liberal and sensible view of their duties and were not too rigidly insisting that "work of (national) import-ance in their special fields" must be available before they recom-mended the release of various internees. But that is stretching the provisions of the White Paper beyond its evident intentions.

Men *accepted* for enlistment in the Pioneer Corps will be released. Willingness to enlist is insufficient. Finally "persons engaged in refugee organisations which are still functioning, such as officers of voluntary organisations, hostels and training establishments," will be released, but "only in cases in which the loss of the alien's services is seriously hampering the work of the organisation or establishment." Thus workers in an organi-sation like the Austrians' *Laterndl* theatre, which was killed by in-ternment, will not be released because it is not still functioning.

The July White Paper failed in particular to provide for three groups of interned refugees : (*a*) Men who have dis-tinguished themselves in their own countries in various fields of scientific or cultural endeavour, but for whom "work of (national) importance in their special fields" is *not* available at the moment. (*b*) Those who have suffered from Nazi perse-cution for "racial," political or religious reasons. (*c*) Those who have distinguished themselves as opponents of Hitler and Mussolini and have even fought on Spanish and other battle-fields against them. The August White Paper made no change for the first two groups, but Sir John Anderson added a nineteenth exempted category which was intended to meet the criticism that he had locked up many of Hitler's most hated enemies :

"Any person as to whom a Tribunal, appointed by the Secretary of State for the purpose, reports that enough is known of his history to show that by his writings or speeches or political or official activities he has consistently, over a period of years, taken a public and prominent part in opposition to the Nazi system and is actively friendly towards the Allied cause."

It was announced in September, 1940, that the tribunal to examine such cases consists of Sir Cecil Hurst (former President of the Permanent Court of International Justice at the Hague), Chairman, Sir Andrew McFadyean (a former Treasury official and expert on German war reparations), Dr. Seton-Watson (the distinguished authority on Central Europe) and Mr. I. Kirkpatrick (formerly First Secretary at

the British Embassy in Berlin).   No man should be permitted
to judge the integrity of refugees claiming to be consistent
opponents of Hitler and Mussolini unless he also has himself
been a consistent opponent of authoritarianism and reaction *in
his own country*.   From this point of view the composition of
the tribunal might have been distinctly worse than it is.
Dr. Seton Watson was an outspoken critic of the Munich
Agreement.   We fervently hope that Mr. Kirkpatrick is not a
man of the same calibre as his chief in Berlin, Sir Nevile
Henderson, who during his whole period as British Ambassador
to Hitler seems to have learned absolutely nothing about
Germany except the personal foibles of the Nazi leaders, for
some of whom—to judge from his reminiscences—he acquired
a distinct liking.   Any man whose intellect is capable of per-
forming the curious feat of regarding Goering as a " blackguard, but not a dirty blackguard " should not be trusted to
judge anti-Nazi refugees.   The majority of Hitler's political
opponents now in Britain belonged to left-wing parties or the
trade union movement in Germany, but there is not a single
person with even the mildest Socialist views on the tribunal
which is to judge them.   We doubt whether even Dr. Seton-
Watson has that intimate knowledge of the German and Austrian
working-class movements which is vital for such a tribunal.

According to the Home Secretary :

> " the tribunal shall be assisted as and when it is thought
> fit by calling upon reliable representative refugees who
> were leaders of German political groups to give them advice
> and information."

Will the tribunal call in representative leaders of working-
class groups to advise it, or will it rely on " sound," " respectable " men from former right-wing German political circles,
who themselves hated the German working-class movements
and whose quarrel with the Nazis had, and has, very little to do
with democracy or the rights of the common people ?   If it
does the latter, the tribunal might do little more than advise
the release of a handful of prominent ex-politicians whose
views could be tolerated by the Conservative Party Central
Office.   This point must be strongly insisted upon, since many
of the former German and Austrian politicians in exile who are
most " actively friendly towards the Allied cause " are men
whose claims to be regarded as democrats and lovers of freedom
are highly dubious—for example, the numerous Fascist-minded,

anti-semitic adventurers who are damaging the reputations of the Polish and Czech National Committees in Britain, and the discredited Austrian Monarchists who organised the notorious " Austria Office." Such men are anti-Hitler and support the Allied cause for highly questionable motives—because Hitler has deprived them of their possessions and positions of power, not because he has stamped out tolerance and decency over half of Europe. Prince Starhemberg, who himself destroyed the Austrian Republic and slaughtered the workers of Vienna, but whose castles and domains in Austria were expropriated by the Nazis, is " actively friendly towards the Allied cause," as an officer in General de Gaulle's air force, for very good reasons of his own ; but he, together with all the similar refugee adventurers now swarming in London, and claiming to be " reliable and representative " leaders of German political groups, might more justifiably be regarded as " enemy aliens " than 99 per cent. of the refugees interned in the camps.

The wording of the definition of a man eligible for release as a political opponent of the Nazis is curious. The emphasis on " writings or speeches or political or official activities " and on " a public and prominent part in opposition to the Nazi system " strongly suggests that it is only intended to apply to men who were well known political leaders in the Republican period, and that the mass of men who worked in Germany illegally under the Nazi terror will be excluded. For no one who worked against the Nazis illegally could produce evidence of writings or speeches or official activities, nor could he have taken a *public* part in opposition to the Nazis. He could no doubt prove that he had played some part in illegal opposition work but might find it very difficult to show that that part was a *prominent* one, precisely because his activities were illegal. After the exodus of well-known political opponents of the Nazis (or of the Dollfuss-Schuschnigg dictatorship in Austria), the majority of whom gradually got cut off from the remnants of the movements they formerly led, there grew up both in Germany and Austria a new cadre of political leaders, leaders precisely because they were unknown, operating against the Nazis on the greatly reduced scale and with the small bands of followers that alone were possible. These men came mostly from the rank and file and junior officers of the Labour movement and from its youth sections. The White Paper makes little provision for releasing the " illegals " or for a closely allied group, the Germans and Austrians who fought in the International Brigade in Spain, but had not become prominent in their own countries (perhaps because they were too young) by their speeches, writings and activities as opponents of the Nazis.

A second bad feature of this category is that it imposes as a condition that the anti-Nazi applicant for release must be "actively friendly towards the Allied cause." Superficially this does not appear very objectionable, but it is a test which may be misused in a most dangerous fashion. Many refugees, if asked about their attitude to the Allied cause, are likely, as the Indians do, to reply :

"What is this Allied cause? The most important of Britain's allies, France, has abandoned the struggle ; the British Government will not say what it is fighting *for*. First it locks us up, and then it says it will release us if we support the Allied cause. Our experiences as German citizens since 1918 have taught us to be sceptical about Governments, including democratic ones, which call for support for a cause which they are unable or unwilling to state in plain and concrete terms. If Britain is really fighting, *not* for Europe *before* Hitler (to which no German will ever willingly return), but for the political liberation and social and economic reconstruction of Europe on super-national and democratic lines, then we are with Britain. If the Government will not speak, except in the vague platitudes of 1914–18, then we remain well-disposed but critical, if not (after internment) sceptical."

Many of the disillusioned refugees, who may argue as we have suggested, may remain locked up if they say frankly what is in their minds. There is one whole class of former fighters against Hitler who are definitely excluded from release : those who do not support Britain's war effort—the pacifists and the various Socialist groups who regard the war as a struggle of rival imperialisms in which no decent man should take sides. These groups correspond to the Quakers, the Peace Pledge Union, the Independent Labour Party, the Communists and other groups in England, but are more numerous among the refugees than among the British people (the same groups would be among the refugees from British Fascism). Ossietzky, the German pacifist who was awarded the Nobel Peace Prize when in a Nazi concentration camp, one of the noblest characters

of Republican Germany, who used his journal to conduct a
life-long struggle not only against the Nazis but against all
forms of militarism and intolerance in Germany, if he had
escaped to Britain would have been locked up again for the
duration of the war as an " enemy alien," because he could not
honestly say he supported the " Allied cause." All the various
German Socialist groups who refuse to fight either for the British
Empire or the Nazi Reich have their representatives among
the refugees in Britain, who will remain under lock and key.
One of these groups, the Communists, Sir John Anderson
explicitly promised (on August 22) not to release. (The term
" Communist " may have, as we know, quite as all-embracing
a scope in Britain as the term " Bolshevist " on the lips of Hitler).
Although most English people strongly disagree with their
attitude to the war, neither the Quakers, nor the Pacifists,
nor the I.L.P., nor the Communists in Britain have had their
organisations declared illegal, nor are conscientious objectors
automatically sent to prison. Why, then, apply such methods
to German and Austrian refugees holding similar minority
opinions ? Is it not time we fully recognised that a community
is enriched by the presence of men and women of high character
who hold unpopular views, and acknowledged the fact that we
cannot fight a war for freedom if minority views are to be
suppressed ? Only in Britain would it be possible, in the
middle of a war, for an Army officer at a Conservative Party
Conference to oppose a resolution attacking conscientious
objectors, on the grounds that to refuse to acknowledge the
freedom of the individual conscience is to put ourselves on
the same plane as the Nazis and to destroy Britain's claim to
be fighting for superior moral ends. For Englishmen the
tolerance of minorities has been fairly completely accepted,
although in war-time intolerance tends to grow. But once
again what holds for Englishmen should hold for refugees
and other foreigners, too. If Englishmen are not interned for
not supporting the war effort, neither should refugees be
interned. If a refugee is to remain locked up if he cannot prove
that " by his writings or speeches or political or official activities
he has consistently, over a period of years, taken a public and
prominent part in opposition to the Nazi system," Englishmen
to whom the same applies should also be locked up. If this
were done, how many members of the Cabinet, the Conservative Party or the House of Lords would remain at large ?

Sir John Anderson's nineteenth category is clearly a tricky business. If the Home Secretary really wishes to bind refugees " more closely to our common cause," he would do well to listen to the advice of the Bishop of Chichester (House of Lords, August 6, 1940) :

> " I have no doubt whatever that the first step towards maintaining the morale of refugees from Germany and Austria, refugees from Nazi oppression, is not to speak to the world in general terms about ideals of freedom, but to convince them that you will do justice : that the upholders of freedom, as we are proud to be, the fighters against evil things—brute force, bad faith, injustice, oppression and persecution—are doing justice to the men and the women who have already suffered bitterly from these things in Germany and have fled from them to us."

In particular Sir John might try to persuade his Government to take positive steps clearly to demonstrate to neutral opinion, to the peoples of Germany, Austria and Italy, and to refugees that the Allied cause includes a concrete and constructive plan for the future of Europe, a plan which is infinitely preferable to Hitler's unified Europe under Nazi domination, a plan in support of which the suppressed millions of the Greater Reich will be prepared to struggle against Hitlerism to the death.

As a whole Sir John Anderson's release policy remained narrowly utilitarian. It is easy to demonstrate that internment put under lock and key large numbers of men of skill and ability who were anxious to be " used " by an intelligent Government. This was in fact one of the main arguments advanced by all who objected to wholesale internment. But the argument, used by itself, has its dangers, because it is certain that the majority of internees are not " useful " in Sir John's narrow sense, although the majority of internees capable of work are able to contribute something of value—in a much wider sense—to the economic, social or cultural life of the community. The utilitarian argument has succeeded in getting internment policy placed upon an entirely wrong basis. Refugees are not cattle or horses to be kept locked up in stables—however hygienic or comfortable—and only taken out when their owner has some use for them. The whole approach which this attitude implies is wrong. It entirely overlooks the depressing effects, not only on the refugees themselves, but on the anti-

Nazis and anti-Fascists both in powerful neutral countries and inside Germany, Austria and Italy, whose support the Government is anxious to win. The utilitarian argument also tends to dissociate entirely the internment of refugees from the internment of British citizens and other encroachments on their liberties. As we have shown in Chapter IV, Section 4, these two problems are by no means isolated from one another ; but the utilitarian attitude tends to imply that, whilst every effort should be made to use as many refugees as possible in work connected with the war effort, no great harm is done in keeping the unusable remainder locked up. Why such treatment should be applied to *any* non-Briton who has been persecuted and repudiated the Nazis, simply because he does not happen to be useful, is not at all clear. If non-Britons are to be treated thus why not Britons too ? Why not lock up all Britons who are either doing no work at all or who are doing work that is not useful to the war effort, however respectable, loyal and eager to fight for freedom they may be ? The idle rich and the idle poor, the unoccupied women, the children, the millions of workers who are still engaged in occupations necessary for daily life but not for waging war, are after all a nuisance and an encumbrance to the military machine and its industrial foundations. They ought to be locked up and forced to subsist on a bare minimum of consumption goods until the war is over. This crazy reasoning is a logical development of the utilitarian attitude to internment, if sole or main emphasis is placed upon it to the quasi-exclusion of considerations of morale, human liberties and common decency.

What should be done.—The great majority of internees do not fit into any of Sir John Anderson's categories—they are *victims* of Hitler, but are neither old, nor ill, nor "useful," nor well-known political opponents of the Nazis. Sir John Anderson made it clear that internment for the duration was to be their fate. Mr. Herbert Morrison, the new Home Secretary, may think differently. Public opinion in August, 1940, was completely divided on the question, " Intern or release ? " Against the Government's policy many M.P.s on August 22 urged a different view. For example :

" I want no refugee to be refused the right of being released simply because he does not come under any particular category. I want there to be an individual Committee . . . who will examine the request of an individual on its merits." (Major Cazalet.)

This view was also advanced in the House of Lords on August 6 by Lord Cecil:

> "We say each case must be considered on its merits. If it can be shown that there is the slightest suspicion that a person is not a trustworthy and honourable citizen of the country, of course he must· be interned. What we want is to reverse the principle of 'intern the lot.' That is the foundation mistake which was made. We have got to say, 'No.' As to refugees who are not under the protection of an enemy alien State, primarily they should not be subject to internment. If you want to intern any of these, you must make out a case for internment in special circumstances."

This is the view of the present writer:

1. It is high time an end was put to this scandal by the only practical method open to the Government: *to order the release without delay of every single interned refugee who is not in any way suspect*. By the end of September, 1940, at the latest every non-suspect internee, man, woman and child, should be free again to pick up the threads of their broken lives. Even if this involves a certain slight risk to national security, the gain in morale from a frank admission that a colossal blunder has been made and that justice will be done far outweighs all other considerations. This is the only method of doing justice, of proving to the world that we have recovered our senses, and of making the camps tolerable to those who will have to stay in them.

2. All internees against whom the police have some real grounds for suspicion (not just overheard gossip and fabricated tales) should remain interned until their cases can be considered. But their cases should be considered without delay by attaching a tribunal to each camp to review all such cases. And these tribunals should be conducted as proper courts of law with evidence presented, legal representation for the defendant, and a right of appeal. The tribunals should have the power of ordering a suspect's internment if they decide that the suspicions of the police are well founded.

3. In future " enemy aliens," " friendly aliens " and British citizens should all be treated alike. The principle of internment of *classes* of men must be dropped. Each man must be judged individually, irrespective of his race, language or birthplace, on the basis of his past record and present conduct.

The grounds for internment are that his past record or his present conduct arouse strong suspicions of pro-Nazi or anti-democratic views. In general only suspects should be interned ; the decision to intern them should not be in the hands of the police and those who control the police ; a proper trial with a right to appeal are essential.

4. " Enemy aliens " who fear that they may be lynched because of mass air-bombing, and who wish to be interned for their own safety, can be provided for by the *voluntary* internment of individuals and families in mixed centres under tolerable conditions, with easy access to the outside world. The refugee organisations could organise such centres themselves and could make arrangements for protection with the local police and the Home Guard.*

5. A clear understanding about the legal status and rights of refugees is needed. How this can be effected is discussed in Sections 2 and 3.

6. Positive measures to rehabilitate released internees, and especially to promote welfare and employment, will be needed. These are discussed in Section 4.

It is pointless and futile to discuss at great length the welfare of interned refugees. Even if they are locked up in beautiful luxury hotels and live on the best the land can supply, it would still be an outrage to treat them thus. They want their freedom back, their dignity, their humanity. They want to get back to their families and do a useful job of work. It is not a question of good or bad internment conditions, nor a question of whether there should be one, two or three dozen exempted categories, nor even a question of whether internees could be used, but a question of elementary human rights and decencies, of democratic solidarity and common kindness. There is only ONE exempted category : all who are opponents and victims of oppression, whose records and conduct prove them to be lovers of freedom and tolerance. They must *all* be released. The OTHER category, the foes of freedom, the would-be suppressors of the common people, the aiders and abettors of reaction, are those who should be locked up. This group includes many Englishmen and Frenchmen, but not many refugees.

* No anti-refugee disturbances were reported following the Nazi bombing of London in September, 1940. Londoners were far more concerned about the lack of adequate air-raid shelters than about possible Fifth Columnists masquerading as refugees.

In April, 1940, Sebastian Haffner wrote in his book, *Germany :
Jekyll and Hyde* :

" Whilst in England there has been no change in policy,
France has declared war on the German emigrants no less
than on Hitler.   Immediately after the outbreak of war, all
adult male German emigrants, with few exceptions, were
arrested.   The fact was deliberately ignored that they were
exiles and they were treated like the Nazi agents, with whom
they were imprisoned.   An army of valuable allies has been
destroyed in order to get, at small cost, a number of prisoners
of war.   Something much worse than an injustice has been
perpetrated ; a grave, a catastrophic defeat on the psychological battlefield.

" . . . It is useless to regard the affair as one of bureaucratic routine, or to justify it by necessity of increased
measures of state protection in war time, or the argument
that among the thousands of emigrants there might be
concealed a couple of spies.   One can surely depend on the
French counter-espionage and police to be fully acquainted
with aliens who have been living in France for many years,
and to be in a position to divide the black sheep from the
rest. . . .

" No, the matter cannot be thus explained away.   The
internment of German emigrants is not a trifling bureaucratic lapse, but a deliberate political gesture.   It says more
clearly than any ministerial speech that the war is being
waged against the German people, including those who have
proved themselves anti-Hitlerian. . . .

" The policy of France, embodied in its hostile treatment
of German emigrants, can only be directed towards a war of
annihilation against the German nation, whilst England has
always clearly repudiated such intentions. . . . I would
wish that my voice would be strong enough to penetrate the
deaf ears of those responsible for this error and make them
realise that what happens to German emigrants is important ;
important not on its own account, but because it is exposed
to view, and the eyes of Germany are directed towards it as
otherwise they are directed towards Hitler ; because it is a
symbol, and symbols—mark this, you professional politicians
—occupy the very first rank among political realities. . . .
The fate of these exiles arouses a more vibrant echo in
Germany than what you speak into the microphone over the

ether (you might as well save yourselves that trouble if at
the same time you contradict your speech by your conduct
to the German emigrants)."

" You professional politicians " took no notice. Haffner is
an " enemy alien " living in England. They interned him two
months later. Is it not time someone paid attention ?

Why General Internment is still the Rule.—Cabinet Ministers
have read and praised Haffner's book, but they have paid no
attention to this solemn warning. On August 22, 1940, the
Home Secretary had again to justify his policy before the House
of Commons. He began by stressing the fact that refugees
were " of enemy alien nationality as a matter of law and national
status," a doctrine which is probably bad law and certainly bad
sense (*see* Section 2). He and Mr. Peake advanced the following
fresh arguments for sticking to their policy of general internment:

" (1) Can we be sure that in the 60,000 ' C ' category aliens
there is not a proportion—it may be a small proportion
—who are enemy agents deliberately introduced by a
very determined and resourceful enemy ? I cannot
say we can be sure that there is not a proportion of
people of that description among these friendly enemy
aliens."—(Anderson).

" We have had definite cases, not of refugees committing
hostile acts . . . but of German agents, impersonating
refugees, who have been so detected, and it is, therefore, not impossible that there are some people whom
we honestly believe to be refugees in category C who
may be enemy agents."—(Peake).

" (2) Is it not the case that a fair proportion of those friendly
aliens still have friends and relations in Germany, still
have material interests in Germany, and as a result
might be subject to pressure which would lead them,
perhaps at the hour of our greatest peril, to take
action, on an impulse it may be, which afterwards they
might greatly regret ? "—(Anderson).

" (3) Is it not the case that these enemy aliens include quite
a large number who, perhaps because of the experience
they have gone through, are fundamentally defeatist,
who, if it appeared that the enemy was making progress
in an attempt to land on our shores or by parachute,
would lose heart, would be a source of weakness, and

would tend to lower the morale of the people around them, and might be tempted in the last resort to try to make terms ? "—(Anderson).

" (4) What we are not certain about in relation to a great number of these refugees is whether they are actively loyal to the British cause. After all, there is no very great reason why all of them should be. Many of them came here in transit to the United States of America and other overseas destinations. . . . They came here, no doubt, because their primary object was to secure freedom from oppression, and not because they wished from this country to carry on a war against the régime in Germany."—(Peake).

1–3.—Earl Winterton, with the approval of the Home Secretary, backed up statements about enemy agents masquerading as refugees with the following remarks :

" (a) Again and again in the countries on the Continent which were invaded by Germany it was found that refugees aided Nazis in their march." (For proof of this he referred to the Bland broadcast).

" (b) After these people were interned there was much less leakage of information from this country to the Continent than before they were interned."

(To this latter point we need only remark : after the surrender of France to the Nazis there was much less leakage of information from this country to the Continent than whilst France was still fighting.)

We have no doubt that there *are* a few Nazi agents masquerading as refugees and that they have caused leakages of information. But as we have pointed out, the most dangerous Nazi agents do not masquerade as refugees, because it is not the best disguise for a Nazi spy. The Nazis are thorough enough to select as their agents men who speak English perfectly or who are apparently in no way connected with Germany. But the presence of a few Nazi agents masquerading as refugees is *not* an argument for general internment. The French Government locked up all " enemy aliens " on the first day of war and "took no risks," but France was betrayed to the Nazis—by Frenchmen ; the German refugees were kept shut up at a stadium near Paris and their gaolers waited at the gates to hand the keys over to the Gestapo and the men inside to torture

and massacre. As Haffner has said, France lost her first battle
when the German refugees were interned. Wholesale internment of refugees amounts to an admission that the C.I.D., the
Military Intelligence and the counter-espionage services are
failing to do their work of tracking down suspects properly.
The Fifth Column that really matters is composed of
" patriotic " potential traitors of British nationality. To deal
with them on the same lines as refugees who are really spies
would involve the immediate internment of the whole of
Mayfair, the entire membership of the Conservative Party, the
Federation of British Industries and other employers' associations, the whole daytime population of the City of London,
half the Army officers ranking as Generals or higher, and every
man who lives on unearned income. That is the implication
of this hit-and-miss method of immobilising enemy agents,
preventing leakages of information and preventing treason.
Some M.P.s realise this. In the debate of August 22 Mr.
Pickthorn said :

> " If an archangel appeared before all the members of the
> War Cabinet at once and said, ' There is one red-headed
> man in England who, unless care is taken, will do something
> to injure the State,' I think it would be the duty of the War
> Cabinet to see that all red-headed men were interned. I should
> say it was their duty to do this at whatever cost in human
> misery, or at whatever risk to what is called British prestige."

That is precisely what " interning the lot " amounts to. Yet
the French Government, which was so zealous in rounding up
refugees, failed to apply these methods to its own traitors.
Our own Government does not do so either. Without pre-
suming to be archangels we can appear before the War Cabinet
and inform it that there are far more potential traitors to be
found among the wealthier classes of Britain than among the
refugees from Nazi oppression. If some refugees " still have
material interests " in Germany, are there not British men
who have material interests in this country which they might
seek to preserve—to the " sympathetic consternation " of Lord
Elibank—by betraying their country to the Nazis if the only
alternative were conscription of wealth and a people's war ?
That is what happened in France. For every " enemy alien "
refugee who has become " fundamentally defeatist " and would,
if Nazi invasion showed signs of succeeding, " lose heart . . .

and might be tempted in the last resort to try to make terms," there are a hundred Englishmen who certainly would do the same. It happened not only in France but even in Czechoslovakia, and the men who did these things were natives of their own countries. If *this* is to be the basis of internment, Mr. Norman Angell has estimated that a minimum of 250,000 British subjects, British-Italians and Dutch and Belgian refugees would have to be locked up forthwith to immobilise potential Quislings.

Interning anti-Nazi refugees does not mean security. Security is achieved by interning *suspects*, whether English or " alien." " But how can you decide who is a genuine refugee and who isn't ? " How do you decide who is a genuine British democrat and who is not ? The method is the same and the attitude ought to be the same : you judge them both by what they do and have done, by their records, including the statements of people who know them well and have no reason for being biased. If you are suspicious of a man he is watched, the police make inquiries and searches. If they find evidence, he may be brought before a court and charged ; or they may simply intern him.

4. Mr. Peake's argument that refugees may be dangerous *because many of them were not intending to stay here anyway*, but are planning to go to the U.S.A., is contemptible. These refugees were only admitted into this country on condition that they should *not* stay here permanently, but should proceed elsewhere as soon as possible. Having admitted them on sufferance and made them feel *de trop* the Government now uses its own past policy as a reason for locking them up ! But the situation in which this large group of refugees find themselves is undoubtedly embarrassing. However much many of the younger men may be eager to see Hitlerism smashed and to play a part in the struggle against the Nazis, they also have a definite chance of getting away from the muddle and misery of Europe and of starting a new life as free men overseas. In Britain they are now offered the choice of remaining interned until their boat sails for America or joining the Pioneer Corps in which they will serve the British Government, *without weapons in their hands*, under armed British officers and N.C.O.s, forsaking all their personal hopes for the future. It is a hard and cruel dilemma which does not confront the British soldier, who is conscripted without regard to his personal wishes. In such circumstances most Englishmen would have

a long and tough wrestle with their consciences before making up their minds. Can we really blame refugees who hesitate?

Internment Conditions in August, 1940.—In the debate of August 22, 1940, Mr. Peake's stock answer to M.P.s who complained about bad conditions in the camps was that all these abuses were things of the past, and that, since the Home Office took over the camps on August 5, rapid improvements were taking place. It was not, however, quite so simple as that. In August some of the worst camps—Wharf Mills, Prees Heath, Sutton Coldfield, Kempton Park—were closed down or about to be closed down. The process of transferring internees to the Isle of Man continued and relieved pressure on the mainland camps. But all our evidence goes to show that conditions in the camps were improving at little more than snail's pace. It is idle to present the reader with a full list of matters that needed remedying. These are obvious to anyone who has read Chapter III. We shall pick out only a few major issues.

(1) *Nazis and non-Nazis all through August*, 1940, *were still interned in the same camps*. On September 17, 1940, Mr. Peake explained that the Home Office was finding out from camp commandants (!) who were Nazi sympathisers, in order, " as soon as practicable," to put them all together in one camp. No steps were taken to define the legal status and rights of genuine refugees. It was reported from Huyton Camp that the commandant invited internees to claim the protection of the Swiss Legation. Out of 2,500 only 200 men did so, and thereby identified themselves as Nazi sympathisers. A report in mid-August stated:

" Many groups have been formed, e.g. a group of non-German and non-Austrian origin, a group of physicians without English diploma, a group of Dachauer and Buchenwalder,* a group of English residents, a group of students and research workers, a group of German Aryans, groups of members of different Churches, the Zionists, the Orthodox Jews, etc. Few realise that the formation of these groups entails the danger of splitting up the unity of the camp representatives. Several times the commandant put the question to the German group and the Church groups whether they felt themselves terrorised by the Jews. The Commandant also declared he does not expect loyalty but discipline ; . . . The German group, under the protection

* Men who had been in Dachau or Buchenwald concentration camps in Germany.

of the Swiss Consulate, consists of Nazis, Nazi sympathisers and a number of German civilian internees (*Auslandsdeutsche*), who are under a certain amount of moral pressure. All together they are only about 5 per cent. of the camp inhabitants. The Commandant would like it best to see the internees divided in companies of about 600 persons and each company surrounded by barbed wire. They would even be provided with separate kitchens. Two rows of houses form a company under the command of an officer. Practical considerations were an obstacle to this separation. But as the unity of the camp inhabitants showed unwelcome results for the commandant an attempt was made to enforce the above-mentioned regulations. But it remained a mere attempt. . . ."

A report of about the same date from one of the Isle of Man camps stated that a small group of Nazis and sympathisers had not been deported with the rest in July, 1940, mainly because a number of them were camp officials. These men remained in key positions in the camp administration (e.g. they had access to the lists and the mail) until pressure culminating in a street demonstration forced their resignation.

(2) *Families remained separated.*—All through August and September there was still no news that husbands and wives interned separately were being brought together, or even allowed to visit one another except in the most exceptional circumstances. Nor were there any provisions for reuniting families split up by internment (e.g. by allowing non-interned wives to join their husbands).

(3) *Postal delays.*—After the Home Office decision to apply a hit-and-miss censorship of correspondence (censoring as many letters as possible each day, and then forwarding *all* the day's letters), there appears to have been a definite improvement in the communications from the middle of August, although there were still many complaints in September.

(4) *Information and Records.*—Progress in clearing up this muddle was less rapid. The Information Bureau which was opened in London on Monday, August 12, with a totally inadequate staff, made a poor start. From the moment it opened its doors it was completely snowed under with women inquiring about their interned menfolk. What the Bureau needed was a quadrupled staff, consisting of people who speak German and Italian, and adequate records from the Home Office. Cases have come to our notice of men who were said

by the Bureau to be in Canada, but when their refugee organisations cabled inquiries the reply came back that no persons with those names had arrived in Canada. We hope that by the time this book is on sale this particular muddle will have been cleared up. It is totally inexcusable.

(5) *Material Conditions.*—Latest reports show that camp conditions began to improve after the Home Office took over, but at an incredibly slow and unsatisfactory rate.

(6) *Cultural Facilities.*—Most reports show considerable improvements in this respect, although, if genuine refugees are to be kept locked up, far more is needed to make internment tolerable. The Government has never spent a single penny on assisting cultural organisations of the refugees to develop their work. It has at least a clear duty to assist the efforts of the refugees in the camps to turn them into cultural centres of which they can be proud.

(7) *Medical and first-aid facilities.*—Slight improvements in these are also reported from most camps, but at the end of August the provision in all camps still appeared totally insufficient and disgraceful.

(8) *Machinery.*—A major cause of the unsatisfactory state of affairs which still existed in August was the apparent total lack of adequate official machinery to deal with the situation. In spite of a considerable expansion of staff, every branch of the administrative apparatus dealing with internment and release from internment appears to have been grossly deficient in personnel. If the Home Secretary does not decide (*a*) to release large numbers of non-suspects rapidly, and (*b*) to expand his staff enormously for the time being, the administrative muddle is bound to be prolonged and improvements in internment conditions are bound to be extremely slow. To make internment really tolerable can only be done by a rapid reduction of the camp populations through large-scale releases. The Home Office hopes to make internment conditions tolerable by reducing camp populations (*a*) by speeding up release of exempted men, (*b*) by recruiting men into the Pioneer Corps, (*c*) by releasing men about to proceed to America. We doubt whether enough men will be drawn out along these channels before winter sets in even if speeding up of releases of exempted men really takes place. On September 17, 1940, Mr. Peake was only able to announce that 2,516 internees had been released (the interned invalids alone probably numbered as

many as this). Innumerable suggestions for improvements in the official machinery dealing with internees have been suggested. We do not propose to discuss them. If the Home Office were working in the right spirit creating the appropriate machinery would present no difficulty. If the will were there the means could be found.

2. *The Legal Status of Refugees*

If it is the Government's entire internment policy that is wrongly conceived, and not simply the conditions under which internment took place, if it would still be wrong to keep locked up thousands of refugees against whom there are no grounds for suspicion at all, even if they are locked up in nice hygienic prisons, what is the right basis for a constructive " enemy aliens " policy ? Let it be understood at the outset that we do not question the necessity of interning or deporting against their will German or Italian soldiers, sailors or airmen captured in the course of the war ; nor do we object to similar treatment for German civilians who are clearly and willingly citizens of Nazi Germany or betray Nazi or nationalist sympathies (similarly in the case of the Italians). These two groups, however, constitute a very small minority of the " enemy aliens " in this country. The great majority of German and Austrian " enemy aliens " fall into three groups : (1) those who have lived in England for many years and are therefore not technically refugees, although they are non-Nazi or anti-Nazi, and have no wish to return to Nazi Germany or definite reasons for fearing to do so ; (2) refugees who came to England and have settled down here and wish to stay ; (3) refugees who came to England as visitors for a period, intending to re-emigrate as soon as their arrangements were settled. The third group is the largest; the first group is quite small. Each of these three main categories can be subdivided into many smaller groups differing from one another in their exact legal status according to the part of the Reich from which they came, the date of their departure, the nature of their travel documents, the conditions under which they were allowed to enter Britain, or for some other technical reason. There are in consequence many complications about deciding whether a *technical* " enemy alien " is a *real* " enemy alien."

The clear intention of the Convention of 1938 on the status of refugees coming from Germany (since extended to Austrians and Sudeten refugees and provisionally to Czech refugees until the League takes a final decision) was that its provisions should apply to all genuine refugees. But the definition of a " refugee coming from Germany " is not an easy matter. The Convention excludes " persons who leave Germany [Austria, Czechoslovakia, the Sudeten territory] for reasons of purely personal convenience," and defines refugees as follows :

" (*a*) Persons possessing or having possessed German nationality and not possessing any other nationality who are proved not to enjoy, *in law or in fact*, the protection of the German Government.

" (*b*) Stateless persons not covered by previous Conventions or Agreements who have left German territory after being established therein and who are proved not to enjoy, *in law or in fact*, the protection of the German Government."

The two main snags about this definition are : (*a*) the phrase " in law or in fact," which may mean a great deal or very little ; (*b*) the fact that the Convention does not indicate who is to be the *defining party* who shall decide whether " in law or in fact " a person claiming to be a refugee does not enjoy the protection of the German Government. Although the League Commissioner has to see that this Convention is applied, it is clear that his office cannot take on powers of definition since his staff (for the entire world) is limited to three assistants, four typists, and an office keeper. In practice the British Government has been the defining party for refugees in this country so that, as far as Britain is concerned, the groups of refugees technically placed under the High Commissioner's protection have depended entirely on the way in which the British authorities have treated refugees. Before the outbreak of war there is no doubt that the British Government behaved reasonably and fairly, and genuinely considered that the great bulk of refugees, whatever the complications of individual cases, were covered by the Convention of 1938. When war broke out, however, it gradually began to disregard the Convention, which it could quite properly do because of the Convention's vagueness about the authority responsible for defining a refugee. When general internment began all refugees once again became " enemy aliens " and prisoners of war. Sir John Anderson's description of *all* internees as " aliens of enemy nationality " (when he announced the formation of the Asquith Committee) and the repeated statements in August that the Dominions Governments were applying the

Prisoners of War Convention to the internees, coupled with the fact that even C Class internees sent to Australia had to be written to via the Prisoners of War Bureau, Melbourne, are all indications of an immense retreat on the part of the official mind from the former fairly clear distinction between Nazi or Fascist subjects and refugees from the Nazis or Fascists.

The British Government, which had created through the tribunal an officially recognised class of " refugees from Nazi oppression," later proceeded to ignore its own distinction, interning all and sundry alike. It should be clearly understood that the power of defining a " refugee from Nazi oppression " should not appertain to the British Government at all. The Government has no power to decide who is a Canadian and who is not. That is a matter for the Canadian Government. If a Canadian in Britain gets into difficulties with the authorities he can claim the intervention and protection of the Canadian High Commissioner, behind whom stands the Canadian Government. Similarly with a man who claims to be a refugee : *it is not the British or any other Government that should define a refugee, but the High Commissioner for Refugees behind whom stands (in theory only) the League of Nations*. But because the Convention defines a refugee in a very narrow and difficult manner, because the High Commissioner's powers of definition are very obscure, because the League of Nations is an idea rather than a reality at present and has, for practical purposes, become dematerialised into an aura of the British Government, things have not worked out according to theory. In the absence of any clearly acknowledged defining and protecting authority the British Government had to set up its own defining machinery. The tribunals were given not only the legitimate function of sorting out the sheep (C) and the goats (A) and the animals of dubious parentage (B) among the " enemy aliens," but the further function of deciding who was and who was not a refugee. In theory this should have been none of their business ; in practice it was inevitable that they should be given defining powers. Yet, since the tribunals' definitions were later completely ignored, it is difficult to see why anybody ever bothered to invent a category of " refugees from Nazi oppression," unless it was a mere political gesture that has since served its purpose.

Before examining the 1938 Convention on the Status of Refugees it is necessary to state why the Prisoners of War

Convention should *not* be applied to interned refugees. It is *only* the humanitarian provisions of the Prisoners of War Convention, prescribing standards of material comfort and of freedom of communication with the outside world, that should be applied to interned refugees, not as a norm, but as a rock-bottom minimum above which they should be raised as quickly as possible, precisely because they are *not* prisoners of war. It would be highly dangerous and harmful, however, officially to apply the Prisoners of War Convention to interned refugees for the following reasons :

1. Because they would come under the protection of the Swiss Government acting on behalf of the Nazi regime. The British Government is required to supply all necessary information about prisoners of war either to the Protecting Power or to the International Red Cross, both of which are obliged to pass on such information to the Nazi Government. In 1938 the Nazi Government attempted to trace the whereabouts of refugees by instructing all holders of German passports living abroad to register at the nearest German consulate without delay. Thousands of refugees refused to do so because they had no desire for the Nazis to know their whereabouts. If the British Government itself is to pass on information about these same men, now interned, to the Nazis, is it not a clear case of helping the enemy ? (The *Arandora Star* lists—but only the names of the drowned and the missing—were passed on to the Nazis, through the Swiss Legation, without, it appears, any attempt to distinguish between Nazis and anti-Nazis. Similarly the Italian lists were passed on, via the Brazilian Embassy, to Mussolini. He, no doubt, was gratified to learn that Mr. Anzani had been drowned.)

2. Another provision of the Convention is that prisoners of war shall be sent to their own country as soon as possible after the conclusion of peace. But few refugees would wish to return to Germany or Austria unless there were definite guarantees that their lives would be safe. Many have started new lives in this country and would in time become valuable British citizens ; many more intend to go overseas with their families to make a fresh start. Are all such men to be re-patriated willy nilly ?

3. Finally, the treatment of all refugees as prisoners of war is a gratuitous insult to the thousands of internees who have never acknowledged any allegiance to Hitler and the Nazi

state.   To treat them as " enemy aliens " is flying in the face of all the facts, and has had, and will continue to have, a highly damaging effect upon their morale and their opinion of Britain generally.

Whether interned or not, therefore, all genuine refugees must be clearly distinguished from Nazis, Nazi sympathisers and suspected supporters of the Nazis, and must be treated quite differently from prisoners of war.   Prisoners of war have a clearly defined legal status and a Protecting Power ; refugees have not, but must have.   Leaving aside the question of how to decide who is and who is not a refugee, the first need of genuine refugees is for a charter of rights.   Although they were becoming part of the British community by sharing in its fate, because they are foreigners they are denied, in common with all other foreigners, certain liberties which only Englishmen enjoy ; because they are citizens of no existing State which can insist on their proper treatment, they are denied certain liberties which all other foreigners (including " enemy alien " prisoners of war) enjoy ; because they are regarded as " aliens of enemy nationality " without being subjects of an enemy State, the British Government is more or less free to do what it likes with them.

Clearly the first thing to do is to rule out all distinctions made between non-Britons in this country that are based solely on place of birth or former citizenship.   A man who is a genuine anti-Nazi should not be interned without trial, whether he was born in Berlin, Vienna or Prague, Brussels, Amsterdam, Paris, Camberwell, Winchester or Glasgow.   As Mr. Peake himself remarked in the debate of July 10 :

" I think it is extremely important for the House to bear in mind that labels of nationality in Europe have meant very little in the last twenty years. They are no guide, or very little guide, to the sympathies of the individual or to his reliability."

Belgians, Dutch, Norwegians, Poles, Czechs, Austrians, Germans, Italians who are genuine refugees are all victims and enemies of the same evil thing, and it is futile and harmful to discriminate between them on the basis of the particular country of which they were once citizens or in which they were born.   All refugees alike suffer from the absence of a clearly defined and generally accepted Charter of Refugee Rights, which will ensure that they are not left entirely in the hands of the Government of the country in which they are living.

The basis for such a Charter of Rights already exists in the Conventions of 1933 (for " Nansen " refugees) and 1938 (for German, Austrian, Sudeten and Czech refugees from the Nazis). The two Conventions are very nearly identical in their wording, but we quote the provisions of the 1938 Convention. The Convention was signed, according to the preamble, by Governments who were

" desirous that refugees shall be ensured the enjoyment of civil rights, free and ready access to the courts, security and stability as regards establishment and work, facilities in the exercise of the professions, of industry and commerce, and in regard to the movement of persons, admission to schools and universities."

Chapter I defines refugees. Chapter II, in cautious language, guarantees refugees a " right of asylum " :

" *Without prejudice to the power of any High Contracting Party to regulate the right of sojourn and residence,* a refugee shall be entitled to move about freely, to sojourn or reside in the territory to which the present Convention applies, in accordance with the laws and internal regulations applying therein."

According to this the British Government cannot abolish the " right of asylum," but can only *regulate* it. Chapter III provides for Governments to issue travel documents to refugees. Chapter IV provides that :

" In every case in which a refugee is required to leave the territory of one of the High Contracting Parties to which the present Convention applies, he shall be granted a suitable period to make the necessary arrangements."

It adds that refugees may *only* be expelled if " such measures are dictated by reasons of national security or public order." The British Government, however, added a reservation to this clause to the effect that it would not apply to refugees admitted only temporarily—i.e. as transit immigrants.

Chapter V makes provision for the legal standing of refugees. Article 6 is very carefully worded :

" The personal status of refugees who have retained their original nationality shall be governed by the rules applicable in the country concerned to foreigners possessing a nationality. . . . The personal status of refugees having no nationality shall be governed by the law of their country of domicile, or, failing such, by the law of their country of residence."

In view of the highly complicated position of the majority of refugees who have never been formally deprived of their nationality by Hitler, especially of that great number who came into Britain after the pogrom of November, 1938, many of whom may still possess valid German passports, it is extremely difficult to decide which refugees have still retained " their original nationality " and which refugees possess no nationality. Everything depends on the British Government's own interpretation of these categories. It is not clear whether the 55,000 officially recognised " refugees from Nazi oppression " are officially regarded as still possessing " their original nationality." Apparently, since May, 1940, at any rate, they are. But Article 8 of the Convention is much more explicit :

" Refugees shall have, in the territories to which the present Convention applies, *free and ready access to the courts of law.*

" In the countries in which they have their domicile or regular residence, *they shall enjoy in this respect*, save where otherwise expressly provided by law, *the same rights and privileges as nationals.* They shall on the same conditions enjoy the benefit of legal assistance and be exempt from *Cautio judicatum solvi.*"

No doubt there are legal loopholes even in this provision, but there are no loopholes for a Government which seeks to act wisely and humanely. The whole spirit of Article 8 is in flat contradiction to the way interned refugees were treated from May, 1940, onwards. And the British Government has not, as far as we know, " otherwise expressly provided by law." The sole question here is whether Britain is still a territory " to which the present Convention applies."

Chapter VI deals with the right to work and is accepted by the Government except for refugees holding transit visas (the majority) :

" 1. The restrictions ensuing from the application of laws and regulations for the protection of the national labour market *shall not be applied in all their severity* to refugees domiciled or regularly resident in the country."

" 2. They shall be *automatically* suspended in favour of refugees domiciled or regularly resident in the country, if one of the following conditions is fulfilled :

(*a*) The refugee has been resident for not less than three years in the country.

(*b*) The refugee is married to a person possessing the nationality of the country of residence.

(*c*) The refugee has one or more children possessing the nationality of the country of residence."

Clause 2 is explicit enough, but it is doubtful whether, prior to November, 1939, its provisions were put into operation in any systematic way for refugees fulfilling those conditions. Chapter VIII, Article 13, states :

" Refugees shall, as regards the setting up of associations for mutual relief and assistance and admission to the said associations, enjoy in the territories of the High Contracting Parties to which the present Convention applies the most favourable treatment accorded to the nationals of a foreign country."

In view of the many reported attempts of Chief Constables to prevent refugees from meeting together to promote their common interests, it is not clear how far this provision is observed.

Chapter IX makes a provision to which the British Government refused to put its name, " owing to the special position of schools and universities in the United Kingdom " :

" Refugees shall enjoy in the schools, courses, faculties and universities of each of the High Contracting Parties treatment as favourable as other foreigners in general. They shall benefit in particular to the same extent as the latter by the total or partial remission of fees and charges and the award of scholarships."

Why should the British Government refuse to treat refugees as well as " other foreigners in general " ?

Chapter XII is highly important :

" The enjoyment of certain rights and the benefit of certain favours accorded to foreigners subject to reciprocity shall not be refused to refugees in the absence of reciprocity."

It is precisely this absence of reciprocity—i.e. the absence of counterparts to our refugees in Nazi territory against whom reprisals can be applied—which has made it possible for the Government to disregard many of the provisions of this Convention and to treat refugees in a way in which it would not dare to treat the citizens of any State not at war with Britain or even Nazi prisoners of war.

The British Government, however, made one reservation to the whole Convention (and to the 1933 Convention on " Nansen " Refugees) which can, if the Government so decides, render its provisions nugatory as far as most refugees in Britain are concerned. As to the definition of a refugee contained in Article 1 of the Convention, the Government stated :

> " His Majesty's Government in the United Kingdom regards the definition *as applicable only to refugees coming from Germany as defined, who at the date of ratification no longer enjoy the protection of the German Government.*"

This vague phrase, as Sir John Hope Simpson points out,*

> " is open to an interpretation that refugees who come to Great Britain after the dates referred to [October, 1936, for " Nansen " refugees, September, 1938, for refugees from the Nazis] would not be considered by the British Government as refugees to whom the Conventions apply."

The Government thus has as many loopholes as it could wish for to evade almost all the provisions of the Convention so far as almost all refugees are concerned. That it should do so is contrary to the spirit of the Convention and to common decency ; but there can be no doubt that it has done so.

Nevertheless, if this Convention were clearly operated in the spirit in which it was intended, it could be made into the foundation of a Charter of Refugee Rights. But in itself the Convention is insufficient, and needs supplementing by a number of other provisions which could conveniently be put into a short Act, Order in Council or formal declaration on the part of the Government. The most important additional points of such a Charter are :

(1) An explicit restoration into British law of the " right of asylum."

(2) The explicit according to refugees of certain common rights of Englishmen, most of which derive from the principle of *Habeas Corpus*. Especially :

(a) Right to trial with legal assistance and presentation of charges with evidence before a properly constituted court of law. No refugee to be interned except by order of such a court.

* *The Refugee Problem* (1939).

(*b*) Right to appeal against internment.

(*c*) Right, if released from internment, to sue for wrongful imprisonment and to claim redress and damages for injury to health or capacity to work and for loss of property, employment opportunities or business connections.

(These basic liberties seem to be implied in Article 8 of the Convention.)

(3) Refugees to be permitted the same rights of meeting together in private or in public as are accorded to all British citizens.

(4) No compulsory deportation of *classes* of refugees, but only of individuals who have been interned by order of a properly constituted court after examination of the evidence against them. (This is implied in the " right of asylum.")

The " right of asylum " does not exist in British law, except in so far as the British Government cares to apply the Conventions on Refugees of 1933 and 1938. It is in any case nôt strictly speaking a right, but a privilege conferred by the State on non-citizens. So confused is the whole position of nationality both in " international law " and in British legislation, that a refugee without any valid passport and possessing a British travel paper, issued in accordance with the provisions of the Conventions of 1933 and 1938, can still be regarded as possessing the nationality of the country of which he used to be a citizen, even if he enjoys the protection of the government of that country neither in law nor in fact. Even John Heartfield, formally deprived of his German citizenship, can still be called an " enemy alien." The issuing of travel documents to stateless persons implies no administrative distinction in British law between "aliens " and refugees. In practice, as Hope Simpson (*op. cit.*) points out, the distinction implied in the Conventions of 1933 and 1938

" has been made at the discretion of Government officials concerned, who have given sympathetic attention to the claims of the refugee and to the representations of private organisations helping refugees."

As we have seen, as the war progressed, Government officials have gradually used their discretion almost completely to abolish the distinction they at one time recognised fairly explicitly. Yet the privilege of asylum is not only an ancient and honourable tradition of most democratic countries, but *in Britain it was given explicit recognition in the Aliens Act of 1905 which expressly provided that admission should not be refused to persons who sought shelter purely on religious or political grounds.* This generous expression of British liberalism was swept away by the first world war and has never reappeared in subsequent legislation. Its abolition is something to be ashamed of. Even a country like Mexico before war broke out was putting the British Empire to shame in this respect. Right now, in the midst of the second world war, no finer gesture to demonstrate the sincerity of Britain's intentions could be made than to make a public declaration restoring the " right of asylum " by some provision such as that of the Act of 1905.

Our second point, based mainly on the principles of *Habeas Corpus*, needs little amplification. Neither Sir Oswald Mosley nor Welsh Communists, neither Czech Legionaries who object to anti-semitic officers, nor French Foreign Legionaries who refuse to serve under semi-Fascist Pétainist officers of the French regular army, neither anti-Nazi refugees nor Italian café proprietors should be interned without trial or presentation of evidence before a court. Interned refugees have no right of appeal at all, although they may now apply for release, if apparently falling in one of the exempted categories. In this respect they are worse treated than Sir Oswald Mosley and Sir Barry Domvile, who can appeal to the Advisory Committee under Mr. Norman Birkett. But appeal to an Advisory Committee which can only recommend release to the Home Secretary is insufficient. Internees, whether British, " friendly " or " enemy aliens," should have a right of appeal to a court or tribunal with powers to *order* their release, and should have the right to appear personally and to be legally represented before such a body. All this may sound like " old-fashioned liberalism," but Britain is supposed to be fighting to preserve the very modern and progressive principles that are the strength of " old-fashioned liberalism." If a military emergency arises the Government has power to sweep aside in a moment all our traditional checks and guarantees against oppressive action by the executive. If this is clearly done in the interests of the nation the people will accept it without a murmur. But it should not be done before such an emergency does arise. The right of redress for wrongful imprisonment and of damages for injury to person, property, business connections, working capacity or personal reputation is again a liberty which has been encroached upon both for British subjects and for " aliens " of all sorts. But especially in the case of interned refugees is it urgently necessary to insist on the need for such a guarantee. It is nothing short of a scandal that released refugees, whose luggage, money and papers have been mislaid during internment, are compelled to sign a statement that they make no claims against the camp authorities. Because they have been interned under laws permitting the locking-up of all " aliens of enemy nationality " they can make no claims whatever for compensation for damaged health or ruined business, let alone the general suspicion that surrounds a man who has been released from internment.

Our third and fourth points (the right of meeting together and no deportation except after proper trial before a court) need no explanation. Refugees cannot protect their interests unless they are free to meet. The peace-time practice which obliged the police to obtain a deportation order from a magistrate, before whom the " alien " in question had to be produced, should be restored without delay.

3. *A Protecting Power for Refugees*

For the enforcement of a Charter of Refugee Rights an authority independent of the Government is required to protect and defend refugees and to ensure that the Government lives up to the spirit of its undertakings. But, before discussing the question of a Protecting Power for refugees, it is necessary to see how refugees can be identified and who should identify them. In theory, we have argued, identifying refugees should be no business of the British Government, which should only be concerned with classifying refugees (and British subjects) from the point of view of security. But in the present position, in the middle of a war in which the League of Nations, which should be responsible for refugees, has ceased to function effectively, it is obvious that the Government had to create machinery which would attempt to identify genuine refugees. It is not in fact a difficult matter to decide —as far as the great majority of " enemy aliens " are concerned —who is and who is not genuinely a refugee from Nazi oppression.

Although we have criticised the work of the tribunals which examined " enemy aliens " in individual cases, on the whole there can be no doubt that in a rough-and-ready manner their classification of " enemy aliens " into refugees and non-refugees was broadly correct.   Unless a hair-splitting legalistic definition—the kind of definition Governments like to have—of the term " refugee " is attempted, the genuine refugee can be found quite easily, because so much more is known about him than about almost any British citizen. Let all non-suspects be released. Let all against whom the police have a shred of evidence remain interned until, as suggested in Section 1, new tribunals have reviewed their cases. Let any released internee against whom the police develop any suspicion be brought before another tribunal and re-examined. If the tribunals are properly constituted, and are assisted by the refugee organisations and other people who know about " enemy alien " problems, if they work as courts of law and allow the " enemy aliens " to hear the evidence and reply to it, the sorting out of genuine refugees should be fairly simple. The difficulty is not about identifying the genuine refugees, but about disentangling the precise legal status of the many groups that exist among refugees. Yet the present muddle over the legal status of refugees can be very simply cleared up by putting all genuine identified refugees in to a clearly distinct category of non-Britons who are *not* " enemy aliens " or prisoners of war, but simply *refugees under the protection of the High Commissioner for Refugees*. If this is done there is no particular reason why one group of refugees from Nazi terror or *Blitzkrieg*, namely, those who came from Germany or Austria, should be singled out for exceptional treatment, while other groups of refugees, from Belgium or Holland, for example, are treated a good deal better. If all genuine refugees, whatever their origin, are clearly understood to be under the High Commissioner's protection, their status guaranteed by an honest acceptance of the provisions of the 1933 and 1938 Conventions, and if the British Government offers facilities to the High Commissioner to develop his work of protection, one of the major difficulties of the outcasts from Nazi occupied territories will be well on the way to solution.

The League of Nations High Commissioner for Refugees is Sir Herbert Emerson (until recently Governor of the Punjab). His mandate from the League of Nations instructs him :—

(*a*) To provide for legal and political protection of refugees ;

(*b*) To superintend the entry into force and application of the legal status guaranteed to refugees under the Convention of 1938;

(*c*) To facilitate the co-ordination of humanitarian assistance ;

(*d*) To assist the Governments and private organisations in their efforts to promote emigration and permanent settlement.

In Chapter II, Section 2, we have already described some of the limitations under which the High Commissioner has to work—a staff restricted to one office in London, severely restricted funds, nothing but diplomatic standing, not even the full backing of the League, which accepts no responsibility for his actions but leaves him very free to act as he thinks fit. The League itself in war-time is in a rather similar position to the High Commissioner, so that Sir Herbert's whole status is uncertain and curious and his world importance not as great as it might be. Willy nilly, the course of the war has increasingly restricted the scope of his activities to the English-speaking countries and he seems to be developing, with the League itself, out of an international authority into a semi-official of the British Government. Thus, in addition to being High Commissioner and Director of the Evian Committee, he sits on the Asquith Committee to advise the Government on internment policy, is Vice-Chairman of the Lytton Council to advise the Government on the control of " aliens " and the welfare and employment of internees, and is Chairman of the Central Committee for War Refugees, which advises the Ministry of Health on matters relating to the welfare of " alien war refugees from Holland and Belgium," of whom there are about 20,000 in the country. Dr. Kullmann, Sir Herbert's Deputy, is honorary secretary of the latter body.

It is gratifying to see how willing the Government is to obtain the advice of an important League official, but are all Sir Herbert's new commitments compatible either with his status as High Commissioner or with the international work he has to do ? The High Commissioner has not had his mandate extended to cover war-time refugees from Belgium and Holland, but he and his deputy occupy the key positions in the committee which advises the British Government about them, and everything points to the fact that they are doing excellent work. The High Commissioner's membership of the Lytton Council can also be justified, since it gives him an opportunity of pressing for a clear recognition of the rights of refugees under his protection.   But it does not seem very easy to explain his presence on the Asquith Committee, the functions of which are clearly outside his League mandate.   In any case, is it wise for an international authority who has the duty of protecting refugees to associate himself, with the best intentions of the world, so closely with one of the most important Governments against which he should at present be protecting refugees and fighting stubbornly—and, if necessary, in public—for a clear recognition of the status of refugees ?   If he has to intervene with other Governments on behalf of refugees in the course of his duties as High Commissioner, will they regard him as an international authority of independent standing or as an unofficial representative of the British Government ?

In practice, of course, the collapse of the League of Nations and the gradual abandonment by the British Government of any pretence of acting in the spirit of the 1938 Convention have cut the ground from under the High Commissioner's feet.   His eagerness, as a patriotic Englishman, to make himself useful in other ways can be perfectly well understood. Nevertheless we feel that he has the task of dissociating himself from the British Government and of asserting himself as official protecting power for refugees.   But he cannot successfully carry out such a task without a big change of attitude on the part of the British Government.   For it is perfectly clear that the Convention of 1938 and the reservations added to it by the Government are so full of loopholes and escape clauses that the Government can perfectly well recognise the Convention in theory and totally disregard it in practice.   In peacetime officials did use their discretion very much in the spirit of the Convention ; but they did have discretion in the matter.   It is not generally realised by Englishmen (who usually resent absurd formality when they travel in countries where they are " aliens ") how great is the power concentrated by British Aliens Acts in the hands of the Home Secretary. Even in peacetime, according to the most recent study of the law relating to foreigners (C. F. Fraser : *Aliens in the British Empire*, 1940), the Home Secretary has the power vested in him, at his own discretion " without giving reasons or public indication of his intention, to effect the exclusion of any and every class of alien."   Such being the case, there is no hope of the High Commissioner getting the Convention of 1938 enforced in Britain unless the Government itself is once again prepared to act in the spirit of the Convention and to recognise the High Commissioner as the supervising and protecting power.   This change of attitude will have to be forced upon the Government by pressure of public opinion, in fostering which the High Commissioner could play an important part.

Supposing the Government *did* change its attitude, and was anxious to see that every genuine refugee did get the rights guaranteed under the Convention, and was willing to assist the High Commissioner to act as the refugees' protector—what could be done ?

(1) The Government could inform all interned refugees that they can place themselves under the High Commissioner's protection, and can appeal for his intervention.   The great majority of interned refugees still have to rely for protection on occasional visits to their camps from a Bloomsbury House liaison officer.   If the High Commissioner insists on being the internees' protecting power the Government would have to help him.   He would need a considerable staff to organise regular and thorough visits to the camps.   His mandate restricts his staff to a quite inadequate degree, but there is nothing to prevent the British Government itself providing the means whereby the High Commissioner could build up an Interned Refugees' Department attached to his office.   The Swiss Legation enforces the Prisoners of War Convention ; what internment standards would the High Commissioner enforce ?   It is evident that a programme of minimum intern- ment conditions for refugees is required.   The High Commissioner in collaboration with the voluntary organisations, the organisations of the refugees, and with the men in the camps themselves should draw up such a programme and insist on its enforcement.   He should also take over the Information Bureau for internees set up by the Government in August, 1940.

(2) All this is only the most immediate step.   If camp- visiting and providing information about interned refugees were the only functions of the High Commissioner, it might as well be left to him as a member of the Asquith Committee and the Lytton Council.   His next step should be to insist on rapid release of all non-suspect internees, in accordance with the personal liberties guaranteed in the Convention.

(3) His third step should be to aim at building up a service of advice and information for refugees on questions relating

to their legal status. Foreigners in difficulties usually go to their nearest consulate or legation for assistance. The High Commissioner should aim at setting up bureaux in the largest towns which would enjoy quasi-consular functions in relation to refugees. These services could also be planned in co-operation with refugee organisations of all types.

(4) The High Commissioner should aim at setting up in Britain an organisation on lines similar to the Nansen International Office for Refugees, possessing quasi-consular functions and powers of definition. It should aim once and for all at getting identified all those persons in this country who are refugees coming under the High Commissioner's protection. Provided some simple and not too legalistic definition of a refugee were adopted all persons who claimed to be refugees, and who could produce sufficient evidence to arouse no doubts in the minds of the tribunals, could be automatically put under the High Commissioner's protection. As at present, any doubtful individual should be brought before an appropriate court or tribunal which should consider the evidence against him and give him a chance to defend himself. A representative of the High Commissioner's Office might watch such proceedings in order to satisfy himself that the tribunals were functioning fairly. In all cases of doubt the organisations of and for refugees and the police should furnish the High Commissioner's Office with information to assist it to decide whether or not a given person is a refugee. We are confident that the task of identifying genuine refugees is a relatively simple matter provided the will to do so is there. Once a refugee is identified all talk about " enemy aliens " should be dropped. The High Commissioner's Office should itself have the power to issue " Emerson Passports," identity and travel documents which make it clear that their holders do not enjoy the protection of any state but are refugees under the protection of the League High Commissioner.

(5) So much the High Commissioner, if encouraged and assisted by the British Government, could do as protecting power for refugees. He is completely free to appoint advisory bodies of every kind to assist him in his work. We see no reason why he should not bring together—quite apart from his consultations with the voluntary societies—representatives of the Czech Working Committee, the Council of Austrians, the Free German League of Culture, the *Notgemeinschaft* and

other organisations of refugees. They represent large sections of the people he protects and he should work with them and know their wishes. Owing to the peculiarities of the situation we have treated the High Commissioner as if he were simply operating in Great Britain. It would be well to start such an organisation in Britain, but it would have to expand overseas and become international as and when circumstances permitted.

(6) To begin with, the Emerson Office, if it took its protecting powers seriously, would have to open up departments for the welfare of interned refugees in Canada and Australia. The need for something of the sort is evident, since in August the Home Office both refused to send a liaison officer to Canada or Australia to watch over internment conditions and refused to allow welfare officers to be sent over by the voluntary organisations. In due course the Emerson Office organisation could be extended to all parts of the British Empire and the " Emerson passport " might be accepted as a travel document within the Empire. A little tactful pressure from London should ensure that the Dominions provide the necessary facilities. The U.S.A. and other American States might next be approached, and asked to co-operate with the Emerson Office and to recognise its passports.

These developments take us into the speculative future, but they are not impracticable. The League of Nations wound up the Nansen Office in 1938 ; yet the urgent need to-day is for a new Nansen Office embracing all refugees. The Nansen Office grew out of the refugee problems that followed the last war. May there not be need for a new and better Nansen Office when this war is over ? It is not fashionable in England to think when there is a war on, especially to think about what will come after the war. To say the least, it is highly probable that this war will also produce a large-scale refugee problem in addition to the one already on our hands. A Nansen Office will be needed. The sort of development of the High Commissioner's work we have proposed would create within the Empire, and possibly in America, the structure of an organisation which would rapidly be extended to other countries when war ceased and the post-war refugee problem began. The High Commissioner therefore has important and difficult tasks before him if he takes his duties as protector of refugees seriously, and if he can envisage the possibilities of winning support, especially in America, for the elaboration during the war of an

Emerson International Office to function on a world scale immediately the war is ended.

We have suggested that in themselves the provisions of the 1933 and 1938 Conventions are insufficient to guarantee to refugees the full rights they should be entitled to enjoy. To complete the Charter of Refugee Rights four further guarantees are necessary : (*a*) the " right of asylum," (*b*) the right to a fair trial, appeal and redress for wrongful imprisonment, (*c*) right of assembly, and (*d*) no compulsory deportation (which is implied in the " right of asylum "). These guarantees will again only be given by the Government when forced to do so by pressure of public opinion, which the High Commissioner could assist in promoting. The second and third points affect British citizens just as much as refugees and other " aliens." Since they are integral elements of British liberty, the British public cannot afford to stand aside and see these liberties filched away from foreigners who have sought sanctuary in this country. If *Habeas Corpus* is the Englishman's birthright, can he deny it to fellow members of the British community, which is what the refugees were becoming prior to May, 1940, simply because they do not, as non-Britons, enjoy full citizen rights in this country ? For the sake of their own liberties Englishmen must insist on the guaranteeing of the principles of *Habeas Corpus* and the right of assembly to refugees ; for the sake of England's good name they must insist on an explicit recognition by the Government that refugees are a distinct group not to be confused with " enemy aliens " at all, and that they are a group of non-Britons to whom a " right of asylum " shall be afforded without question.

These matters are the concern of British citizens. If they neglect them the refugees will come to feel that they are not wanted in Britain, but are in the way and only tolerated on sufferance, and will seek to get away from England at the earliest possible opportunity. This *British* problem, the problem of the British attitude to " aliens," has got to be solved quickly. People must make up their minds about civil liberties and see to it that all unnecessary encroachment on the freedom of refugees, other " aliens " and British subjects alike are not tolerated. If the Charter of Refugee Rights is to be enforced we must have a public opinion in this country which insists that the Government shall operate the 1933 and 1938 Conventions in the spirit in which they were intended ; shall proclaim the fact that it recognises the High Commissioner as protector of all refugees (irrespective of the muddle about the exact position of different groups of refugees in " international law " and the High Commissioner's rather obscure connections with a League of Nations that has ceased to function) ; shall publicly state its intention of assisting and facilitating the work of the High Commissioner in every way and shall do all in its power to ensure him an independent and authoritative standing ; and that the Government shall publicly announce the guaranteeing of those other necessary liberties of refugees that are not clearly stated in the Conventions.

For the enforcement of these additional points in the Charter of Refugee Rights a number of methods are possible. The Government could, if it wished, add them to the 1938 Convention ; it could issue them as amending Acts or Orders in Council ; it could produce a complete Charter of Refugee Rights of its own and entrust the High Commissioner with the responsibility of watching over its carrying into operation. Whatever method were adopted, it is important that something like a Watch Committee, consisting of British citizens of the highest repute, should be set up to supervise the enforcement of such guarantees of liberties. Possibly it might be a Committee to watch over civil liberties in general, including the liberties of refugees and other foreigners. Such a body should consist of members enjoying a status similar to that of British judges, irremovable unless they fail in their duties and independent of the Government, with a constitution ensuring them definite powers of intervention in defence of civil liberties. Failing this, an unofficial Vigilance Committee might well be established by the numerous organisations that are concerned with refugee problems and with personal freedom—ranging from the Church Assembly and the Parliamentary Committee on Refugees to the Trades Union Congress and the Council for Civil Liberties. Certainly some type of influential and independent body of trustees, consisting of men and women whose reputation as champions of personal freedom is beyond dispute, might become a very valuable protector of the liberties of refugees and British subjects alike.

4. *Constructive Measures*

The " Refugee Problem " as an aspect of the war. We have argued that the " refugee problem " is in fact a *British* problem closely connected with the whole question of British civil liberties. In an important sense the " refugee problem " is also indissolubly linked with the whole character and conduct of the present war. In approaching the question of constructive measures it is therefore necessary to say a little about the British war effort and, because of the collapse of France, it is necessary to speak with the utmost frankness.

At present Britain runs the risk of losing the war by default, because the vigour and ingenuity of the Government in the *technical* tasks of waging warfare are cancelled out by its neglect of those moral and political factors which, as Haffner argues so powerfully, are far more important than tanks, artillery, barrage balloons or bombers. To the world at large the stand of Britain appears to be a stand for the old order in Europe, the order which preceded Hitler and gave rise to him. Nazism and Fascism offer no solution to the muddle into which Europe drifted in 1914, but in essence are movements designed to avert a solution by the most desperate and inhuman of means. But neither does Britain appear to offer any solution. Our statesmen proclaim one war aim in which all people heartily concur—victory over Hitler and Mussolini. But they give no clear answer to the question, " What comes after Hitler and Mussolini ? " This question needs a plain and concrete answer, because everyone remembers what came after the defeat of the German Kaiser and the Austrian Emperor in 1918. If our statesmen are not simply clinging to the old order which was so advantageous to British Imperialism and so harmful to the peoples of Germany, Austria and India, at least their behaviour inspires little confidence that they can conceive of any better European political and social order. The Nazis are victoriously imposing a new, but spurious, barren and desert-like order upon Europe, and Britain appears in contrast to offer nothing more inspiring than a return to the muddle and confusion of Versailles Europe, the state of affairs which was the breeding ground of Nazism and Fascism. The mass of people in all European countries have no desire to get back to the Europe of Versailles with its unemployment of men and resources ; still less do they wish to live under the new Hitlerian regime. All over the world there is instinctive support for Britain, not because Britain is known to stand for anything new, but simply because Britain is at war with Hitler and Mussolini. But the barrenness of the Allied cause as expressed in official utterances has become so evident since the collapse of France that this negative support of Britain is not becoming converted into positive enthusiasm.

It is important to realise that people in other countries, especially neutral countries, do not see the British Government in quite the same light as it sees itself. This difference of vision is most sharply present in India, where there is profound hatred of Nazism and fervent hope for its ultimate destruction, but where the most representative and important organisations of the people have been making support of the war on their part conditional on concrete proof that the British Government lives up to its professions of democracy and freedom by applying them to India without delay. (A number of their most important leaders have been imprisoned without trial for taking this view.) Perhaps less strongly and less clearly than the Indians, the peoples of the most important neutral countries have similar feelings. There are millions in all countries (including the countries under Nazi tyranny) who are waiting for a clear sign, not merely that Britain is fighting Nazis and Fascists and not Germans, Austrians and Italians, but also that Britain is beginning to understand *how* to fight Nazis and Fascists and knows what it is fighting *for*. A bold and concrete statement of British post-war aims, *on condition that it is accompanied by positive measures on the home front* (especially a real purging of our social and economic life of undemocratic privileges and institutions) *and in international affairs* (particularly in relation to India, China and Spain), might transform the whole character of the war, and would establish once and for all the fact that Britain, by putting its own house in order, is not only fighting against every kind of political and social oppression, but clearly understands what is needed for the construction of a liberated Europe and the organisation of world peace.

This requires a Government which will take as its object the regeneration of Britain and the economic, social and political reconstruction of its Indian and African dependencies, and will show by its behaviour in war time (not merely by promises or declarations) that it is pushing ahead as fast and as far as it can in war conditions, and is ready to join hands with all in Europe who will work for its regeneration once we have purged ourselves and Europe of the pestilence of militarism and anti-democratic reaction. In this vital sense our attitude to the burning problems of the reconstruction of Britain, the Empire and Europe is not a matter which we can put aside and only think about and act upon *after* the war, but is a vital factor in the winning of the war itself. It may seem curious to argue that moral and political factors are a major weapon against *Blitzkrieg*, but it is in fact so. It was moral political factors that made possible the thirty-one months' resistance of the men of Madrid, under-equipped and half-starved as they were, and moral and political factors of a different order that led to the surrender of Paris without a struggle, despite arms and resources far superior to those of Madrid. If the siege of Britain is hard pressed we shall be faced ultimately with the same choice. The conscription of every man, woman and child in the country will not make up for the lack of a positive, constructive policy. The war will not be won if we fight for the past ; it is not yet clear that we are fighting for the future.

If this analysis is accepted it is evident that the whole character of the war needs revolutionising, and that such a revolutionary transformation of the war will involve a transformation of our methods of conducting the struggle against authoritarianism and reaction, of our ideas about the nature of the ultimate victory and above all of our concepts of the peace that is to follow. The kind of victory we should envisage is not so much a military victory of one nation over another, but a triumph of the peoples of all belligerent countries both over Nazism and Fascism and over the old order of Versailles Europe which breeds Nazism and Fascism in *all* countries, including our own. The kind of peace to look forward to is not a dictated peace imposed on one nation by another nation following a military defeat, but a peace based upon the working together of the free peoples of a unified Europe in the tremendous tasks of rebuilding the civilisation of Europe upon planned, co-operative and democratic lines. It must be admitted that we are far away from such a conception of the British war effort. Our leaders are not rising to the heights imperatively demanded of them by events. That is why they tend to take the easier path of suppressing criticism, locking up refugees and restricting instead of extending democracy. And yet the lesson of France is plain : if our plutocratic democracies do not transform themselves into revolutionary democracies they cannot ultimately destroy Fascism, because the germs of Fascism are lurking within them. Not even the highest degree of *technical* efficiency in waging warfare can, in the long run, make up for the fact that our leaders appear to stand for the old, discredited order which Hitler claims to be abolishing, that they do in fact behave like an " old gang," with no positive aims to oppose to those of Hitler and Mussolini and to arouse active enthusiasm among the hundred million people on the Continent who might be Britain's allies, and whose active co-operation is indispensable for the destruction of international reaction. In the present war Allied statements of post-war aims have never attained the lucidity and precision of the " Thirteen Points for which the Spanish Republican Government is Fighting " ; they have not risen above the level of platitudinous generality of the Fourteen Points promulgated by President Wilson in 1918. In fact, the Churchill Government refused in August, 1940, to make any statement at all about its intentions after the war. If the war continues to be conducted as a war of Britain against Germany, or as a war of the British Empire against the Greater Reich, it does not make sense. That, after all, is what the French have discovered. It can only make sense if it becomes—what it is not at present —a people's war of liberation in which there are no " aliens " except the destroyers of freedom and the preservers of privilege and social injustice in every country, including our own.

To revolutionise the war in such a way is not a matter of adjusting our propaganda or of *saying* the right things, but a matter of *doing* the right things here and now, of showing by our conduct that Britain has once and for all made up its mind to finish with all those features of its home life and imperial structure which made British professions of democracy seem hypocritical to foreigners. The foreign propaganda we need is not a propaganda of promises or threats but a propaganda of deeds which speak for themselves. In such a propaganda of deeds, of bold democratic measures which are necessary if the war *is* to be made into a people's war and Britain's cause *is* to become the cause of the oppressed millions of Europe, the treatment of " enemy alien " refugees plays a very important symbolic part, as " enemy alien " Haffner has pointed out. If, as *one* among other measures to revolutionise the war, the Government were publicly to announce that it recognises the serious blunder and injustice it has committed and now proposes to repair the damage by releasing all non-suspect refugees, this would be no mere negative step. *The release of the interned refugees would be a positive action of the highest significance, one of a series of positive measures which would demonstrate to the world that Britain had undergone a genuine change of heart and would, more than anything else, ensure that refugees and neutrals alike become " actively friendly towards the Allied cause."*   That is why such a symbolic gesture, directed especially to the peoples of the Nazi Reich, is first in our list of constructive measures.

Releasing refugees is not in itself enough, if they are to be let loose into an atmosphere of suspicion which will make life unpleasant and employment impossible.   Measures will be needed to dispel such an atmosphere and to ensure that refugees fit into British life as really welcome members of the community whose fate has become their own.   The main measures indicated are :

(1) Public proclamation of the " right of asylum " for all genuine refugees.

(2) The dropping of all talk about " enemy aliens " as far as refugees are concerned, and a plain statement by the Government that it does *not* regard all " aliens of enemy nationality " as enemies.

(3) Some sort of reparation of the damage done to refugees by internment.   (It is especially important to ensure that the large numbers of refugees who will go to the U.S.A. in the coming months should not go there (*a*) with a stigma attached to them because they have been interned, or (*b*) with a sense of grievance which will lead them to spread stories in America which will damage Britain's good name.)

(4) Above all, the promotion of schemes of all sorts for the employment of refugees, on the lines suggested in the conclusion of Chapter I :

" That as far as possible we should create opportunities for our ' alien ' friends (whether officially ' enemy ' or officially ' friendly ') to develop and use their ability, skill and man-power both for our war effort and generally to enrich our economic, social and cultural life."

What Refugees could do.—We do not intend to labour the question of the " useful " refugee groups, since it has become generally accepted that no good is done to Britain by locking up and wasting refugee talent.   Sir John Anderson has to a considerable extent recognised this fact in the utilitarian basis of his exempted categories (which now release Einstein, though probably not Toscanini). The prospect for the "useful" is fairly bright since Mr. Churchill has himself said (August 20, 1940) :

"We may be able to do to the enemy quite a lot of things that they have not thought of yet. Since the Germans drove the Jews out and lowered their technical standards, our science is definitely ahead of theirs."

In general the release of "useful" men was already proceeding, though slowly, in August, 1940, and their absorption into employment in their special fields, especially as regards the scientists and technicians, should present no overwhelming difficulties if Mr. Churchill means to live up to his brave words. There was, however, from July, 1940, one major obstacle preventing the employment, not so much of eminent scientists but of the general mass of skilled technicians and scientific workers. This was the new Order issued by the Home Secretary in the middle of July, 1940, greatly extending the range of occupations prohibited to all foreigners unless their employers secure permits from the Aliens War Service Department (formerly Auxiliary W.S.D.). The scope of this Order is so wide as to apply, if the A.W.S.D. so interprets it, to any work which is directly or indirectly undertaken for the Government. In August, 1940, the A.W.S.D. appears to have been still following the rule of only issuing permits to foreigners of any description in the most exceptional circumstances. More important still was the fact that employers had become so excessively cautious as a result of the official attitude to "aliens" that they would often refuse to take on any foreign technicians at all, even when it meant holding up essential war production. This is a situation which applied not merely to "enemy aliens" but to *all* foreigners, including even Irishmen, and not merely to scientists and technicians but to almost every type of "alien" worker. A new attitude to the employment of foreigners is evidently needed. The Convention on the Status of Refugees guarantees to refugees certain rights to seek employment (*see* Section 2). The most sensible way to enforce its provisions is probably to revert to the position of the Aliens Employment Order of November, 1939, and to allow local employment exchange officials themselves some latitude in deciding what is and what is not a prohibited job. Apart from reverting to the general employ-

ment policy of November, 1939, the selection of the " useful "
of all types for employment is essentially a matter for such
placing agencies as the Central and Supplementary Registers
(which do record foreigners willing to offer their services), the
University Appointments Boards, the special registers of the
various professional bodies, and for the Society for the Protection of Science and Learning, the *Notgemeinschaft* and similar
bodies which might be officially recognised as placing agencies.
Alternatively, Mr. Bevin's International Labour Branch might
be entrusted with the task of compiling a central register of all
foreigners available for work requiring special qualifications.

The refugee doctors, dentists and medical specialists form
a group which exemplifies the present under-utilisation of
refugee ability.   No fewer than 1,500 German and Austrian
doctors and dentists were examined by the Aliens Tribunals,
1,413 were officially recognised as refugees, and of these 1,359
were placed in C Class.   The Medical Department of Bloomsbury House, which assists refugee doctors from other countries
besides Germany and Austria, had on its register in May, 1940,
no less than 809 refugee general practitioners, 485 specialists
and 238 dentists.   (All these figures exclude Czech doctors,
of whom there are over 200 in this country)   Seven out of
every eight of these medical practitioners are idle, wasting
their time because they are not permitted to practise, two out
of every three dentists are idle, and even among the specialists
four out of five are wasted because they are " aliens."   In
July, 1940, only 460 foreign practitioners of *all* nationalities,
refugee and non-refugee, " friendly " and " enemy " alike,
had Home Office permits to practise.   Britain is not apparently
capable of taking advantage of one of the few benefits Hitler
has bestowed on us !   The chief reason for this paradox is the
narrow and unworthy craft-union spirit of the practitioners
organised in the British Medical Association, who have shown
more anxiety about foreign competitors than concern to welcome colleagues persecuted for their " race " or their democratic opinions, as if medicine were a business rather than a
public service.   Sir John Anderson explained the position to
the House of Commons on May 28, 1940 :

> " I have no doubt that the majority, if not all, of the
> foreign doctors would be willing to undertake some form of
> national service in their own profession, but my information
> is that the medical profession would not look with favour

upon this proposal. In pursuance of the Emergency Powers (Defence) Act, 1940, these foreign doctors, like other people, may be required to place their services at the disposal of His Majesty, and there will be power to utilise their services in any way which may be found appropriate in the national interest."

Prior to the Austrian *Anschluss* permits to practise were granted to German refugee doctors and dentists without insuperable difficulties. But when the influx of refugees from Austria and Czechoslovakia began, the medical profession hardened its attitude and would only agree that fifty Austrian and fifty Czech refugee doctors should be permitted to practise (after acquiring a British qualification in the usual way). The number of Austrian dentists was similarly limited to forty. The doctors accorded this favour were selected by a special medical committee appointed by the Home Office. In July, 1940, four of the Austrian doctors had finished their qualifying work and were in practice, and nine other refugee doctors had enlisted in the Pioneer Corps. Including Czechs and Poles there must be 900 to 1,000 refugee practitioners in this country with nothing to do, over 400 specialists and nearly 200 dentists. If the Home Secretary can find no other appropriate use for them under the Emergency Powers Act he might do worse than to send them all into the Indian Medical Service, which could absorb twenty times that number of medical men to meet the needs of India. (England has roughly one hospital bed per 400 inhabitants ; each Indian hospital bed has to serve ten times as many people.) But we are confident that every one of them could be used with advantage to enlarge our own medical services.

With regard to another special group of refugees, the writers, political leaders, military experts, economists, business men and all kinds of men with expert knowledge of one or another field of German life, much has been written about the ways in which they could be " used " for assisting Britain's war effort as advisers, propagandists, experts and so on. It is a point that should hardly need demonstrating that the men who understand the enemy best are capable of rendering powerful assistance in the conduct of the war. It requires no elaboration here. But the advocates of this particular " utilitarian " argument (including even the intelligent Sebastian Haffner), tend to forget that such men cannot be " used " just because the Government is willing to use them. Most of the men in this group are refugees on account of their progressive democratic views, and their opinions about the nature and conduct of the war do not necessarily coincide with those of the present Government. Many of them would not be willing to serve, for example, under Ministers who cherish the idea of splitting up Germany into small states ruled by princelings or of restoring the Hapsburg Monarchy in Austria ; many of them emphatically repudiate the curious view of the war put forward by Lord Lloyd (and commended by Lord Halifax, the Foreign Secretary) in his pamphlet *The British Case*. A very large number of the refugee political and economic experts view with alarm the way in which the British Government makes use of the refugee adventurers who possess not the slightest trace of democratic instincts and who are fighting Hitler for castles in Austria or Poland. Refugees who want their freedom back in their own countries are not anxious to collaborate with refugees who only want their privileges and their money back and are not interested in human values. If the Government really wants to secure the assistance of democratic refugees it will have to convince them, by taking the necessary steps to revolutionise the character of the war, that it has for Europe a constructive and democratic counter-policy to Hitler's unification of a Europe enslaved to German economic interests. If it does this it will have refugee co-operation without having to ask.

These considerations apply equally to another " useful " group, the men of military age. On August 22, 1940, Sir John Anderson explained that interned refugees aged 19–50 will be released if accepted for the Auxiliary Military Pioneer Corps. There is no doubt that German and Austrian refugees are quite as capable of military prowess as any other body of men, if they are given a chance. Before the collapse of France the unarmed refugee battalions of the Pioneer Corps were used exclusively for labour work behind the lines of the B.E.F. Col. Arthur Evans (M.P. for Cardiff South) described in Parliament on July 10, 1940, what the refugees under his command did when the *Blitzkrieg* swept over Northern France :

" It happened not many weeks ago that I had the honour to command a force of some 6,000 men, known as the Havre

Defence Brigade, and I had in the force two such companies [of refugees] each 281 strong, roughly 600 men. When we were ordered to take a position in the line these men were not armed. They were composed largely of professional men . . . and there was a certain percentage of technical and experienced artisans. We were very hard up for men at the time, and I decided to arm those men 100 per cent. on the spot. I issued them with 50 rounds of ammunition per man. I am pleased to say that they conducted themselves in a manner worthy of the best traditions of the British Army. Within a few hours, and certainly in less than two days, not only did they learn to load their rifles and handle them, but they were manning machine-guns and anti-tank rifles at the side of the road and at points, and were prepared to meet and to deal with any armoured vehicle column that came along in their vicinity.

" I heard the other day when I came back that these two companies . . . were returned to the United Kingdom because of their alien character, were again disarmed and put into a particular category, not exactly dissimilar from British Companies of the Auxiliary Pioneer Corps."

After withdrawal from Dunkirk M.P.'s persistently pressed for the Pioneer Corps to be armed, and Mr. Eden finally announced on July 30, 1940, that it had been decided to arm the *British* members of the Corps.

The position in August, 1940, was that the Government was in effect saying to the interned refugees :

" You can choose between remaining locked up or joining the Pioneer Corps. If you volunteer and we do not accept you, you remain locked up. But you will be released when your turn comes to go to the U.S.A. on the immigration quota. But if you sacrifice your chance of making a new start as free men in America by joining the Pioneer Corps, we trust you so little that we will allow you to serve only in this one minor branch of the Army, without weapons, but side by side with British members bearing arms and, of course, under British Officers and N.C.O.'s who are also armed. Your satisfaction will be that we trust you sufficiently to allow you into our Army at all. Your compensation for abandoning all hopes of a new free life is that we should condescend to use you at all in our war against Germany."

This is *not* the way to win recruits among refugees. No self-respecting Englishman would volunteer for military service under such conditions. Many of the best types of refugees will probably prefer internment to such humiliation. It is in any case not very accurate to describe such recruiting methods as volunteering. As Sir John Anderson remarked in the debate of August 20, a young man who joins the Pioneer Corps as an alternative to remaining interned is hardly a volunteer in the ordinary sense. The Government must genuinely conscript refugees, as it could do if it wished, or it must release them and invite them genuinely to volunteer. If conscription is to be genuine, all the conditions which apply to British conscripts (reserved occupations, hardship committees, postponement of service for students, etc.), must apply to refugees. If volunteering is to be genuine, refugees must be allowed to volunteer for every branch of the armed forces in the same way as Englishmen. And if Sir John Anderson and Mr. Eden are really anxious to recruit refugees into the armed forces, they might appreciate the fact that many Austrians, for instance, are not willing to serve side by side with men like Prince Starhemberg who turned many of them into refugees. They might also make it clear to refugees whether they are being asked to fight for a dismembered Germany, a Hapsburg Austria, a semi-feudal, anti-Semitic Poland, or whether the Government's plans for Europe's future are more constructive and more freedom-inspired.

The humble majority of refugees, German, Austrian, Dutch and Belgian alike, fall outside these special groups and are distinguished mainly by being simply victims of Nazi aggression. We have already argued that reversion to the employment policy of November, 1939, would be a desirable step to help them become economically independent. In itself, because of what has happened since May, 1940, this would be insufficient. Positive work-promotion and placing schemes are needed, both in the interests of the nation and of the refugees. Mr. Ernest Bevin, Minister of Labour, showed in his statement of August 1, 1940, that he fully understood the position :

" I have decided, with a view to organising the man-power of Allied nations and of other well-disposed persons of

foreign nationality in this country, to set up an International
Labour Branch, as part of the Employment Department of
my Ministry.   This branch will have its headquarters at a
separate office in London.   The staff will include persons
able to speak the languages of the countries concerned, and
I am confidently expecting to secure the co-operation of
representatives of the different nations in making a success
of this new organisation.   In particular, I hope to have the
advice and assistance of an advisory committee, including
trade union representatives from foreign countries.   It is
my hope that we shall thus get valuable assistance in establishing the *bona fides* of well-disposed foreigners and in
bringing sympathetic consideration to bear on individual
cases.   It will be part of the functions of the new International Labour Branch to obtain .full knowledge of the
persons available for employment and to seek suitable
openings for them in industrial or other work."

Mr. Bevin went on to explain that there was no intention of
employing refugees in the place of British workers, but that

" I am extremely short of skilled men at present, and in
utilising the skill and ability of a number of these men, I
shall actually be putting Britishers to work."

He added :

" I shall have nothing to do with the people who are
interned.   The question of release is one for my right hon.
Friend the Home Secretary.   My duty will begin when he
has completed his, and has passed them on to me to utilise
their services. . . . I do not propose to use the term
" aliens " or " refugees."   As far as this part of the work is
concerned, it is my intention to call them, once they are
passed on to me from the Security Department, the International Labour Force, and neither aliens nor refugees."

The possibilities of Mr. Bevin's new department, under the
energetic direction of Mr. Scott, former head of the Maritime
Division of the International Labour Office, are immense.   Its
main function would be that of a sifting and placing agency for
all foreign workers.   If the deadlock over release from internment can be overcome, we have no doubt that Mr. Scott will
be able to hold an occupational census of all the non-suspect
men and women interned in the camps, to build up a complete
register of all refugee and other foreign workers, to fill up

labour shortages wherever they occur with foreign workers, and actually to promote work schemes for their employment. All these things were done in the' last war, and opportunities to-day are even greater. Thus in March, 1918, the Ministry of National Service inaugurated an Enemy Alien Workers Scheme for uninterned Germans and Austrians on lines analogous to the War Work Volunteers Scheme. It built up a card index of 8,800 men. Mr. Bevin clearly intends to compile such a placing register again, but without making distinctions between " friendly " and " enemy " foreigners, refugees and non-refugees. A vigorous prosecution of such a policy should once again set the " refugee problem " on the road to liquidation.

In addition to such measures there are many possibilities of group employment of refugees of all nationalities which ought to be considered. The refugee farm colonies which were crippled or closed down by internment might be re-opened. This will probably be done in time, since the Home Secretary is prepared to release key workers in agriculture and food production. A bold Minister of Agriculture would take the further step of equipping new farms entirely with refugee workers, or of inviting farmers in need of labour to take on a refugee staff. Forestry workers could also be employed in groups living on their own, as were the Danish forestry men during the last war. The refugee-owned factories on the Trading Estates and elsewhere should all be reopened, if doing useful work, and should be encouraged to use refugee labour. All these types of group employment, developed out of existing refugee enterprises, would be congenial to refugees and convenient for those who insist that " aliens " must be kept under special supervision for security reasons. But group employment might be developed much further than this, mainly along two lines.

(1) Entire factories or departments of factories might be staffed by refugee workers, under their own or British supervisors or employers. During the last war Messrs. Vickers at Erith and Messrs. Armstrong at Newcastle staffed entire departments of their arms factories with Belgian refugees ; two Belgian firms making shells (Messrs. Pelabon at Richmond and Messrs. Kryn and Lahaye at Letchworth) used Belgian refugees almost exclusively ; and in 1916 a national shell

factory started at Birtley was staffed entirely by Belgian workers who formed a complete community of their own. Employment on these lines need not necessarily be in munition trades. The Table in Chapter II, Section 1, shows, for example, the large number of German and Austrian refugees who are available for work in the textile and clothing trades.

(2) Another and, for German and Austrian refugees, more promising type of group employment would be the promotion of co-operative production schemes on the lines of the Austrian Studio for Arts and Crafts, concentrating mainly on the export trades. The Studio itself, which was beginning to develop export connexions in fancy goods of all sorts, might be assisted to get back on its feet. In addition there exist among the German and Austrian refugees many workers capable of organising co-operative workshops for the production of fancy leather goods, Gablonz ware, fine glass work and many other kinds of arts and crafts. The Nazi persecution of the Jews and the war itself have transferred to London a large proportion of the international fur trade and many of the world's leading fur experts, who came here as refugees. This gives Britain a chance to develop her fur trade which should not be missed. Equally important for Britain's export trade is the fact that Vienna and Paris have ceased to be international centres of fashionable dress production. There are in Britain scores of expert Viennese dressmakers and tailors of first-class quality, most of whom are idle. The most far-sighted are aiming to get away to the U.S.A. as quickly as possible, where they know there is a big market for their products. Why not encourage them to get busy now, in co-operative workshops, sending their products to America?

Of the Birtley shell factory during the last war the late Mr. Humbert Wolfe wrote:

" Here was created, in the most remarkable way, not only a great producing unit, but what was even more surprising, a complete Belgian community on British soil. A village was constructed in the neighbourhood of the factory, which developed into a small but completely typical Belgian town. It was governed by a Belgian administration with Belgian police."*

* *Labour Supply and Regulation* (1923), in the Carnegie Endowment Series on the Economic and Social History of the World War.

There is no inherent reason why German and Austrian refugee volunteers should not be invited to build up a productive community of their own, possibly including a farm colony, and administered by their own elected representatives. The Kitchener Camp at Richborough was a highly successful community experiment, the implications of which have been completely ignored since the outbreak of war led to its dissolution.

Another idea which Mr. Bevin's new department will undoubtedly take up (it was developed during the last war) is the formation of flying squads of skilled refugee workers, especially of engineering workers, who are moved around the country as required. Lady Astor in July, 1940, put forward some similar proposals for the organisation of women refugee workers. The advantage of refugees in this respect is that, because they are for the most part propertiless and penniless, they are more mobile than ordinary British workers.

In all such schemes it goes without saying that refugee workers should be paid the normal trade-union rates, should be encouraged to join trade unions and should be entitled to all the usual social service and insurance benefits available for British workers. It also goes without saying that the existing organisations of refugees should be invited to collaborate in the planning of work schemes, and that their views should be taken into account. Mr. Bevin recognises this principle, and we only hope that he will be able to get back from internment or deportation the refugee trade-union representatives he will require as collaborators, and that he will bear in mind that organisations like the Council of Austrians and the Czech Refugees' Working Committee are in a very real sense the representatives of the refugees they protect. The Central Committee for War Refugees held a conference on July 31, 1940, to discuss, *inter alia*, employment schemes for Dutch, Belgian and other wartime refugees. There is no particular reason why the scope of this Committee's work should not be extended to all refugees. But it should always be borne in mind that for the majority of German and Austrian refugees who, unlike the new arrivals from Holland and Belgium, are acclimatised in Britain and know their way about, group employment is probably not the main solution. For most of them individual absorption into employment is the best way of putting them on to their feet and of ensuring that they are able to use their ability, skill or labour power to the best advantage of the community and of themselves. That is where the International Labour Branch, if accompanied by a new attitude to " enemy alien " refugees, should prove so valuable.

There remains the question of the employment of interned refugees. The Home Office's plans were stated by Mr. Peake on August 22, 1940 :

> " These people are well provided with books and organisation of all kinds for recreation and study, but that is no existence by itself for civilised man. Employment is the most crying need, and the Isle of Man does offer exceptional opportunities for the employment of men outside the camps. There is work available for them in agriculture, in reclaiming land, in public works, cutting peat on the hillsides, and so forth which would not be available near or around the internment camps in this country."

It is *not* employment of *any* kind that is the " crying need " of " civilised man," but employment of a kind for which he is suited and in conditions of personal freedom. No doubt many internees will enjoy " cutting peat on the hillsides, and so forth " as a physical exercise, but how many of them will not be yearning to do the real work, whatever it may be, for which each of them has been trained and can do best ? If general internment is to be persisted in, there are several questions about the employment of interned refugees which have to be clearly answered. (1) Are genuine non-suspect refugees to be separated from genuine prisoners of war ? (2) Are non-suspect internees to receive trade-union rates of pay for the work they do (less *reasonable* deductions for board and lodging) ? (3) Are they to enjoy the normal social service benefits available to British workers, especially the right to workmen's compensation for injuries ? (4) Will their working conditions be subject to control and inspection in the ordinary way ? (5) Will the work be compulsory or voluntary ? In particular will the work offered be of such a character as to train refugees for useful work as free men once the war is over ? Will the refugee organisations be allowed to continue their industrial training scheme for refugees, drawing men from the camps as required ? (Or alternatively will the International Labour Branch have power to recruit men from the camps for training in Government engineering centres ?)

These questions will have to be answered before judgment

can be passed upon the Home Office's new plans. Mr.
Morrison may be able to give clear answers ; we doubt whether
Sir John Anderson could have done.   If non-suspects have
to be interned, is it not evident—since security is *not* the prime
consideration—that they should be interned in places where
the best opportunities for employment exist ?   We doubt
whether schemes for employing internees on the Isle of Man
will be more successful in 1940 than they were in 1914–18,
when it seems to have been largely a matter of " finding work
for idle hands."   During the last war prisoners of war—
mostly German soldiers of peasant origin—were used mainly
on the land, in limestone quarries, and unsuccessfully in the
ironstone quarries on the Island of Raasay.   Such work may
be suitable for genuine prisoners of war, but to compel non-
suspect refugees who could do far better and more useful work
if released, to do such work is not only unjustifiable but plainly
idiotic.   The refugees are a welcome addition to the nation's
labour force, but they will never be properly utilised unless
they are released to find work in the normal way.   Many
ingenious proposals for the employment of interned refugees
have been advanced.   We will not discuss them here.   It is
an unnecessary problem which the Home Secretary could
solve with a stroke of his pen, by releasing his prisoners.

A final series of constructive measures relates to the culture
of refugees.   Many of the most eminent scholars and artists
of Germany and Austria are living as exiles in this country.
One of the finest gestures an anti-Nazi Government could ever
have made would have been to take these men and women
under its protection, to have said to them :

> " The Nazis have driven you out, have burnt your books,
> destroyed your works of art, banned your music and songs,
> because they have declared war on German culture.   Nazi
> scientists have renounced the international Republic of
> Learning, and spat on ' Jewish ' mathematics and ' Bol-
> shevist ' physics.   You wish to keep a free German culture
> alive in exile until the day when Germany and Austria are
> again free.   We also have this wish and will give you all the
> help you need."

Such a Government could have assisted in the founding of a
German University in Exile (one was in fact started in the

U.S.A.), an Academy of Free German Arts (a beginning was made at the Dartington Hall Arts Department through private benevolence), and of centres for free German and Austrian culture in London and other large towns.   What a magnificent demonstration of Britain's championship of the cause of freedom if such institutions had been flourishing in this country at the outbreak of war, when Hitler closed down all but three of the Universities in his Reich!   So far as we know, however, the Government has never spent a single penny on assisting free German culture.   All the splendid work in the cultural field done by the refugees in Britain, as individuals teaching, writing, painting, composing, assisted by private benevolence or the generosity of universities and other institutions, or through organisations such as the Austrian Centre, the Free German League of Culture, the Warburg Institute,* all have been done without the slightest encouragement or assistance from the Government.   Internment has in fact seriously damaged the cultural life which the refugees were building up, although, as we saw, it led to the growth of a new type of cultural life—in the internment camps.   The least the Government can do now is to give the internees every facility for making the camps into strongholds of refugee culture.   If it wished it could go much further ; and could begin to do some of those things which it might have done in peacetime, to ensure that neither the Nazis nor the war shall stamp out all free creative intellectual or aesthetic activity on the part of Germans and Austrians.   As Mr. Wickham Steed has said, there will be need of good Germans in the years to come.   This again is one of those symbolic gestures which count in warfare.   Hitler did not neglect to open a Breton University after his conquest of France.   Britain's only reply to this propagandist gesture is to release the culturally valuable men who can be " used," precisely as the Nazis might release an " economically valuable Jew " for whom they had found a use.

Refugees and the Future.—Of the future of German and Austrian refugees there is little that can be said with certainty. It is doubtful whether the majority of them will ever wish to return to their own countries, even when Germany and Austria are really free.   The iron has bitten too deeply into their

* A world-famous centre of classical studies which was transferred as a unit from Hamburg to London in the early days of the Nazi regime.

souls. Of those who would go back it is also doubtful whether more than a small minority will ever play a leading part in the future life of their own countries. The men and women who will lead and regenerate Germany, Austria and Italy are there already, waiting or working for their peoples' liberation ; just as the men and women who will have to reconstruct British life are in our midst to-day. Revolutions are not made by emigrants but, as we have argued, the treatment of emigrants in their countries of refuge plays an important rôle in the fostering of revolutions. The minority of German and Austrian refugees who do not wish to lose their national identity, who do intend to go back one day and do what they can to assist in reconstructing their own countries, should be encouraged in every way to preserve their morale and community life in exile, to develop their own ideas and activities for the future of their countries.

But the majority of " enemy alien " refugees in Britain will probably end up as American citizens, since the large numbers of intending emigrants to the U.S.A. in Britain at the outbreak of war have since been augmented by the transference to refugees in Britain of American immigration quotas which, in war-time conditions, cannot be filled by refugees in other European countries. This outflow will be a major channel for the reduction of Britain's refugee population in the coming twelve months. There is no particular reason why the majority of refugees who remain in Britain should not ultimately become absorbed into the British community as fully-fledged British citizens. The employment situation of refugees in May, 1940, was clearly pointing in this direction. Economically they were becoming part of the British community ; socially they were developing ties and friendships, cultural habits and modes of living that drew them ever more into British life. We hope this process, rudely interrupted by internment, will be allowed to continue, with the clear intention of finally allowing all non-suspect refugees who wish it to become British citizens. The Government in June, 1940, made an offer to the French Government of joint-citizenship for all Frenchmen and Englishmen. Why should it not make an offer of citizenship to the refugees to whom it opened its doors in the past, as in earlier days Britain welcomed the Huguenot refugees who contributed so much of value to British life and culture ? In any case, Britain is suffering from an, as yet, hidden tendency to population decline, which the war will inevitably aggravate and accelerate. This can be overcome mainly by the difficult method of encouraging people to have more children, but another method which would help is to import new citizens from other countries who think they have a superfluity. If ever a nation wanting new citizens was offered immigrants of a desirable character, fully trained for useful, creative work, that country was Britain when Hitler drove out the refugees who sought asylum in this country. Why hesitate ?

If the " refugee problem " develops along these lines it should liquidate itself before the war is over. Admirable though the work of Bloomsbury House and its associated organisations is, we look forward to the day when Bloomsbury House will close its doors for good. With intelligent and imaginative handling the problem of the German and Austrian refugees in Britain—intensified all over again by the recent behaviour of the British Government—could be more or less finally settled within twelve months, so that the charity and welfare services of Bloomsbury House would no longer have any place in British life. As an aftermath of the war there will undoubtedly be many refugee problems in Europe. In the preceding section of this chapter we have outlined possible machinery for dealing with them. But there is no necessity at all for our present problem of German and Austrian refugees to persist into the post-war period. It must and can be finished with now. Mr. Herbert Morrison, the new Home Secretary, has a splendid opportunity to remedy the harm done by his predecessor in office.

We have shown how the British Government has declared war on the wrong people, how its policy of internment and deportation is needlessly discouraging vital progressive forces all over Europe and, maybe, turning friends into enemies. To many Englishmen the British war effort is worth £6–8 millions *each day*, year in, year out. The reader who still has doubts about the thesis of this book, who is not impressed by our concern for British civil liberties or the conduct of the war, might pause to consider, as he finishes the last page, how much of this colossal expenditure is simply being wasted by the frustration of democratic endeavour of which the Government's attitude to " enemy alien " refugees is symbolic.

THE END

APPENDIX

ON THE TREATMENT OF THE SICK

THE seriously ill were normally transferred from internment camps to *military* or *prison* hospitals, where they often had no opportunity whatever of communicating with their families, however dangerous their condition. From scores of reports by invalids about their treatment we select two stories.

(1) *The Wrexham Emergency Military Hospital* is described by a man who passed through it at the end of July, 1940. The man is an internationally famous artist, in whose judgment we have complete confidence :

" The hospital was well equipped, the food excellent, even to the point of extravagance. There were proper beds and hot and cold water—these latter luxuries which the prisoners had not seen since the day they were interned."

The seven men with whom our informant shared a room included :

(1) A man in the last stages of tuberculosis. He coughed and spat the whole time, and never ceased smoking. (His smoking was permitted, since it was clear that he would have gone out of his mind had this not been allowed.)

(2) A diabetic sent over from an internment camp to be tested, with a view to seeing whether he ought to be released. His water was in fact tested thirty-six times, which was quite unnecessary. He was finally sent back to his camp with an elaborate diet sheet which, when shown to the camp doctor, provoked laughter, since none of the items on the sheet was obtainable. The reports on his condition which were to have been sent on to the camp from the hospital never arrived.

(3) An epileptic who, during the whole period, required the bedpan on an average of three times an hour. It should be noted that during the night, owing to blackout requirements, there was no air in the room, and what air there was was polluted by this case and the T.B. case.

(4) A diabetic who had been on insulin for sixteen years. He was receiving sixty units a day. It is common medical knowledge that a diabetic receiving insulin must have a balanced diet of sugar and carbohydrates in order to offset the effects of the insulin. This man had precisely the same diet as the rest of the hospital. The result of such a preponderance of insulin with no balanced diet was an immediate major coma. At intervals during the night he had to be held down by two soldiers and three nurses. During the states of coma he would have periods of screaming, delirium, tears, etc. The inclusion of this man in this small room was desperate for the other patients. These noisy comas were daily and nightly occurrences. A fellow patient asked that a balanced diet be given to the man, and that he be removed. No reply was forthcoming to this request. The doctor visited the man, and his method of treatment was to attempt to shout him down. He told him to " pull himself together," to " lie down," etc.

On the morning that the man was discharged he was given his morning ration of forty units of insulin, but was not given any supply with which to continue the treatment. It is extremely unlikely that this man is still alive.

(5) A man who was operated on three times during his short stay in the hospital. His wife and children were living two miles away in ignorance of his whereabouts. He asked, when very ill indeed after his operations, to be allowed to see his wife. This was refused. A little later he was allowed to write to her to say that he had been operated on three times, but was forbidden to say where he was. His wife was subsequently sent to Carlisle, which involved passing the very doors of the hospital. They were never permitted to meet and she remained in ignorance that she had been so close to him.

Prisoners arriving at the hospital as patients were put to bed, all their own belongings were removed, and they had to wear Army pyjamas. They were compelled to stay in bed all the time, even when this was quite unnecessary. There was a guard in the hospital of young soldiers who marched up and down inside the wards all night. They later took to shaking such prisoners as had achieved a moment's sleep, either to ask them the time or to ask other questions. They sat on the prisoners' beds, smoked, shouted to each other all the time and joked noisily with the nurses. Frequent requests that the prisoners should tell them the time were made since they had four-hour shifts, and were anxious to be off. None of the prisoners in such conditions were able to sleep. Lights Out was at 9 ; at 10 temperatures and pulses were taken ; at 11 the Matron came round, shining a bright torch into each prisoner's face, and asking if he was all right.

This man's experience is by no means out of the ordinary.

(2) *An Outrage.*—We have every reason to believe that the following story is exceptional ; nevertheless it is one of a number all equally ghastly in their different ways :

Josef Jokl (fifty-two, C Class) was an Austrian Jew who smuggled his wife and child into Czechoslovakia in the summer of 1938. When the Nazis seized that country he escaped to Poland and thence to England, where he was supported by the Czech Trust Fund. He was suffering from thyrotoxicosis (a serious glandular condition), and in February, 1940, went into the West London Hospital for five weeks. His condition was too dangerous to permit an operation, so the Czech Trust Fund sent him to a convalescent home to strengthen him for an operation at a later date. Back at home, a police officer came to arrest him on July 9. He was shown a medical certificate, but went away without taking it with him. On July 18 the police officer returned with the story that the hospital considered that Jokl could continue his treatment in internment (the hospital knew nothing about the camps !). Jokl was taken away to the Lingfield Racecourse camp. Here he was unable to eat his food, and suffered from diarrhœa and vomiting. He remained in the camp sick-bay until July 25, and was then transferred to Redhill County Hospital *in a lorry*. He did not expect to survive the lorry journey, but he did. On July 30 his sister was told by the police of his whereabouts, and visited him the same day. She found him in a serious condition, but in full possession of his senses. On August 8 a police officer came to tell her he had died that morning. The Czech Trust Fund had applied for his release.

INDEX

* indicates an internee
Brief identifications have been added where possible to names that might otherwise be unknown.

NOTE ON THE TEXT

The text of this edition has been offset, without alteration save photographic enlargement, from the original Penguin edition of 1940.

Errata
page 37 line 8 up *for* tribunal *read* tribunals
page 79 line 21 *for* Heinz *read* Hein
page 81 line 4 *for* Osborne *read* Osborn
page 95 line 8 *for* blitzkrieg *read* Blitzkrieg
page 119 last line *for* Nunnenmacher *read* Nonnenmacher
page 126 line 16 *for* details *read* details)
page 139 line 3 *for* Burfend *read* Burfeind
page 139 line 3 *for* Woerman *read* Woermann
page 161 line 6 *for* debate itself *read* first debate

Where a name in the above list occurs more than once, its first occurrence only is given.